THE WORLD ENCYCLOPEDIA OF
FRUIT

THE WORLD ENCYCLOPEDIA OF
FRUIT

KATE WHITEMAN AND
MAGGIE MAYHEW

LORENZ BOOKS

First published in 1998 by Lorenz Books
27 West 20th Street, New York, NY 10011

LORENZ BOOKS are available for bulk purchase for sales promotion and for premium use.
For details, write or call the sales director, Lorenz Books, 27 West 20th Street, New York,
NY 10011; (800)354-9657.

© 1998 Anness Publishing Limited

Lorenz Books is an imprint of Anness Publishing Inc.

ISBN 1 85967 757 6

Publisher: Joanna Lorenz
Senior Editor: Linda Fraser
Copy Editor: Jenni Fleetwood
Indexer: Hilary Bird
Designer: Nigel Partridge
Photography: William Lingwood (recipes) and Don Last (fruits)
Food for Photography: Bridget Sargeson (recipes) and Christine France (fruits)

Printed and bound in China

1 3 5 7 9 10 8 6 4 2

CONTENTS

INTRODUCTION

Everything you ever wanted to know about fruit is contained within this fascinating book, from information on the various varieties to advice on buying, storing, preparing, cooking and serving. Snippets of historical data are included, as are useful notes on nutrition. The sections are divided by type of fruit for easy reference: Apples, Pears, Quinces and Medlars; Stone Fruits; Berries and Currants; Citrus Fruits; and Exotic Fruits; with a final section on fruits that do not fit into any other category: Melons, Grapes, Figs and Rhubarb. Beautiful photographs help you to identify—and will tempt you to try—many hitherto unfamiliar fruits.

FRUITS ARE NATURE'S most bountiful and versatile creation. No other foods offer such a variety of colors, textures, scents and flavors. Almost all fruits are pleasing to the senses of sight, smell and taste. Just think of the crispness of an apple, the velvety skin of a peach, the jewellike colors of red currants, the juicy tartness of citrus fruits. There is nothing like the sight of a glorious display of fruit in a market to lift the spirits and whet the appetite. Without colorful, health-giving fruits, our diet would be infinitely more dull.

Fruit is not only good for the soul; it is a supremely healthy food, bursting with natural energy-giving sugars, minerals and vitamins. When energy levels are low, a few grapes, a banana or an apple revitalize us in moments. Fruit provides the perfect guilt-free snack, since most varieties are completely fat-free and contain very few calories. Nearly all fruits have a high proportion of water—between 75 and 90 percent—which makes them wonderfully thirst-quenching in hot weather. Picture the pleasure of eating a large wedge of chilled watermelon or a

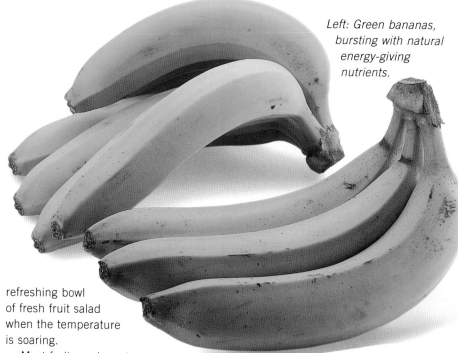

Left: Green bananas, bursting with natural energy-giving nutrients.

refreshing bowl of fresh fruit salad when the temperature is soaring.

Most fruit can be eaten raw, just as it is (be sure to wash it first), although some varieties may need peeling. Nothing beats a simple dessert of perfectly ripe juicy fruit, perhaps served with a scoop or two of vanilla ice cream or a dollop of cream, or with some good cheese—try crisp apples with a wedge of farmhouse Cheddar or Lancashire cheese, juicy, ripe pears with either blue Stilton or Gorgonzola, or raspberries and sliced peaches with mascarpone cheese.

All fruits can be served on their own, or used to create sweet and savory dishes of infinite variety, from pies to puddings, cakes, muffins, ice creams, mousses, soufflés and featherlight fruit-topped meringues.

You could easily base an entire meal on fresh fruit without repeating any colors, textures or flavors. The meal might begin with the classic combination of melon with prosciutto, or a refreshing fruit soup, followed by Normandy pheasant with apples and cider, then a platter of cheese, fresh and dried fruit and nuts and finally a tropical fruit salad, a bowl of bright red berries or a lemon tart.

Fruit is enormously rewarding to cook with and is very versatile. Almost all fruits complement each other, so you can create all manner of interesting combinations. Although the recipes in this book concentrate on the use of fruits in sweet dishes, they have an important role to play in savory ones too. Tart fruits like gooseberries, rhubarb and cranberries cut the richness of fatty fish like mackerel and can also enhance the sometimes insipid flavor of poultry. Dried fruits are used extensively in North African and Middle Eastern cooking—the combination of meat and sweet, sticky dates, prunes or

Below: The vibrant seeds from ripe pomegranates can be eaten raw as they are or added to both sweet and savory dishes.

dried apricots is superb. Most fruits also marry well with exotic spices, such as cinnamon, ginger and vanilla, and even those fruits that are relatively bland can be lifted by the addition of a squeeze of lemon or lime juice.

The hundreds of different kinds of fruit can be divided into four main categories: soft fruits, such as raspberries, strawberries, blueberries and red, black, and white currants; stone fruits, including peaches, apricots, cherries and plums; "pome" fruits of the apple and pear families; and citrus fruits. In addition there are several that do not fit into any other category. These include figs, grapes, melons and rhubarb (which is actually a vegetable, but is always treated as a fruit).

Fruits are no longer the seasonal produce they once were. Nowadays, thanks to sophisticated transportation methods, all types of fruit from every country are available almost all year round. Travelers who have enjoyed exotic produce abroad now find it gracing the shelves of their local

Above: Orleans Reinette apples—one of the pome fruits.

Left: Watermelons, like other melon varieties, are in a category of their own.

greengrocer or supermarket, giving less fortunate stay-at-homes a taste of the tropics. The disadvantage of this is that we no longer wait with eager anticipation for a particular fruit to come into season; somewhere in the world it will be grown year-round. So strawberries, raspberries and peaches have ceased to be exclusively summer treats, but can be bought in almost any season, although they will never taste as good as when freshly picked, and are still always at their best and cheapest in the summer.

There are many other ways of savoring fruits throughout the year. They can be frozen, canned, or preserved in other ways—as juices, liqueurs or macerated in alcohol; dried or candied; or made into jams, jellies, curds, chutneys and relishes. There is no time of year when fruit is not readily available in one form or another, so you need never go without nature's most precious bounty.

EQUIPMENT

Although most fruits can be prepared with the aid of a good sharp knife, a wide variety of special implements is available to make the task easier, safer and more efficient. The following items are very useful—provided you have space for them in your kitchen.

Peeling and Coring

Paring knife The most useful item in any kitchen. Choose a really sharp knife with a short blade and a handle that is comfortable to hold. Always use a stainless steel knife for preparing fruit; the acids may damage other metals.

Apple corer This utensil removes apple and pear cores in one easy movement. Place over the core at the stem end and push down firmly right through the fruit, then twist slightly and pull out the core and seeds.

Apple segmenter Use this handy device to core and slice an apple into twelve even-size segments in one simple operation.

Apple peeler Perfect for people with a huge glut of home-grown apples, this hand-cranked implement peels, cores and neatly slices the fruit into rings in seconds. This tool is expensive to buy, but worth it if you have apple trees that bear abundantly.

Above right: Apple corer
Below left: Paring knife
Below right: Apple segmenter

Above: Fixed- and swivel-blade vegetable peelers

Pineapple slicer Cores and slices a pineapple in one easy corkscrewlike action. This simple-to-operate utensil is useful for keeping the pineapple shell intact for use as a serving container, but only works with smaller pineapples.

Swivel-blade vegetable peeler Use this tool to pare off the thinnest possible layer of peel or skin so that no nutrients are lost.

Fixed-blade vegetable peeler This type of peeler takes a thicker strip of peel or skin than the swivel-blade version.

Grating and Zesting

Box grater Choose a stainless steel grater with four different grating

Below: Citrus zester and channel knife
Right: Box grater

Left: Pineapple slicer

surfaces and make sure it will stand firmly on a chopping board or in a bowl. Most include a flat blade suitable for slicing lemons or limes.

Citrus zester The row of holes at the top of the zester shaves off thin shreds of zest, leaving behind the bitter pith.

Channel knife This tool has a toothlike blade that pares off the zest in ribbons or julienne strips. Combined zesters/channel knives are available.

Juicing

Lemon squeezer Hand-operated squeezers catch the juice in the base. Basic models can also be used for limes and small oranges. Some have interchangeable heads to accommodate citrus fruits of various sizes.

Left: Citrus press
Below: Reamer

Citrus press These hand-operated chrome juicers have a geared mechanism to enable as much juice as possible to be extracted. When the handle is pulled forward, the juice is squeezed into a container.

Electric juice extractor These machines will extract juice from other fruits besides citrus. They take up a lot of space, but are invaluable for lovers of fresh fruit juice.

Pitting and Preparing

Cherry pitter The bowl of this implement has a hole through which the cherry pit is ejected when the fruit is pressed. Useful for large quantities.

Grapefruit knife A curved knife serrated on both sides. Run it between the membranes and pulp to release the segments.

Left: Cherry pitter

Below: Grapefruit knife

Grapefruit segmenter This curved implement has a V-shaped blade. Position with the point against the inside of the rind and push down, around and inward to cut out the segments.

Melon baller Insert this small, round scoop into the melon flesh and twist to remove neat balls of fruit. It comes in various sizes and can also be used for other fruits. Tiny ones sometimes double as a cherry pitter.

Preserving

Funnel Essential for pouring hot jams and jellies into jars. Stainless steel funnels will withstand heat better than plastic ones.

Jelly bag A heavy muslin filter bag for straining jellies and juices. Suspend it from the legs of a chair placed upside down or, far better, buy one on a stand.

Preserving pan Especially designed for preserving, this is a thick-bottomed double-handled pan. The heavy bottom prevents the fruit preserve from burning and sticking.

Sugar thermometer Use this for checking the temperature of a syrup or to determine whether the setting point of a jam and jelly has been reached.

Above: Sugar thermometer
Below: Funnel with strainer

Reamer This wooden device enables you to squeeze the fruit directly into a bowl or pan. Insert into the cut fruit and twist.

Lemon tap A simple gadget that turns citrus fruit into a "juice jug." If only a small amount of juice is required, leave the tap inserted in the fruit to keep the juice fresh between squeezings.

Below: Lemon squeezer

Above: Melon baller

PURCHASING, PREPARING AND COOKING

BUYING FRUIT

Obviously, the best time to buy fruit is when it is fully ripe and at its peak. The exceptions are fruits, such as bananas and pears, that ripen quickly and should therefore be bought at different stages of maturity so that they are not all ready at the same time. You are most likely to find top-quality fruits in markets and shops that have a quick turnover of fresh produce, preferably with a daily delivery. Although most fruits are now available almost year-round, they are best and cheapest when in season in the country of origin. Only buy as much fruit as you need at one time so that it remains fresh and appetizing.

PREPARING FRUIT

For some fruits, the only preparation needed is washing or wiping with a damp cloth; others must be peeled or skinned, cored, pitted or seeded. Wash fruit only just before using. If necessary, cut away any bruised or damaged parts.

Firm Fruit

Peeling

Some firm fruits, such as dessert apples and pears, can be eaten raw without peeling. For cooking, peeling is often necessary. Pare off the skin as thinly as possible to avoid losing the valuable nutrients under the skin.

1 Wash the fruit and pat dry using paper towels. Use a small, sharp paring knife or a vegetable peeler to pare off the skin in long, thin vertical strips. Pears are best peeled by this method.

2 Alternatively, for apples, thinly peel all around the fruit in a spiral.

Coring

1 To core whole apples and pears, place the sharp edge of a corer over the stem end of the fruit.

2 Press down firmly, then twist slightly; the core, complete with seeds, will come away in the center of the corer. Push out the core from the handle end.

Storing

Storage methods depend on the type of fruit, but there are some basic guidelines:
- Do not wash fruit before storing, but only when ready to use.
- Store fruit at the bottom of the refrigerator in the salad crisper.
- Do not refrigerate unripe fruit; keep it at room temperature or in a cool, dark place, depending on the variety (see individual fruits).
- Fragile fruits, such as berries, are easily squashed, so spread them out in a single layer on a tray lined with paper towels.

Segmenting

1 Halve the fruit lengthwise, then cut into quarters or segments.

2 Cut out the central core and seeds with a small, sharp knife.

Preventing discoloration

Some fruits, such as apples, pears and bananas, quickly oxidize and turn brown when exposed to the air. To prevent discoloration, brush cut fruits with lemon juice. Alternatively, acidulate a bowl of cold water by stirring in the juice of half a lemon. Drop the cut fruits into the bowl immediately after preparing.

Citrus Fruit

Peeling

It is very important to remove all of the bitter white pith that lies just beneath the rind of citrus fruits.

1 To peel firm-skinned fruits, hold the fruit over a bowl to catch the juice and use a sharp knife to cut off the rind.

2 For loose-skinned fruit, such as tangerines, pierce the skin with your forefinger at the stem end and peel off the rind. Pull off all the white shreds adhering to the fruit.

Segmenting

Use a small serrated knife to cut down between the membranes enclosing the segments; carefully ease out the flesh.

Grating

Citrus zest adds a wonderful flavor to many dishes. If it is to be eaten raw, grate it finely, using the fine side of a grater. Remove only the colored zest; if you grate too deeply into the peel, you will be in danger of including the bitter white pith. For cooking, pare off long, thin strips of zest using a zester.

Garnishing

1 To make thick julienne strips of zest, cut downward, using a channel knife.

2 To make twists, slice the fruits thinly, cut to the center, then twist the ends in opposite directions to make an S-shape.

Soft Fruit

Peeling

Fruits such as peaches, nectarines and apricots can be peeled with a sharp paring knife, but this may waste some of the delicious flesh. It is better to loosen the skins by dipping them *briefly* in boiling water.

1 Make a tiny nick in the skin.

2 Cover with boiling water and leave for 15–30 seconds, depending on the ripeness of the fruit. Remove the fruit with a slotted spoon and peel off the skin, which should come away easily.

Removing stones and pips

1 To pit peaches, apricots etc., cut all around the fruit through the seam. Twist the halves in opposite directions, then lever out the pit with a knife.

2 To pit cherries, put the fruit in a cherry pitter and push the bar into the fruit. The pit will be ejected.

3 To remove grape seeds, cut the grapes in half, then pick out the seeds with the tip of a small, sharp knife.

COOKING FRUIT

Most fruits can be cooked and in a great variety of ways.

Poaching

Apples and pears, stone fruits, figs, rhubarb and even grapes can be poached whole, halved or in segments. The classic poaching liquid is a syrup and usually consists of 1 part sugar boiled with 2 parts water for about 2 minutes, or until clear. The syrup can be flavored with lemon, orange or spices, such as cinnamon or vanilla. Red or white wine can also be used for poaching, usually with added sugar. Alternatively, use fruit juice.

Bring the poaching liquid to a boil. Lower the heat and add the fruit. Simmer gently until the fruit is just tender.

Stewing

This method is suitable for all fruits that can be poached.

Cut up the fruit. Put in a saucepan with just enough water, wine or fruit juice to cover. Add sugar to taste. Simmer gently until tender. Stir only if you want the fruit to become a pulp.

Broiling

Any firm fruits can be broiled, with or without sugar. Tropical fruits, such as pineapple and bananas, are particularly good for grilling. For desserts, they can be cut into 1-inch wedges or chunks and threaded onto skewers to make kebabs. Brush the fruit with honey before broiling.

For savory dishes, halve the fruit or cut into pieces, removing the core if necessary. Brush with melted butter and broil under medium heat, turning occasionally, until tender and browned on all sides.

Baking

Apples and pears; stone fruits such as peaches, nectarines, apricots and plums; and figs and rhubarb can be baked whole or in halves, wedges or slices, according to type.

1 Put the fruit in a shallow ovenproof dish, add a little water and sprinkle with sugar to taste.

2 Top the fruit with small pieces of butter. Bake in a preheated oven at 350°F until tender.

Microwave Cooking

All fruits that can be conventionally cooked can be microwaved with excellent results, although the skins on some fruits, such as plums, may not soften sufficiently in the short cooking time. Whole fruits, such as apples, should be scored, or they may burst. Place the fruit in a suitable dish, cover and cook on High for the time recommended, or until tender.

Sautéing

Slice or dice the fruit (peel it or not, as you wish) and toss quickly in hot butter until lightly browned all over. Add sugar and flavorings to taste.

Deep-Frying

For fruit fritters, such as pineapple, apple or banana, peel the fruit and cut into chunks.

Heat oil for deep-frying to 360°F, or until a cube of dried bread sizzles when it is added to the pan. Coat the pieces of fruit in batter and deep-fry until the fritters rise to the surface of the hot oil and are golden brown. Drain the fritters on paper towels and sprinkle with sugar.

Puréeing

Fruit can be puréed for sauces, fools, ice creams and sorbets. Some types must be cooked first; others, like berries, can be puréed raw.

1 For berries, wash briefly and push through a fine nylon sieve, using the back of a large spoon or ladle. If you prefer, purée the berries in a food processor, then strain the purée to remove any seeds.

2 For cooked peeled fruit, mash with a potato masher for a coarse purée.
3 For a finer purée, process cooked, peeled fruit in a food processor or push through a food mill.

Caramelizing

Fruits look pretty when caramelized. Small fruits like cherries can be used whole. Larger fruits should be cubed.

1 Combine scant 1 cup sugar and ¼ cup water in a small, heavy saucepan. Stir over low heat until the sugar has dissolved. When the mixture boils, add 1 teaspoon lemon juice and boil until the syrup turns a deep golden brown.

2 Carefully add 1 tablespoon hot water (protecting your hand with an oven mitt, as the mixture will "spit") and shake the pan to mix.
3 Spear a piece of fruit on a fork and dip it into the caramel to coat. Place on an oiled baking sheet until the caramel cools and hardens.

Candying

Also known as crystallized or glacé fruits, candied fruits make a delicious end to a meal. Suitable fruits include citrus (slices and peel), cherries and other stone fruits, physalis (cape gooseberries) and pineapple. For professional results, the candying process is a lengthy one, but this simplified method works well for candied citrus zest or for fruit that is to be eaten within a few days.

1 Cut the fruit into slices or chunks. Make a syrup using 1 cup sugar and 2/3 cup water; follow the instructions under Caramelizing. Immerse the pieces of fruit in the syrup. Set aside in a cool, dry place to soak for 2 weeks. Drain.

2 Place the fruit on a rack over a baking sheet. Dry for 3–6 hours in a very low oven (no higher than 125°F). Cool, then store in an airtight container.

Frosting

Try this technique with grapes, red and black currants and cranberries. Eat on the day they are prepared.

1 Leave the fruit on the stem. Dip in lightly beaten egg white, then roll in sugar until frosted all over. Let dry before serving.

Drying

Suitable fruits include apples, pears, stone fruits, figs, grapes and bananas. Commercial dehydrators are available, but you can dry the fruit in a low oven.

Prepare the fruit: Peel, core and slice apples; peel, core and halve pears; halve and pit peaches or similar fruits. Leave smaller fruits whole. Lay the fruit on clean wooden slatted trays, cut side up. Dry in an oven preheated to the lowest possible temperature. Cool completely before storing.

Preserving in Alcohol

All fruits can be preserved in alcohol. In the eighteenth century, seafarers discovered that their cargoes of exotic fruits could be preserved in barrels of rum. Dark rum is still the classic preserving spirit, but brandy and other spirits can also be used.

The ideal container is a purpose-made *rumtopf*, but a wide-mouthed preserving jar will do. Start with summer fruits, then add other fruits as they come into season.

1 Wash and dry the fruit. Place in a bowl and cover with an equal weight of sugar. Set aside for 1 hour.

2 Tip the fruit mixture into a *rumtopf* or preserving jar. Pour in just enough rum to cover the fruit completely. Cover the jar with plastic wrap and store in a cool, dark place.
3 Continue to fill the jar with fruits as they come into season, using only half as much sugar by weight as fruit; cover the fruit with rum each time. When the jar is full, leave for at least two months before using the fruit.

APPLES, PEARS, QUINCES AND MEDLARS

A bowlful of apples, polished to shiny perfection, is one of life's pleasures—beautiful to behold, delicious and healthy to eat. Pears are almost as popular, with juicy flesh whose scent is almost as tempting as its taste. Quinces are even more aromatic, while medlars are intriguing—not least because they can only be eaten when they are on the verge of rotting. They are all pome fruits, with an indentation in the stem end and the coarse brown remains of a flower at the other, and a tough central core containing a number of brown seeds.

APPLES

Ever since Adam bit into the fruit of the Tree of Knowledge, apples have been the stuff of myth and legend. The ancient Greeks and Romans believed them to be aphrodisiacs, and for the Celts crab apples were a symbol of fertility. In the Middle Ages, the cult of the apple continued in such customs as apple bobbing at Halloween and wassailing at Christmas.

The most popular of all fruits, apples are also convenient, perfect for eating raw as a nutritious snack and ideal for making into a multitude of hot and cold desserts. There are thousands of named varieties worldwide, but the choice of those available to buy is, sadly, decreasing year by year. However, because apples are now grown in every temperate country in the world, some varieties can be found in the shops all year round. Delicious as they may be, no store-bought apples can ever beat the flavor and crisp texture of local apples that have been freshly picked.

Apples come in many shapes and sizes, from tiny cherry-sized crab apples to huge cooking varieties like Howgate Wonder, Reverend W. Wilkes and the unbelievably warty Knobby Russet, which looks remarkably like a huge toad. They can be round, oval, or "cornered," with four distinct corners around the calyx, like the Catshead, which is shaped like the face of a Siamese cat.

Left: Granny Smith apples—first cultivated in Australia in the twentieth century.

Colors range from bright, shiny red through vivid greens, yellows and pale creamy-white to golden russet, while the skins may be ultra-thin or unpalatably thick. As for taste and texture, there is an almost infinite variety—something to suit every palate, from crisp and sour to soft and sweet.

History

Apples have been eaten since prehistoric times, when only crab apples existed. The Romans adored apples and were the first people to cultivate the fruit; by the first century AD they were growing at least a dozen varieties throughout the Roman Empire.

The most famous of all British apple growers was the nineteenth-century English nurseryman Thomas Laxton. With his sons, he hybridized hundreds of varieties of apples, many of which still exist today and bear his name.

The Pilgrims introduced apples to the New World, planting seeds that they had taken with them from England. They proved so popular that in the eighteenth century John Chapman (popularly known as "Johnny Appleseed") planted apple orchards across about 10,000 square miles of North America, using discarded apple seeds from cider-making plants.

A century later, apple growing in Australia took off when Mrs. Maria Smith cultivated the first Granny Smith apple in her garden in Sydney.

Above: Laxton's Fortune

Below: Braeburn—crisp, juicy apples that make excellent eating.

Varieties

With over 7,000 named varieties of apples, it would be impossible to list more than a tiny fraction. In any case, only about a dozen varieties are readily available in stores, although nurseries can supply many more to people who wish to grow apples in their gardens.

Growing your own apples will allow you to enjoy exotically flavored fruit, like the pineapple-flavored Pine Golden Pippin or Ananas Reinette, or the Winter Banana, which develops a creamy texture and a banana flavor when stored. D'Arcy Spice is a small golden apple with the flavors of cinnamon and allspice, while Anisa is one of several aniseed-flavored apples. Other apples are redolent of melon, strawberries, raspberries, peaches, lemon, and even fennel.

In some countries, including Britain and the United States, apples are categorized as eating or dessert fruit, or cooking apples. Other countries regard all apples as suitable for both eating or cooking. As for cider apples, many are disagreeably sour, but some are very pleasant to eat.

Below: Beauty of Bath

EATING APPLES

Ashmead's Kernel: These late-variety apples were first cultivated in Gloucestershire in the seventeenth century. Their flesh has a good acid/sugar balance and develops a strong, spicy, aniseed flavor in some seasons.

Beauty of Bath A beautiful, small, flattish green apple extensively flushed with red, with sharp, sweet, juicy flesh. Beauty of Bath apples should be eaten straight from the tree, as they rot almost as soon as they are picked. Consequently, you are unlikely to find this apple in stores.

Blenheim Orange This apple was discovered growing out of a wall in Blenheim Palace in England in the nineteenth century and was named by permission of the Duke of Marlborough, but it also has sixty-seven other names! It is a dual-purpose apple, good for both cooking and eating, with a pleasantly nutty flavor. It is suitable for cooking in dishes, such as apple charlotte and apple crumble, and for serving as a dessert fruit.

Braeburn This crisp, juicy apple with a smooth, pale green skin, heavily flushed with red, makes excellent eating. Braeburn apples need plenty of daylight to grow.

Above: Empire

Above left: Egremont Russet—this sweet, crisp apple is delicious served at the end of a meal with a wedge of strong-tasting cheese, such as farmhouse Cheddar or Lancashire.

Above: Cox's Orange Pippin

Cox's Orange Pippin A greenish yellow apple of medium size, with some orange-red russeting. The firm, crisp, juicy flesh of this sweet fruit, with its overtones of acidity, make it one of the world's best and most popular apples. Cox's Orange Pippins are excellent for cooking as well as eating raw.

Crispin Large, pale yellowish green apples with firm and juicy creamy-white flesh and a pleasant mild flavor.

Discovery Bred from the Worcester Pearmain, Discovery was the first apple to be commercially grown in Britain. It is particularly attractive for its highly colored bright red skin and contrasting hard, crisp white flesh. Best eaten straight from the tree.

Egremont Russet Russet apples have rough, porous skins that allow the water to evaporate, giving a denser flesh and intensifying the nutty flavor. Egremont Russet is the most readily available. It is golden russet in color, sometimes with a bright orange flush, and has a crisp texture and very sweet taste. It can be used for eating or cooking and goes superbly with cheese.

Elstar This sweet, crisp and juicy apple is a cross between Ingrid Marie and Golden Delicious. Originally bred in Holland, it is now grown extensively throughout Europe and in North America. Picked in mid-autumn, Elstar apples will keep for 3–4 months.

Empire A dark red American apple with a shiny skin, best for eating raw, but suitable for cooking. It has crisp, green, juicy flesh and a slightly tart flavor.

Left: Jonagold—these dual-purpose apples have a superb flavor.

Fuji This sweet apple has greenish yellow skin with a rosy blush and crisp, juicy white flesh. It is also suitable for cooking.

Gala This colorful eating apple from New Zealand has a yellow ground color flushed with bright orange and red. The yellow flesh is very sweet, juicy and crisp. It is at its best when absolutely fresh. Good for either cooking or eating. **Royal Gala** is similar, but red all over.

Golden Delicious Originally grown from a chance seedling in the United States, this conical, freckled, golden apple has become ubiquitous. At its peak, the cream flesh is juicy and crisp with a mild flavor; unfortunately, most commercially grown Golden Delicious are sold when they are under- or overripe and are consequently tasteless and mealy in texture. Golden Delicious are suitable for cooking or eating.

Granny Smith First grown in Australia by the eponymous "Granny" Smith, this largish

Right: Golden Delicious

all-purpose apple is bright green, becoming yellow as it ripens. Usually sold underripe, it has firm, crunchy flesh and a tart flavor.

Greensleeves This James Grieve/Golden Delicious cross has more flavor than a James Grieve and better acidity. It is an early-fruiting variety, which should be eaten immediately after picking.

Idared By far the favorite North American apple for making applesauce. American-grown fruits have a good acid flavor that is often lacking in European-grown apples.

James Grieve A Scottish apple raised in Edinburgh in the late nineteenth century, with tart, juicy flesh that bruises easily when handled. James Grieve is good for cooking and eating, but, like most early varieties, it does not store well and should be kept for no more than 2–3 weeks after picking.

Jonagold A hybrid of Jonathan and Golden Delicious, this large, round, green-tinged yellow apple has creamy

Above: Gala are best eaten very fresh, when the flesh is crisp and juicy.

Left: Katy

Right: Orleans Reinette

white flesh and a superb flavor. It can be used for cooking or eating.

Jonathan This smallish, round orange-red North American apple has white, juicy flesh and a fragrant, slightly acidic flavor. It can be used for cooking.

Katy A highly colored early apple bred in Sweden from the Worcester Pearmain. Its small size appeals to children, and its flesh is crisp, sweet and juicy. Katy apples are best eaten immediately after picking.

Kidd's Orange Red A New Zealand apple bred from Cox's Orange Pippin. These deliciously crisp apples are highly aromatic, but need many hours of sunshine to develop their full flavor and color, so they cannot be successfully grown in Northern Europe.

Laxton's Fortune A cross between Cox's Orange Pippin and Wealthy, these apples have yellowish skin heavily tinged with red, and sweet, juicy, lightly aromatic flesh. You are most likely to find them at farm stands.

Laxton's Superb Greenish yellow and partially covered with red, this all-purpose apple has crisp, very juicy flesh. It is sweet, with some acidity.

McIntosh A Canadian apple that is popular throughout North America. It is wonderfully decorative, with deep red waxy skin that can be polished to a

superb sheen, but the skin is quite tough. The pale flesh is melting (and sometimes mushy), with a hint of fresh strawberry flavor.

Orleans Reinette One of the best apples of all, this large orange-flecked russet has a rough skin but juicy, sweet, aromatic flesh. Orleans Reinette is ideal for cooking and eating.

Pink Lady A pretty Australian cross between Golden Delicious and Lady Williams, this large all-purpose apple has a mild flavor and is becoming increasing available in supermarkets and greengrocers.

Pomme d'Apis Also known as Lady Apple, this very attractive fruit has a yellow skin suffused with a bright red blush. Pomme d'Apis is a late apple with good keeping qualities.

Red Delicious This North American apple was first grown in the nineteenth century. It has an exceptionally sweet flavor,

Above: Pink Lady

Above: Spartan—a Canadian apple with a tough skin, but delicious, floral-scented flesh.

Left: Grown mostly in the United States, colorful Red Delicious is another apple with a tough skin that hides juicy, sweet flesh.

but tough skin. Red Delicious apples can be grown in Europe, but not always successfully.

Spartan Another Canadian apple raised in 1926 from McIntosh and Newton's Pippin. It inherits a tough skin from McIntosh, but tastes highly aromatic, with a floral perfume.

Worcester Pearmain A conical yellow apple flushed with bright red. The juicy white flesh has a hint of strawberry flavor. Worcester Pearmain are best eaten straight from the tree, but can also be used for cooking.

Above: Worcester Pearmain

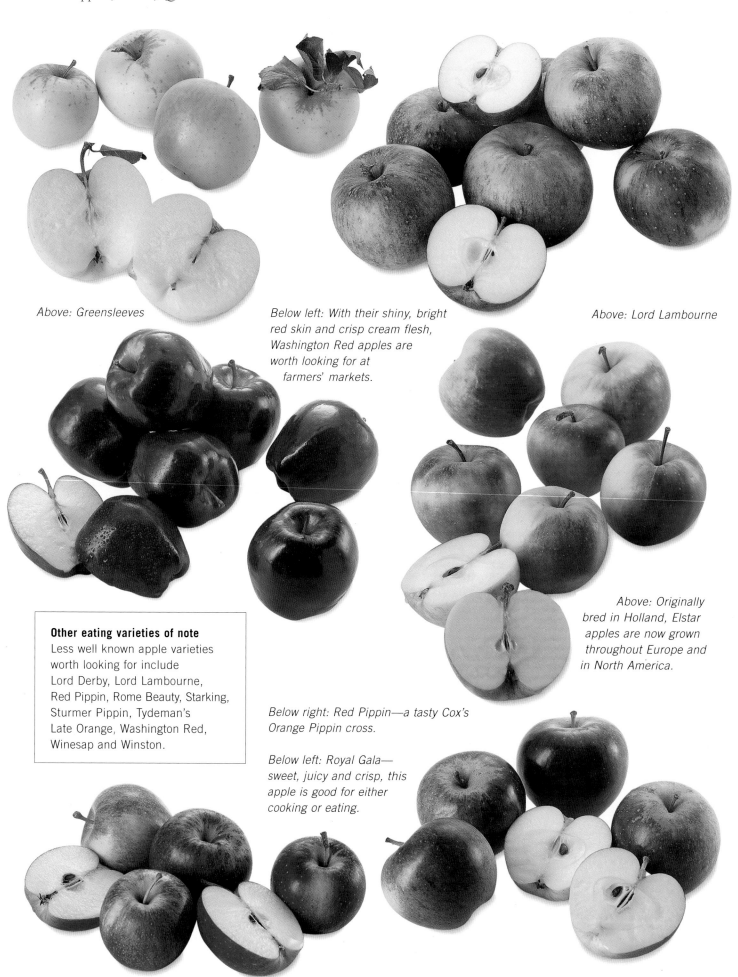

Above: Greensleeves

Below left: With their shiny, bright red skin and crisp cream flesh, Washington Red apples are worth looking for at farmers' markets.

Above: Lord Lambourne

Above: Originally bred in Holland, Elstar apples are now grown throughout Europe and in North America.

Other eating varieties of note
Less well known apple varieties worth looking for include Lord Derby, Lord Lambourne, Red Pippin, Rome Beauty, Starking, Sturmer Pippin, Tydeman's Late Orange, Washington Red, Winesap and Winston.

Below right: Red Pippin—a tasty Cox's Orange Pippin cross.

Below left: Royal Gala— sweet, juicy and crisp, this apple is good for either cooking or eating.

Above: Bramley's Seedling

Below: Howgate Wonder

COOKING APPLES

Bramley's Seedling The nonpareil of cookers, this large, flattish green apple (sometimes faintly flushed with red) has coarse, white, juicy, acid flesh that cooks into a frothy purée. Bramleys are perfect for baking or as the basis for applesauce.

Grenadier An irregularly shaped conical apple with yellow skin. The acid flesh is faintly green, firm and juicy. It breaks down during cooking. Grenadiers do not keep well.

Howgate Wonder This apple can grow to an enormous size—in 1997, the world record was achieved with a specimen weighing 3 pounds, 14 ounces! The juicy white flesh breaks up during cooking and has an uninspiring flavor, so this variety is grown mainly for exhibition.

Reverend W. Wilkes A very large conical apple with pale greenish-white skin. The fine, very white flesh is crisp, juicy and acidic. The apple can be eaten raw, but it is best as a cooker. It keeps well.

Nutrition

Apples were once believed to be the most nutritious of fruits, giving rise to the saying "an apple a day keeps the doctor away." In fact, they have fewer vitamins than many other fruits (although they contain some vitamins C and A), but are high in pectin and are a good source of dietary fiber. They provide 52 calories per 3¾ ounces.

Buying and Storing

Choose apples with undamaged skins, and never buy bruised fruits. If possible, smell the fruits to determine their fragrance (not easy when they are prebagged) and squeeze gently to make sure that they are firm. Do not be seduced by the skin color of an apple; those gorgeous-looking specimens with thick, vivid red, waxy skins often have mealy, tasteless flesh.

Apples continue to ripen after they have been picked, so their color and texture may change during storage. For short-term storage, they can be kept in a ventilated plastic bag in the refrigerator. To store pick-your-own apples, wrap each one in newspaper and place, folded side down, in a single layer in wooden or fiber trays. Keep in a cool, dry, dark place and check occasionally to make sure none has rotted. A bad fruit will taint all the others, so remove it immediately.

Dried Apples These have a sweet, concentrated flavor and are an extremely useful pantry ingredient. Eat them straight from the package

Below: Dried apple rings

Drying apples at home

1 Peel the apples, remove the cores and slice the fruit into rings. Soak in salted water for a few minutes to prevent discoloration.

2 Thread the apple rings onto string. Hang them from the ceiling or suspend across the room until they are completely dry.

3 Alternatively, arrange the rings in a single layer on a wire rack on a baking sheet, making sure that they are not touching. Place in an oven set to 150°F for several hours, until dried.

as a nutritious snack, add them to homemade muesli or soak them in water, then cook them in sweet and savory dishes like fruit compotes, applesauce or casseroles. Dried apples are available commercially, but it is easy to dry your own when there is a glut, and you can choose your favorite varieties. Russets are particularly delicious when dried.

Preparing

Most apples can be eaten with the skin on. To peel, use a vegetable peeler or small, sharp knife, either in a spiral following the circumference of the apple, or peeling downward in strips from stem to calyx. Peeled apples turn brown very quickly; brush them with lemon juice or drop them into water acidulated with lemon juice or cider vinegar immediately.

Cooking

Some apples are suitable only for eating raw, but most can be cooked in such classic sweet dishes as apple pies, crumbles and tarts, baked apples and strudel. Sweet apples combine well with other fruits, like blackberries, quinces and lemon, and dried fruits like raisins or cranberries. Aromatic spices like cinnamon, nutmeg and cloves highlight their flavor. Their high pectin content will help other fruit jellies and jams to set, or they can be made into apple jelly, apple cheese and chutney.

Tart apples make excellent accompaniments for game birds, sausages and rich meats like pork, duck and goose. They go well with red cabbage and are a vital ingredient in Waldorf salad.

To bake apples, core them with an apple corer and score around the circumference to prevent the skin from bursting. Stuff with dried fruit, nuts, butter and sugar and bake in a preheated oven at 350°F until soft.

To cook sliced apples and rings, sauté in butter and sugar to help them keep their shape. To stew, cook in the minimum amount of water or with butter and seasonings.

Making applesauce

1 Peel, core and thickly slice the apples, immediately dropping the pieces into a bowl of cold water acidulated with lemon juice or cider vinegar.

2 Barely cover the bottom of a saucepan with cold water. Add the apple pieces and cook to a purée, adding sugar to taste toward the end.

3 If you are using firmer dessert apples, which will not disintegrate to a purée, cook until very tender, then rub through a coarse strainer.

CRAB APPLES AND CIDER APPLES

Crab apples have grown wild for thousands of years and were eaten in prehistoric times. The fruits are smaller and often more colorful than cultivated varieties. Nowadays crab apples are often grown for their ornamental qualities. The fruits can be vivid yellow, green, orange or bright red.

Crab apples are seldom worth eating raw (and may be completely inedible), although some are perfectly palatable for those without too sweet a tooth. You may find larger self-seeded wild apples, which have grown from the seeds of cultivated apples that have become wild; these can be eaten.

Thanks to their high pectin content, all crab apples make wonderful jellies, either on their own or mixed with other wild fruits, such as hawthorn berries.

Cider apples are closer to eating apples than crab apples, but usually have a bitter or sour flavor due to their high tannin content. There

Below: Crab apples are almost always too sour to eat raw.

are hundreds of different varieties with wonderful names like Strawberry Norma and Foxwhelp, and each local grower will insist that his is the best. Some, like Tom Putt, are sweet enough to eat; these are used to make sweet cider.

Apple Drinks

Apple juice and sweet apple cider, hard (alcoholic) cider and apple brandies, such as Calvados, are the main drinks made from apples. Apple juice is made by crushing dessert apples; the best is pressed from a single variety, such as Cox's Orange Pippin or Russet, but most commercial apple juices are made from a mixture of varieties or, worse, from concentrate.

Cider may have been brought to Britain by the Phoenicians or the Celts; it has certainly been around for thousands of years. It is a fermented drink made from the juice of cider apples and, depending on the variety of fruit and

Left: Cider—the best is still made by artisan producers.

Right and far right: Calvados and applejack are both types of apple brandy.

pressing technique, can range from sweet and bubbly to cloudy and flat. The best ciders are still made by small producers using artisanal methods; some of these ciders can be very strong. The strongest and crudest cider is scrumpy. It is made from the apples of the poorest quality, but can certainly pack a punch!

Apple brandy is made from fermented and distilled apple juice. The best of all is Calvados, the famous apple brandy from Normandy, which is double-distilled and aged in oak. Calvados may only be produced within a defined area; other apple brandies must be labeled *eau-de-vie de cidre* or simply "apple brandy" ("applejack" in North America).

Fermented apple juice can also be made into cider vinegar, which has a strong apple taste and is excellent for making fruit chutneys or adding extra flavor to casseroles containing apples.

PEARS

There are almost as many varieties of pears as there are apples, but only a dozen or so are available commercially. Pears are related to apples, but are more fragile and are more often eaten raw than cooked. They have fine, white, granular flesh and a central core containing the seeds. Most pears have the familiar shape, wider at the bottom than the top, but some are apple-shaped, while "calabash" pears have an elongated neck, like a gourd. Pears are less vividly colored than apples, generally varying from bronze to gold, green or yellow, but there are some beautiful red varieties, too.

History

Wild pears are native to Europe and Asia, where they have grown since prehistoric times. They were cultivated by the ancient Phoenicians and the Romans, and they became a royal delicacy for the ancient Persian kings. Their popularity spread so fast that in medieval Italy over 200 varieties of

Below: Beurré Bosc

Right: Anjou pears are sweet, juicy and aromatic.

pear were cultivated. By the seventeenth century, the French were growing 300 different varieties, inspired by Louis XIV's passion for the fruit. There are now said to be more than 5,000 named varieties throughout the world.

Varieties

Cooking pears (which cannot be eaten raw) do exist, but almost all the pears available in stores are dessert fruit, which can also be cooked. Pears are seasonal, so only a few varieties are available at any one time.

Anjou These large pears have greenish yellow skin with brown speckles or russeting. The flesh is juicy and sweet. Suitable for eating and cooking.

Bartlett These irregularly shaped pears are generally swollen on one side of the stem. The speckled skin is golden yellow with russet patches and sometimes a red tinge. The delicious tender flesh is creamy white and very juicy, and the flavor is sweet and slightly musky. Unfortunately, these superb pears do not keep well. Bartletts are suitable for cooking and eating. (Bartlett is an old English pear also known as Williams Bon Chrétien.)

Beth This modern pear variety resembles the Bartlett in flavor and texture but has the added advantage of keeping longer.

Beurré Bosc and **Beurré Hardi** These elongated pears have an uneven green-gold skin, which becomes yellow and completely russeted as the fruit ripens. The creamy white flesh is firm and juicy with a buttery texture (hence the name, which means "buttered"), and the flavor is deliciously sweet and aromatic, with some acidity. Both varieties are excellent for eating and cooking.

Beurré Superfin These medium-to-large pears are round-conical in shape. Their uneven, almost knobbly skin is pale greenish yellow, which changes to yellow with bronze russeting as they ripen. The creamy-white flesh is firm and buttery and extremely juicy, with a sweet flavor and a hint of acidity. A truly delicious pear.

Comice This large, roundish pear (also know as Doyenné du Comice) is one of the finest of all, with creamy white, melting, very juicy flesh and a sweet, aromatic flavor. The thick, yellowish green skin is covered with speckles and patches of russeting. Comice are best eaten raw, and are delicious with Brie or Camembert.

Conference First cultivated in Berkshire in 1770, these long, conical pears have remained a favorite in Britain, largely because they keep so well. The yellowish green skin with extensive

Below: Conference are one of the best-loved English pears.

russeting turns yellower when the pears are mature. The granular flesh is tender, sweet and juicy. Excellent for eating and cooking.

Forelle A beautiful golden pear with a dark red flush on one side. The grainy flesh is crisp, with a fresh flavor that goes well with cheese, but is at its best when cooked.

Josephine de Malines A French pear, first raised in 1830. The medium-size fruits are round-conical in shape, with yellowish green skin flushed with red and some russeting, The tender flesh can be white or pinkish and is very juicy, with an aromatic flavor. It has good keeping qualities.

Merton Pride An exceptionally sweet and juicy pear with a superb flavor. The conical fruits have yellow skin with brown freckles.

Onward A cross between Laxton's Superb and Comice, these roundish pears are best peeled before eating, as they have ribbed skin. The yellowish green skin is flushed with red and mottled with pale russeting. The creamy white flesh is exceptionally good—soft, melting, juicy and very sweet.

Above: Doyenné du Comice, also known simply as Comice, are very juicy and aromatic.

Right: Forelle are ideal pears to use for cooking.

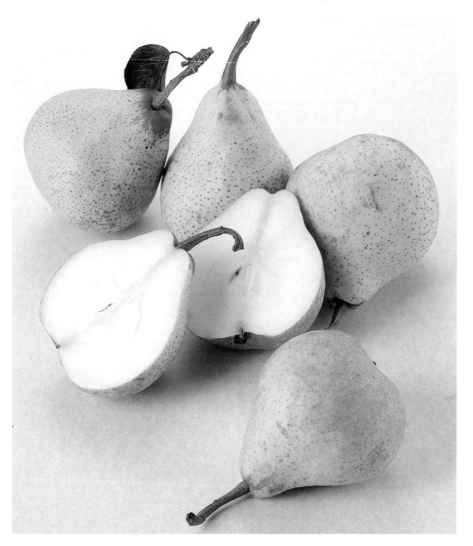

Packham's Triumph The first successful Australian pear was produced by Charles Packham in 1896 and remains a favorite. A largish dessert pear, it has a smooth, green, lightly russeted skin, which changes to yellow as it ripens. The soft white flesh is succulent and sweet, with a touch of acidity.

Passacrena Very plump, roundish pears with russeted greenish yellow skin. The flesh can sometimes be rather gritty, but is very juicy and sweet.

Red Bartlett These pears have shiny, speckled skins, at first green with a red blush, turning to yellow flushed with red. The flesh is sweet and juicy.

Rocha A Portuguese pear with greenish yellow skin with russet spotting and brown markings at the stem end. The firm white flesh has a sugary flavor and unlike many other pears, which pass their prime almost as soon as they reach it, the fruit remains in excellent condition for several days.

Winter Nelis This roundish medium-size pear has thick but tender greenish-yellow skin with cinnamon brown russeting and sometimes a pink flush. The creamy white flesh is soft and very juicy, and the flavor is sweet. These pears can be cooked or eaten raw.

Left: Packham's Triumph

Nutrition

Pears contain a small amount of vitamins A and C and some potassium and riboflavin. They provide about 60 calories per 3¾ ounce.

Pears should always be bought when they are in perfect condition, as they deteriorate quickly. Once past their best, they become mealy or soft and unpleasant. Test for ripeness by pressing the stem end between your forefinger and thumb; it should give a little, but the pear should still be quite firm. Once ripe, pears should be eaten within a couple of days, or they will become overripe. Keep ripe fruit in the bottom of the refrigerator.

Above: Suitable for both eating and cooking, Bartletts have delicious creamy white flesh. They don't keep well, so use them as soon as they are ripe.

Below: Juicy, with a red blush, Red Bartletts make excellent eating.

Above left: The firm-fleshed Rocha will remain in good condition for several days in your fruit bowl.

Dried pears Although dried pears are most often used in winter fruit compotes and savory casseroles, they have a delicate flavor and are delicious eaten raw. They are readily available in stores, but it is easy to prepare your own.

Canned pears Pears are among the most successful of all canned fruit and can be used to make almost any dessert that calls for cooked pears. They are often canned in heavy syrup, but are now available in the healthier alternative of apple juice. Purée drained canned pears, flavor them with pear liqueur, lemon or preserved ginger syrup and freeze for a quick and easy sorbet.

Preparing and Cooking

Most pears are eaten raw, by themselves or with a robust cheese, such as Gorgonzola, Parmesan, Stilton or Roquefort. They also make a good addition to winter salads. Whether or not to peel pears before eating raw is a matter of preference, but they should always be peeled before cooking. Pears discolor quickly once they are peeled, so immediately rub the cut surface with a little lemon juice or place in a bowl of acidulated water. For whole poached pears, simply peel,

Right: Dried pears

leaving on the stem. Use an apple corer to core the pears if you want to stuff them with nuts or dried fruit. Poach in port or red wine spiced with cinnamon, cloves and thinly pared lemon rind, or in a vanilla-flavored syrup. For sautéed or grilled pears, peel and quarter or halve the fruit and scoop out the cores with a melon baller.

Dessert or cooking pears can also be cooked in compotes, tarts, terrines, trifles and the famous Poires Belle Hélène (poached pears with vanilla ice cream and hot chocolate sauce). They make marvelous fritters and go very well with ingredients such as nuts and spices, port and marsala. Cooked pears are also excellent in savory dishes—with game and duck, for example—either made into chutney or braised with game birds or venison. They can be preserved with sugar and vinegar, or pickled with mustard seeds and horseradish. If you are cooking dessert pears, use them while they are still slightly underripe.

Pears can also be dried, canned, crystallized and distilled into spirits like *eau-de-vie de poires* and Poire William. The bottle in which this liqueur is sold sometimes contains a whole pear, an apparent illusion, as the neck is too narrow to allow the pear to pass. The effect is achieved by placing the bottle necks over the infant fruits on the tree so that each pear grows inside a bottle. When it has ripened, the bottle is topped up with the pear-flavored liqueur.

Left: Canned pears

Drying pears

1 Peel the pears and cut them in half lengthwise.

2 Scoop out the cores with a small melon baller, removing all the fibrous part of the fruit.

3 Brush them with lemon juice to prevent discoloration. Spread out in a single layer on a rack over a baking sheet and dry in an oven set to 150°F for several hours, until dried.

ASIAN OR NASHI PEARS

There are many varieties of Asian pear, but their characteristics are very similar. Round rather than pear-shaped, the fruits have a golden brown–russet skin and very crisp, white, juicy flesh. The crunchy texture resembles that of an apple but is more granular. It would be a shame to spoil the crisp texture by cooking. Asian pears are best eaten straight from the refrigerator, to be enjoyed as a "drink on a stalk." They also make excellent additions to fruit salads or savory winter salads.

HOSUI PEARS

These pears have much the same crunch and juiciness of Tientsin pears but look much more like apples, with greeny brown mottled flesh that tastes like a cross between an apple and an unripe pear.

PERRY PEARS

With the demise of the most famous of the sparkling alcoholic pear drinks, perry pears have largely fallen into disfavor. A few small producers still press perry pears into juice, wine or "champagne" perry, but although there

Left: Tientsin pears are best eaten chilled.

are still about 300 known varieties, you will never find these fruit in stores. Perry pears are smaller than their dessert counterparts. Although they look delicious, they contain large quantities of tannin and taste bitter and astringent, whether they are eaten raw or cooked.

TIENTSIN PEARS

These Asian pears from China and Korea are very similar to Asian Nashi pears in taste and texture. They are available when Asian pears are out of season. They look rather like elongated apples, tapering gently at both ends, The skin is pale yellow, slightly speckled with light brown. The pure white flesh is exceptionally juicy and crunchy—perfect for a hot day. Tientsin pears are best eaten chilled to appreciate their refreshing quality, and make the perfect healthy alternative to popsicles.

Left: Asian pears are round rather than pear-shaped, and their crunchy texture resembles that of apples too.

QUINCES

These highly aromatic fruits are known as "apple" or "pear" quinces, according to their shape. Unripe fruits have a downy skin, while ripe quinces have the smooth texture of a pear. Raw quinces are inedible, but they make excellent natural air fresheners—a quince kept in the glove compartment will shrivel but not rot, and will fill your car with the most delicious aroma for up to six months.

History

Quinces originated in Turkestan and Persia. It is said that they were the mythical golden apples of the Hesperides and that the golden apple Paris gave to Aphrodite, the goddess of love, was in fact a quince. To the

Above: Quinces may have been the mythical golden apples of the Hesperides.

ancient Greeks and Romans, quinces were a symbol of happiness, love and fruitfulness. The fruits were widely grown in Britain from the sixteenth to the eighteenth century, but their popularity has declined. In Spain, however, they are still highly prized and are used to make a thick fruit paste called *membrillo*.

Choosing and Storing

Quinces are available in stores in October and November. The skin of ripe quinces should be uniformly golden yellow; unripe fruit may still have patches of down, which can be rubbed off. Quinces keep well—the best way to store them is in a bowl in your kitchen or living room. They will fill the room with their delicious scent.

Preparing and Cooking

Quinces are always cooked. They are prepared in much the same way as pears. For jellies and fruit pastes, the skin is left on, as it contributes valuable pectin, as do the seeds (the word "marmalade" comes from the Portuguese word for quince, *marmelo*). Quince jelly can be spread on bread or served with pork and game. Quinces can be baked whole like apples or pears, stuffed with a rich mixture of butter, sugar and cream. One or two quinces also make a good addition to an apple pie. Peel and slice the quinces (this will be easier to achieve if you

---

Quince jelly
Makes about 4½ pounds

1 Roughly chop 2¼ pounds quinces. Put in a large, heavy pan with 8 cups of water.

2 Bring to a boil, then simmer until the quinces are very tender.

3 Pour into a jelly bag set over a bowl; let the juice run through, but do not squeeze the bag or the finished jelly will be cloudy.

4 Measure the strained juice and pour into a large, heavy pan. Add 2½ cups preserving sugar for each 2½ cups of the juice. Bring to a boil, stirring until the sugar has dissolved completely. Boil rapidly until the setting point is reached.

5 Skim the jelly and pour into sterilized jars. Cover the jars while the jelly is still hot, then label once the jars are cool enough to handle.

parboil them for 10 minutes), then toss them with the apple slices, sugar and cinnamon before layering them in the pie.

In Spain, quince pulp is boiled with sugar to make the fruit paste *membrillo*, which is then cooled, cut into squares and served with soft cheeses or as a sweet. The French equivalent is known as *cotignac*, while quince cheese is similar, but softer and more spreadable.

Quinces marry well with almost all meats, from poultry to beef and game, and also make a wonderful scented addition to spirits such as vodka, grappa or eau-de-vie.

Japonica Quince

As the name suggests, this cultivated quince came originally from Japan. The hard yellowish fruits are virtually inedible raw, but can be cooked and used like quinces. Their perfume is less intense, but they are still sufficiently aromatic to make an excellent addition to pies and tarts. They can also be made into both quince jelly and quince cheese.

Above: Japonica quinces are not edible raw, but they make a wonderful jelly.

MEDLARS

Medlar trees resemble pear trees, but the fruits are quite different. They look rather like large, golden brown rose hips with a russeted skin and a distinctive open five-pointed calyx end. They are eaten when overripe, almost rotten. The process is known as "bletting" and is traditionally achieved by spreading out unripe fruit on straw and leaving it to decay for several weeks, by which time the flesh can be spooned out. To speed up the bletting process, whole unripe medlars can be frozen to break up the cell structure, then left to decay at room temperature. The flesh has a dry, sticky texture. It tastes a little like the flesh of dried dates, but is tarter. Medlars are not to everyone's taste; the nineteenth-century horticulturalist George Bunyard described several different varieties of medlar as "all of equal unpleasantness."

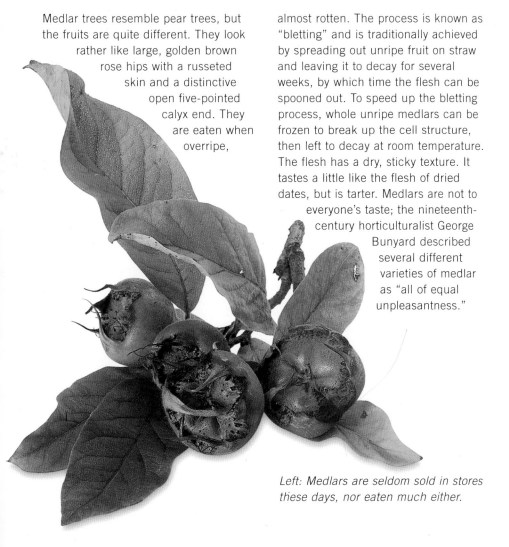

Left: Medlars are seldom sold in stores these days, nor eaten much either.

History

Medlars originated in the Transcaucasus, but are found growing wild in Asia Minor and southern Europe. They were cultivated by the Assyrians, who introduced them to ancient Greece. In Victorian times in England, they were often enjoyed at the end of a meal with the port, but they are seldom eaten today.

Choosing and Storing

Medlars are not available in stores in the United States, but are sometimes cultivated or found growing wild. They are extremely hard and, if left on the tree, are unlikely to ripen sufficiently to be eaten. They are therefore picked in their unripe state and left to "blet." A bletted medlar will be soft and yielding to the touch.

Preparing and Cooking

To eat bletted medlars raw, peel back the skin from the five points of the calyx and suck out the flesh, leaving the five seeds behind, or scrape it out with a spoon. Unripe medlars can be used with bletted fruits to make medlar jelly, or baked to make a thick sauce that goes well with rich meats. Medlar jelly is made in the same way as quince jelly.

STONE FRUITS

One of life's greatest joys is to bite into a perfectly ripe, juicy stone

fruit and savor the wonderful sweetness of the sticky juices.

Stone fruits herald summer—the season starts with cherries,

continues with sun-drenched peaches and apricots, and ends with

plums, from gorgeous greengages to fat, juicy Victorias. Although

stone fruits (or "drupes") may seem very different, they are all

members of the prunus family and share the characteristics of soft,

juicy flesh and a single pit. Stone fruits are often grown in

greenhouses, but nothing beats the taste of a sun-ripened fruit,

so it is worth waiting until they are in season.

PEACHES

Sometimes known as the "queen of fruits," peaches are certainly among the most beautiful. Their downy, velvety skin is yellow flushed with red, and they are voluptuously curvaceous—the French call one variety *tétons de Venus* (the breasts of Venus).

The most familiar peaches are round or "beaked" with a pointed end, but they can also be flat and disk-shaped. The delicate fine-textured flesh, which can be yellow, white or tinged with red, encloses a heavily ridged pit. In some peaches, the flesh clings firmly to the pit; these are known as "clingstone." In "freestone" fruit, the flesh comes away easily and cleanly from the pit.

Peaches and nectarines originated from the same species and are very similar, except that peaches have fuzzy skin, while nectarines are smooth. So alike are they that peach trees sometimes spontaneously produce nectarines and vice versa.

History

Peaches have been grown in China since the fifth century BC and are regarded as a symbol of longevity and immortality. Even today, some Chinese families place peach trees or branches outside their front doors to ward off evil spirits. Peaches were taken along the old silk routes to Persia, where they were discovered by Alexander the Great, who introduced them to the Greeks and Romans; the word "peach" comes from the Latin *Persicum malum* (Persian apple). Immensely popular in Europe, peaches were introduced to America by Christopher Columbus and spread so profusely that they were once thought to be indigenous. Nowadays, so many are grown in Georgia that it is known as "the Peach State."

Varieties

Peaches are seldom sold by variety, but by the color of their flesh—yellow or white. Which you choose is a matter of preference; some people believe that white peaches have the finer flavor.

Above: Mireille, a white-fleshed peach.

Yellow varieties include Elegant Lady, Royal George and Bellegarde. Mireille is a popular white peach. The finest peaches of all are the *pêches de vigne,* small red-fleshed fruits that are grown in vineyards. They do not look particularly attractive, being covered in grayish down, but the flavor is superb. You are unlikely to find them outside markets in France.

Nutrition

Peaches are a source of vitamins A, B and C and provide about 60 calories per 3¾ ounces.

Buying and Storing

Peaches do not ripen successfully after picking, so always buy ripe fruit. The fruits should be handled carefully. Press gently to make sure that they are firm, with some "give." Never buy greenish peaches, except for chutney making, and avoid fruit with bruised skin. Peaches do not keep well. Firm fruit can be kept at room temperature for a day or two to soften; ripe peaches can be kept in the refrigerator for not more than two days.

Left: Elegant Lady—a popular yellow variety of peach.

Dried peaches These are not as widely available as dried apricots, but are becoming increasingly popular. Use them in compotes and cakes, or eat them on their own. Peaches are also crystallized or glacéed (candied).

Canned peaches Available in syrup or apple juice, canned peaches are fine for cooking, but lack the delicate texture and flavor of the fresh fruit.

Above: Dried peaches

Glacé peaches The fruits are coated in a thick syrup, which hardens to a shiny glaze. Glacé peaches are often included in boxes of assorted glacé fruits. They are very sweet, with a melting texture.

Preparing and Serving

A really ripe peach is delicious eaten on its own or in a fruit salad. Peaches combine well with most other fruits and nuts, particularly raspberries, a marriage that inspired Escoffier to create his famous dessert Peach Melba, in honor of the great singer Dame Nellie Melba.

Above: Glacé peaches are coated in a thick sugar syrup and are very sweet.

Pitting a peach or nectarine

1 Slice through the seam line all around the peach.

2 Twist the two halves in opposite directions to separate them.

3 Lever out the pit with a knife.

Left: Canned peaches, available in halves or slices, are fine for cooking but lack the flavor of the fresh fruit.

Fresh peaches feature in ice cream sundaes and can be used to make luxurious drinks like the Bellini (Champagne, peach liqueur and crushed peach pulp) or Champagne cocktails. They are also made into liqueurs and peach wine and brandy.

The fuzzy skin of a peach is not particularly pleasant to eat, so the fruit is best peeled. Nick the fruit, place it in a heatproof bowl and pour boiling water over. Leave for 15–30 seconds, depending on how ripe the fruits are, then drain and refresh in cold water. The skins will peel off easily.

Cooking and Serving

Peaches can be cooked in a multitude of ways—poached whole in vanilla-flavored syrup or wine; macerated in alcohol; in compotes, soufflés, pies,

tarts, pancakes, ice creams and sorbets. They make very good jams and jellies, while spiced peaches are delicious with cured or cold meats. Underripe green-tinged peaches can be made into excellent relishes and chutneys.

Peaches are also good, raw or cooked, in salads, and are natural partners for ham and duck. They can be substituted for mangoes in Southeast Asian dishes and are particularly good with crab and lobster.

To poach peaches in syrup, put 4 cups water in a pan. Add 2 cups sugar, 2 strips of pared lemon rind, a piece of cinnamon and half a split vanilla bean. Bring to a boil, stirring to

dissolve the sugar. Boil for about 5 minutes, then add six to eight peeled peaches (whole or halved) and poach gently until tender, turning occasionally. Let the fruit cool in the syrup.

Peaches make a delicious sweet after-dinner liqueur, Crème de Peche, which can be drunk on its own or combined with Champagne or sparking white wine to make an unusual cocktail. To make a classic Bellini, put some fresh peach pulp in a champagne glass, add a teaspoon of peach liqueur and top up with Champagne.

Left: Peach liqueur

NECTARINES

The botanical name for nectarines is *Prunus persican*, meaning "Persian plum," although these smooth-skinned fruits are a variant of peaches and natives of China. They taste very similar to peaches, with a touch more acidity. The flesh can be yellow, white or pinkish and is delicate and sweet. Unlike peaches, they

do not require peeling, so some people prefer them as a dessert fruit. They can be prepared and cooked in exactly the same way as peaches. Nectarines are sometimes crossed with peaches, but the fuzzy peach skin is generally dominant, so the hybrids are often actually peaches.

Left: Smooth-skinned white nectarines

Nutrition

Nectarines have a lower calorie count than peaches (containing only about 45 calories per 3¾ ounces). They are a good source of potassium and phosphorus, dietary fiber and vitamins A and C.

Buying and Storing

Like peaches, nectarines do not continue to mature after picking, so choose ripe fruit. The skins should be bright and smooth, with no blemishes or wrinkles. Nectarines can be kept at room temperature or in the refrigerator for two or three days.

Left: Yellow nectarines

APRICOTS

These round, yellow-orange fruit have velvety skins flushed with pink. The flesh is firm, sweet and fragrant, and contains little juice. The kernel of the pit (poisonous until it is cooked) is used to flavor jams, cookies and Amaretto liqueur.

History

Apricots grew wild in China thousands of years ago and were introduced to Persia and Armenia, from where they got their Latin name, *Prunus armeniaca.* Alexander the Great brought apricots to Southern Europe; they were prized by the Romans and Greeks, who called them "golden eggs of the sun." They were first successfully cultivated in Northern Europe in the sixteenth century.

Nutrition

Apricots contain the antioxidant beta-carotene, and are a rich source of minerals and vitamin A. An average 2½-ounce apricot provides only 20 calories.

Above: Turkish sun-dried apricots

Below: Dried apricots

Left: Ripe apricots are deliciously fragrant.

Buying and Storing

Apricots do not travel well, nor do they continue to ripen after picking, so those that you buy may be disappointing. Look for plump fruit with a rich color and smooth skin. Do not buy dull-looking or greenish fruit, as their flesh will be mealy. Keep apricots at room temperature for a couple of days, or store in a plastic bag in the refrigerator for up to five days.

Dried and canned apricots Because apricots are so delicate, they are often preserved by drying or canning. The best dried apricots come from Turkey; they are burnished orange and have a rich flavor. Dried apricots can be substituted for fresh apricots and make excellent jams. Use them just as they are in slow-cooked dishes that contain plenty of liquid, like stews and casseroles, but, unless they are plump, soak them in warm water for a couple of hours before using them in sweet dishes.

Preparing and Cooking

Ripe apricots are delicious raw and can be used in fruit salads and platters. Because the flesh is dry, they will not

Right: Canned apricots

disintegrate during cooking, which makes them ideal for tarts and Danish pastries. Apricots can be poached in syrup or sweet white wine and served with yogurt or spice-flavored ice cream; they are also very tasty when halved, stuffed with crushed amaretti cookies and baked, or caramelized and served over French toast. Apricots make wonderful jams and conserves.

Both fresh and dried apricots make frequent appearances in Middle Eastern and North African recipes, where they go particularly well with lamb, poultry and rice dishes.

PLUMS

There are thousands of varieties of plum, all differing in size, shape, color and flavor. These members of the rose family originate from three main types—European, Japanese and Western Asian. The skins can vary from blue-black to purple, red, green and yellow. They have a long season, and one variety or another is available almost all year round. All plums have smooth skins with a bloom and juicy flesh with plenty of acidity.

Dessert plums can be eaten on their own; they are usually larger than cooking plums (up to 4 inches long) and are sweet and very juicy. Cooking plums are drier, with tart flesh that is ideal for pies, tarts and cakes.

History

Wild plums originated in Asia at least 2,000 years ago. They were first cultivated by the Assyrians, then adopted by the Romans, who hybridized them with great enthusiasm; the historian Pliny wrote of the huge numbers of plum crossbreeds available. The Crusaders brought plums to Europe, where they became highly prized. Nowadays they are grown in almost all temperate countries.

Varieties

There are over 2,000 varieties of plum, ripening at different times throughout summer and autumn, although only a dozen or so are available in stores. Japanese varieties are large, round and juicy; they can be purplish red with orange flesh, or orangey yellow

Right: Victorias are the most prolific dessert plum.

with yellow flesh. On the whole, dark-colored plums have bitter skins, while the red and yellow varieties tend to be sweeter. Most dessert plums can be cooked as well as eaten raw.

DESSERT PLUMS

Denniston's Superb An early variety of plum, with medium-size green fruits flushed with red. These plums have an excellent, sweet flavor.

Gaviota These large, round plums have yellow skins deeply tinged with scarlet, and sweet, juicy red flesh. They are best eaten raw.

Marjorie's Seedling These small purple plums with a green flush have bitter skins and sweet, green, almost translucent flesh. They are good for eating and cooking.

Santa Rosa and **Burbank** Large and round, with bright red skins, these two North American varieties of plum are mainly grown in California. They have juicy, deep yellow flesh and a pleasantly tart flavor, which makes them good for both cooking and eating.

Above: Mirabelles—the golden-skinned variety of these small wild plums, which grow on long stems like cherries, are best cooked.

Victoria The most prolific of all dessert plums, Victorias were first cultivated in 1840 from a stray seedling found in Sussex, England. Since then, these large oval fruits with yellow skins flushed with scarlet and sweet, juicy flesh have become ubiquitous. They are good for canning, stewing or eating raw.

Left: Marjorie's Seedlings have sweet, almost translucent green flesh and are good for cooking and eating.

COOKING PLUMS

Beach plums These small plums grow wild along the Atlantic coast of North America, especially near Cape Cod. They have dark purplish black skins and tart flesh that makes them unsuitable for eating raw, but they make excellent jams and jellies.

Cherry plums or **mirabelles** These very small wild plums are round and grow on long stems like cherries. They have black, red or yellow skins, which can taste rather bitter, but all have sweet, juicy flesh. These plums can be eaten raw, but are best stewed or baked, or made into jams, sauces and jellies. Golden mirabelles are delicious in tarts and soufflés, and are also made into a plum eau-de-vie, called *mirabelle*.

Czar Large, rather acidic dark blue-black plums with golden flesh, these can be eaten raw but are more usually used for cooking. They are best eaten straight from the tree.

Nutrition

Plums contain more antioxidant than any other fruit. They provide about 40 calories per 3¾ ounces.

Buying and Storing

Plums are delicate, so make sure that the ones you buy are unblemished. They should be plump and firm, with some "give" (but never squashy), and they should be fully colored for their variety. Plums should always have a pleasant aroma.

These fruit ripen fast and quickly become overripe, so store them in the refrigerator for only a day or two. For cooking at a

Above: Angelino—the skin color varies from red to almost black, but the flesh of these plums is always yellow.

Left: Sweet-tasting Avalon plums.

Below: Red-fleshed Spanish Autumn Rose plums.

Quetsch Also known as *svetsch* or *Zwetschen,* these small purplish black plums have a beautiful bloom. Although their flesh is sweet, they are seldom eaten raw, but are used in Eastern Europe to make plum breads and *pflaumenkuchen, a* yeast bread topped with purple plums. Quetsch plums are also used for making slivovitz and other plum brandies.

Other varieties of note

Angelino, Autumn Rose, Avalon, Circiela Queen Rose, Reeves Seedling, Stanley and Sungold later date, plums can be frozen: Halve the fruit and remove the pits. Place on trays and open-freeze, then pack the fruit into freezer bags and seal.

Preparing and Cooking

Dessert plums are delicious eaten on their own. Dual varieties (suitable for eating and cooking) and cooking plums make excellent pies and tarts, compotes, crumbles, dumplings, sauces, mousses and soufflés. They can be poached, baked or stewed, either whole or in halves or slices. It is not recommended that plums with tough skins be cooked in the microwave, as they will not soften in the short cooking time. Cook plums until just tender; do not let them disintegrate. Plums make tasty ice cream, and the poached fruit goes very well with ice creams flavored with spices like cardamom, nutmeg and cinnamon.

Plums work extremely well in savory dishes. The Chinese make them into a thick sweet-sour sauce to serve with Peking duck, lamb or pork. Spiced stewed plums are good with ham, cured meats, terrines and poultry. Plums add a special flavor to beef or lamb casseroles.

Plums also make superb jams and jellies. They can be preserved in many different

Above: Circiela Queen Rose

Below: Reeves Seedling

Below: Stanley

ways: dried (as prunes), crystallized and candied, bottled or made into wine and liqueurs like slivovitz and plum brandy.

Preserved plums There are many ways of preserving plums, the best known being by drying them as prunes. In Spain, Elvas plums are partially dried, then rolled in sugar. The Portuguese candy sweet greengages, while Carlsbad plums (named after the spa town, now Karlovy Vary) are a speciality of the Czech Republic. These plums (usually Quetsch) are candied in hot syrup until shriveled, then halved and stuffed into dried damsons. The process gives them a very intense flavor. Carlsbad plums are considered a great delicacy and are packed in attractive wooden boxes.

Soaking prunes

Prunes must be soaked for at least 4 hours before using. Place in a bowl and cover with cold water or tepid weak tea for added flavor. Leave overnight if possible to plump up. For compotes and purées it is not necessary to soak the prunes; cook them directly in wine, water or fruit juice until they are very tender.

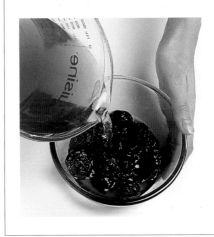

Prunes These wrinkled dried purple or red plums can be prepared in various ways. The plums can be left to dry naturally on the tree, but are more often sun-dried. They can also be desiccated in a low oven. The finest variety of "pruning" plum is the Agen, which is grown in France and California. These prunes are sold complete with pits and must be soaked overnight before being cooked.

Left: Chinese plum sauce has a wonderful sweet-sour flavor and is classically served with Peking duck.

Nowadays, pitted no-soak prunes are also widely available, but they tend to be flabbier than the traditional variety. Apart from their famed laxative qualities, prunes have other healthful properties. They are said to be an excellent cure for hangovers, give a great energy boost, and are purported to be an aphrodisiac.

Culinary Uses

Cooked prunes are traditionally served with custard, but they are equally good with thick cream. They make excellent ice cream, especially when combined with Armagnac. Prunes are often used in savory dishes, particularly in Middle Eastern cooking, and they go extremely well with pork and chicken. They are an essential ingredient in Scottish cock-a-leekie soup. They go well with citrus flavors and can be made into a compote with red wine and orange or lemon zest.

Below: California prunes

Left: Slivovitz—black Madjarka plums are crushed with their pits and slowly fermented to make this eau-de-vie from Croatia.

Puréed prunes can be sweetened, then spiced with a little ground cinnamon or nutmeg and served as a sauce with vanilla ice cream.

Below: French Agen prunes

GREENGAGES

These small members of the plum family have green skins, sometimes tinged with yellow or rose pink, which turn golden as the fruit ripens. There are many varieties of greengage; all have firm flesh and a delicious honeyed flavor. "Transparent" gages have fine, translucent flesh; if you hold the fruit up to the light, you can clearly see the shadow of the pit. These golden gages have a particularly sweet flavor.

History

Wild greengages from Asia Minor were probably introduced to Britain by the Romans, but disappeared from cultivation until Sir Thomas Gage brought them from France in the eighteenth century (and gave them his name). In France, they are known as Reine-Claude after the wife of François I, who adored their sweet flavor.

Preparing and Cooking

The deliciously sweet flavor of greengages makes them ideal for eating raw. They can also be gently poached in syrup, puréed for mousses and fools or made into excellent compotes and jam.

Below: Greengages, named after Sir Thomas Gage, have firm flesh with a deliciously sweet flavor.

DAMSONS

These small, plumlike fruits take their name from Damascus, which is probably where they originated. They have deep blue-black skins with an attractive bloom. The flavor is very strong and tart, which makes them more suitable for cooking than eating raw. Damsons grow wild, but are sometimes commercially available.

Preparing and Cooking

Damsons can be stewed and used in pies, tarts, ice creams and fools, but they are most commonly used for canning or for jams and jellies. Once cooked with sugar, they develop a pleasantly spicy flavor. A traditional old English sweetmeat is damson cheese, very thick fruit pulp boiled with sugar to make a solid jam similar to quince cheese, which can be eaten with bread and butter or biscuits.

The tart flavor of damsons makes them particularly suitable for savory dishes, such as pork or lamb casseroles. The fruit can also be made into wine or damson gin.

Above: Once cooked, damsons have a pleasantly spicy flavor.

Damson cheese

Damson cheese is a traditional English country dish with a very distinctive flavor that is an acquired taste. The "cheese" is potted and aged for several months before being eaten. To make 5½ pounds of damson cheese, put 3½ pounds of damsons in a saucepan, barely cover with water and simmer until the flesh is so tender that it falls off the pits. Strain the pulp, weigh it and return it to the pan with three-quarters of its weight in light brown sugar. Boil until the jam is clear, skimming the surface frequently. Pot the jam in oiled straight-sided containers, seal and store in a cool, dark place for at least two months. Serve with bread and butter, and eat with a knife and fork.

BULLACES

The small round plums known as "black bullaces" have bluish purple skins and mouth-puckeringly acid flesh. So-called "white" bullaces are pale greenish yellow. They can be found throughout Europe in late autumn growing in thorny hedgerows long after the other wild fruits like sloes and blackberries have finished. Although very tart and virtually inedible when raw, bullaces can be cooked with sugar to make pies and tarts. They are also good for jams and other preserves.

Right: The pale greenish yellow fruits known as "white" bullaces are almost inedible raw, but can be cooked with sugar to make delicious jams and jellies or a filling for pies.

SLOES

Sloes are the fruit of the blackthorn, a thorny shrub that grows wild throughout Europe (hence its botanical name, *Prunus spinosa,* which means "spiny plum"). These small wild fruits resemble tiny plums. The blue-black skins have a slight bloom. The flesh is highly astringent and cannot be eaten raw. Sloes ripen late and can be picked from the hedgerows in autumn, but they only become edible after the first frosts. They can be made into jams, jellies, sloe wine and liqueurs, but their chief claim to fame is that they are the principal ingredient of the irresistible sloe gin.

Make sloe gin as soon as the fruit is ripe, and with any luck you'll have a bottle ready in time for Christmas. For each 1¼ pint bottle of gin, you will need 2 cups sloes and a generous ½ cup sugar. Wash the sloes and prick them all over with a darning needle. Pack them loosely into a perfectly clean flagon or bottle, add the sugar and top up with gin. If you like, add two or three drops of pure almond extract and shake well. Seal and store for at least three months before drinking, shaking the bottles three times a week. If pricking the sloes seems like too much trouble, freeze them for several hours to crack the skin. Purists, however, allege that this compromises the flavor of the gin.

Left: Sloes are small wild fruits that grow in hedgerows throughout Europe. They are best picked in late autumn, after the first frosts.

CHERRIES

Cherry trees in blossom are one of the great delights of spring, followed in summer by clusters of bright, shiny fruit hanging in pairs from long, elegant stems. The skin of these small round stone fruits can vary in color from pale creamy yellow to deepest red to almost black. The firm, juicy flesh can be sweet or sour, depending on the variety, of which there are hundreds. Cherries are categorized into three main groups: sweet (for eating), sour (for cooking) and hybrids such as the nobly named Dukes and Royals, which are suitable for eating raw or cooking.

History

The original wild sweet cherries, known as *mazzards,* were found in Asia Minor and were cultivated by the Chinese 3,000 years ago. Mazzards were known to the ancient Egyptians, Greeks and Romans, and still exist today. Sour cherries were brought to Rome from Greece, and all modern varieties derive from these early specimens.

Varieties

Sweet cherries fall into two main groups: **bigarreaus,** with firm, crisp flesh, and **geans** or **guines,** with a softer texture. Today, there are also many hybrids. Sour cherries range from almost sweet to bitter and tart; they are full of flavor and are mainly used for preserving or in the manufacture of liqueurs.

SWEET CHERRIES

BIGARREAUS The best-known of these are the **Napoleons,** large pale yellow cherries tinged with light red. Their crisp fragrant flesh is slightly tart. **Bing** cherries are large, heart-shaped deep red fruit with a superb flavor. They are widely grown in North America.
GEANS/GUINES These fruits have soft, juicy flesh and come in many colors. **Black Tartarian** are deep purplish black from the skin right through to the pit. **Early Rivers** have dark purple skins and flesh, and very small pits. They are fragrant, sweet and juicy. **Ranier** has golden skin with a pink blush. The famous Swiss black cherry jam is made from intensely dark guines.

Above: Bright red Colney cherries.

Left: Napoleons are one of the sweet cherry varieties, with slightly crisp, tart, fragrant flesh.

Left: Widely grown in North America, sweet Bing cherries have a superb flavor.

SOUR CHERRIES

Most sour cherries are too tart to eat but are ideal for cooking. The two main types are **morello** and **amarelle**. Morellos have dark juice, and amarelles have light, almost colorless juice. The small, dark red morello cherries (known in France as *griottes*) are inedible raw, but are delicious preserved in either brandy or syrup.

Montmorency These are bright red cherries with a sweet-sour flavor. They have given their name to a range of dishes that include the fruit, from duck to pastries and ice creams.

English cherries are small, bright orange-red fruit with soft translucent flesh. They are mainly used for preserving in brandy.

Above: Dried sour Montmorency and Bing cherries

Left and below: Maraschino cherries may be bottled with their stems.

Right: Morello cherries, which are often preserved in brandy.

Maraschino cherries

These small wild fruit from Dalmatia are *damasca* or *amaresca* cherries. They are distilled into a colorless sweet, sticky Italian liqueur called Maraschino. The familiar bottled Maraschino cherries beloved of bartenders were originally damasca cherries preserved in Maraschino liqueur; nowadays, the vibrant red fruits sold as "maraschino" tend to be ordinary cherries tinted with artificial coloring and steeped in syrup flavored with bitter almonds. Check the label before buying.

Nutrition

Cherries contain vitamins A and C and some dietary fiber. Their calorie content varies with the type; sweet cherries provide about 77 calories per 3¾ ounces, while the same quantity of sour fruit provides about 56 calories.

Buying and Storing

Choose plump cherries with shiny, unblemished skins. It is best to buy them still on the stem. As a rule of thumb, pale cherries are very sweet, while dark cherries tend to be more acidic; if possible, taste before you buy.

Unwashed cherries will keep for a few days in the refrigerator; wash them just before serving. They can also be removed from their stems and frozen.

Preparing and Cooking

Sweet cherries often need no preparation other than washing and are best eaten on their own or in fruit salads. They make unusual sweets when left on the stem and dipped into melted dark chocolate. Pitted fresh cherries make a delicious filling for sponge cakes and meringues, or an attractive decoration for cakes and desserts. There is no reason not to cook with sweet cherries, but they may not have much flavor, due to their low acidity. Although fresh cherries can be served as they are, for cooking they should be pitted.

Cherries can be preserved by drying in the sun or in a low oven, by preserving in sugar or in brandy. Candied—or glacé—cherries are a popular ingredient in baking.

Dual-purpose and sour cherries can be cooked in tarts, pies, compotes and sauces. They go well with sweet spices, citrus flavors and chocolate; the classic combination of cherries and chocolate is found in Black Forest Cake. In Eastern Europe, they are made into a sweet-sour soup or pickled in spiced vinegar as an accompaniment for rich meats. Cherries go well with all game and are classically served with duck. Amarelle and morello cherries are used for making jam and preserves, or for crystallizing as glacé cherries.

Below: Brightly colored, sweet and sticky glacé cherries are a popular baking ingredient.

BERRIES AND CURRANTS

*Small wonders—that sums up the splendor of berries.
The glowing colors and delectable flavors of strawberries and
raspberries, gooseberries, currants, loganberries and blackberries
(to name but a few of the many varieties) give us immense
pleasure. Whether you brave the brambles or pick up a basket
at your local supermarket, these wonderful treats
are there for the taking.*

STRAWBERRIES

For centuries, strawberries have been the most highly prized soft fruit. A sixteenth-century enthusiast, on tasting his first strawberry, summed up their eternal appeal: "Doubtless God could have made a better berry, but doubtless He never did." Nowadays, greenhouse-grown strawberries are available all year round, but these fruits are at their seductive best when grown outdoors.

History

Cultivated strawberries derive from the small wild fraises des bois, tiny fragrant woodland fruits that grow in all temperate countries and were transplanted into kitchen gardens as early as Roman times. By the fourteenth century, the French had become strawberry enthusiasts, but it was another hundred years before the first bowls of strawberries and cream were served in England, at a banquet given by Cardinal Wolsey in 1509.

The cultivated strawberries we enjoy so much today were developed in the nineteenth century from small, scarlet wild strawberries from Virginia. These were crossed with the larger yellow Chilean pine strawberries, which the aptly named French Captain Frézier (the French word for strawberry is *fraise*) had brought to Brittany in 1712. Once the perfect balance of flavor and size had been achieved, enthusiasm for cultivated strawberries blossomed, and they remain one of the world's favorite fruits.

Varieties

Strawberries come in many different sizes, colors and shapes, ranging from conical to globular to oval or heart-shaped. New varieties are constantly being developed.

Left: Fraise des Bois liqueur is a wild-strawberry version of crème de fraise.

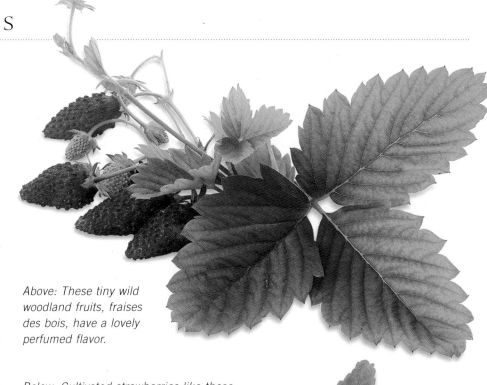

Above: These tiny wild woodland fruits, fraises des bois, have a lovely perfumed flavor.

Below: Cultivated strawberries like these are now one of the world's favorite fruits.

Below: Fragrantly scented and vanilla-flavored white fraises des bois.

Above: Gorella—conical-shaped and deep red when ripe.

Left: Cambridge Favorite—medium-size strawberries that are popular with both commercial growers and gardeners.

Below: Elsantas have a great flavor.

FRAISES DES BOIS

The smallest wild strawberries are the **Hautbois** (or wood) varieties, whose tiny red fruits taste wonderfully fragrant. **Alpine** strawberries are generally a little larger and less juicy, with a highly perfumed flavor. Yellow and white varieties look less appealing, but have a delicious flavor of vanilla.

SUMMER STRAWBERRIES

Cambridge Favorite Medium-size berries with an attractive color and flavor, this variety is indeed a favorite with strawberry growers large and small.
Elsanta Largish, firm berries with attractive glossy flesh and an excellent sweet flavor.
Elvira These Dutch strawberries were developed in the 1970s. The oval berries are a deep glossy red.
Gorella A deep red conical berry with paler red flesh. This is an extremely consistent variety.
Perpetual and remontant strawberries As their name implies, these late-season strawberries go on to fruit continuously throughout the autumn. Although they are juicier than summer berries, they are not as sweet, so are better for cooking than other varieties. They can be picked while they are still green and made into jams, sauces and compotes.

Preparing strawberries

1 Wipe the strawberries with a piece of damp paper towels.

2 Hold the strawberry between your thumb and forefinger and twist off the green frill and stem. Try to remove the central hull in the same movement.

Below: Chocolate-dipped strawberries make a delectable after-dinner treat, or a delightful decoration for chocolate cakes and desserts.

Nutrition

Strawberries are rich in vitamins B and C and contain considerable amounts of potassium, iron and fiber. Three and three-fourths ounces of strawberries provide fewer than 30 calories.

Buying and Storing

Size and color are not necessarily indications of quality. Some smaller, greenish varieties taste succulent and delicious. Try always to buy locally grown fruits and check those at the bottom of the pint, making sure they are not squashed or moldy.

Strawberries should ideally be eaten the day they are bought. If necessary, keep the berries in the refrigerator for a day or two, covering them with plastic wrap to prevent them from drying out and from permeating other foods with their scent. Remove from the refrigerator at least an hour before serving.

Frozen strawberries are never as good as fresh, as the texture collapses after freezing, but they are fine for sauces and ice cream. To freeze whole strawberries, sprinkle with a little sugar and pack in a single layer in a plastic box, or open-freeze on a tray, then pack in a rigid container. Puréed strawberries can be frozen with or without added sugar.

Preparing and Serving

It is best not to wash strawberries, as they easily become waterlogged. If they are very dirty, wipe them gently.

Really ripe strawberries need no other accompaniment than cream or crème fraîche and perhaps a little sugar. Improbable though this may sound, a grinding of black pepper or sprinkling of balsamic vinegar will bring out the flavor of the fruit. Strawberries are seldom improved by cooking, although they make delicious jam. They are best used in their raw state in such desserts as strawberry tartlets, shortcake and meringues. They have an affinity with chocolate and make a fine decoration for chocolate terrines and mousses, or they can be dipped into melted chocolate and served as petits fours.

To "dress up" strawberries, macerate them in red wine, Champagne or orange juice. The classic dish Strawberries Romanov simply consists of fresh strawberries macerated in orange juice and orange liqueur. Puréed strawberries can be served as a coulis or made into ice creams and sorbets.

Arbutus (tree strawberry)
The arbutus is a tall shrub whose bright red fruits look like strawberries but have a different taste. The sweet, spiky berries have a soft, slightly mushy texture and a faint flavor of vanilla. You will not find arbutus berries in stores, but the shrubs can be found growing in Europe, as far north as western Ireland (where they are known as Killarney strawberries), and in the United States and China. The berries are unexciting to eat raw, but are used to make jellies and liqueurs.

RASPBERRIES

Perhaps surprisingly, raspberries are a member of the rose family, as you might guess if you have ever been pricked by a raspberry thorn. Native to hilly areas of Europe and Asia, they grow best in a cool, damp climate and can be found even in Alaska. The deep red (or sometimes yellow) jewellike fruits have a sweet, intense flavor, and indeed many people prefer them to strawberries.

History

Wild raspberries have been eaten since prehistoric times, but perhaps because they were so plentiful in the wild, the fruits were not cultivated until the Middle Ages. Nowadays, in colder climates, raspberries are cultivated from native European raspberry varieties, while in North America, they derive from an indigenous species better suited to the drier, hotter conditions that prevail there.

Varieties

Although there are many different varieties of raspberry, and new ones are constantly being developed, those sold in stores and markets are not identified specifically. Gardeners have their own favorites:

Heritage is a late-fruiting variety with outstanding flavor.

Malling Jewel, which fruits in mid-season, is a heavy cropper.

Wild raspberries You will often find these tiny, fragrant fruits growing in

Above: Raspberries— deep red fruits, with a wonderfully intense flavor.

Above: Arctic raspberries, grown in the chilly climes of Alaska.

Below: Yellow or golden raspberries are worth seeking out, because they have a delectable flavor.

cool, damp areas of woodland. They are full of seeds, but their exquisite flavor makes up for this deficiency.

Yellow and golden raspberries Clear golden berries, not widely available, but worth seeking out for their fine flavor.

Nutrition

Raspberries are a valuable source of vitamin C, potassium, niacin and riboflavin, and dietary fiber. They contain 25 calories per 3¾ ounces. Raspberry juice is said to be good for the heart, while the leaves have long been renowned for their beneficial effects during childbirth; raspberry-leaf tea is said to prevent miscarriages, ease labor and help the uterus to contract after the birth.

Buying and Storing

Raspberries are ripe when they are brightly and evenly colored. They are always sold hulled, but if you are picking your own, they should slide easily off the hulls. When buying raspberries in a basket, check the bottom to make sure it is not stained red or leaking—a sure sign that the fruit is soft and past its best.

If possible, always eat raspberries the day they are bought or picked; if necessary, they can be stored for up to two days in the bottom of the refrigerator, but bring them out at least an hour before serving.

Raspberries freeze very well; whole berries emerge almost as good as fresh. Open-freeze the fruit in a single layer

Left: Raspberry vinegar makes a sharp, yet refreshingly fruity addition to home-made salad dressing.

on a baking sheet, then pack into rigid cartons. Less than perfect raspberries can be puréed and strained, then sweetened with a little granulated sugar or confectioners' sugar before being frozen.

Preparing and Serving

Do not wash raspberries unless this is unavoidable; they are seldom very dirty, and washing will ruin the texture and flavor. All you need do is gently pick off any bits of leaf or stem.

Good raspberries have such a wonderful flavor that they are best eaten on their own, with a little sugar and cream. They go well with other fruits, like oranges, apples, pears, figs and melon. In the classic dish Peach Melba, raspberries are used as a coulis to coat a lightly poached peach. They also make delicious fillings for pastries, meringues and tartlets, and, because they look so attractive, they are ideal for decoration.

Raspberries can be crushed with a little confectioners' sugar, then pushed through a nylon or stainless strainer strain to make sauces, coulis or bases for ice creams and sorbets. They can be cooked in pies; apple and raspberry is a classic combination. They are rich in pectin, so make excellent jams and jellies. Raspberry vinegar is delicious and makes delectable dressings and sauces.

Preparing a raspberry coulis

1 Put the raspberries in a bowl and crush to a purée with a fork.

2 Pour the purée into a strainer set over a clean bowl. Rub through, using the back of a large spoon.

3 Sweeten to taste with granulated or confectioners' sugar; stir well.

CLOUDBERRIES

These deep golden relatives of the raspberry grow on boggy land in the cold northern climates of Scandinavia, Siberia, Canada and even the Arctic Circle. Because they lack warmth, the berries ripen slowly, allowing the flavor

Left: Popular in Scandinavia, cloudberry jam makes a colorful topping for chocolate mousse or soufflé.

to develop to an extraordinary intensity and sweetness, almost like honeyed apples (Canadians call cloudberries "baked apple berries"). These unusual berries are particularly highly prized in Scandinavian countries, where they are made into excellent jams and desserts, and also into wonderful fruit soups.

Cloudberries are also distilled into a nectarlike liqueur that tastes delicious with bitter chocolate. The berries have a particular affinity for chocolate; try topping a chocolate mousse or soufflé with a spoonful of cloudberry jam.

Above: Brightly colored cloudberries have an amazingly intense flavor.

BLACKBERRIES AND DEWBERRIES

These two relations of the raspberry and the rose are virtually indistinguishable, the main difference being that blackberries are larger and grow on thorny upright bushes or brambles, while dewberries trail. The shiny purplish black berries are made up of a number of segments (drupelets), each containing a hard seed. They grow wild almost everywhere in the world, but are also cultivated to give a larger, juicier berry with better keeping properties. Buying cultivated blackberries, however, is not nearly as much fun as picking your own.

Below: Large, cultivated blackberries

History

Archaeological excavations show that man has eaten blackberries since Neolithic times. The ancient Greeks prized them as much for the medicinal properties of their leaves as for the fruit, and they have remained popular throughout the centuries. Not everyone appreciates the qualities of wild brambles, though; after they had been introduced to Australia by the early settlers, they were declared a noxious weed in some areas!

Nutrition

Blackberries are rich in dietary fiber and vitamin C and are often used to make health drinks. They also contain some calcium, phosphorus and potassium. Blackberries typically contain about 30 calories per 3¾ ounces.

Choosing and Storing

Whether you pick or buy blackberries, they should be plump and tender, but not wet or mushy. Look for large, shiny fruit, and if you are buying a basket, check that the underside is not stained. Legend has it that blackberries should not be picked after September, or the Devil will be in them and they will taste impossibly sour.

Blackberries do not keep well. If you cannot eat them immediately, store them for no more than one day in the bottom of the refrigerator.

Preparing and Cooking

If you must wash blackberries, do so just before serving and drain them well on paper towels.

Freezing blackberries

Blackberries freeze well. Open-freeze perfect specimens in a single layer on a baking sheet, then pack into rigid containers. Damaged berries can be puréed and strained, then sweetened with sugar or honey.

Above: Wild blackberries—also known as brambles.

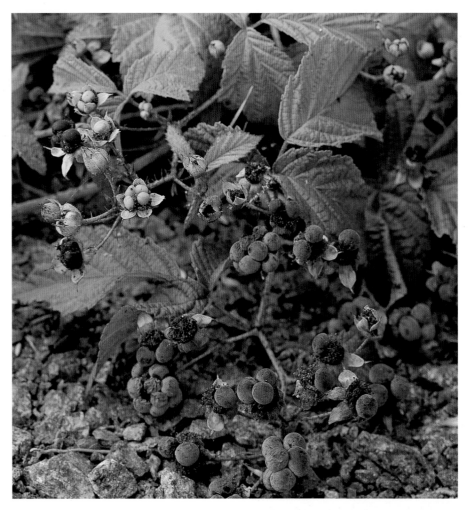

Right: Crème de mûre—this richly flavored blackberry liqueur is seldom drunk on its own. It is more often used as a colorful flavoring for cocktails.

Left: Dewberries—smaller than but very similar to blackberries—grow on long, trailing branches.

Blackberry Kir Royale

Ripe, juicy blackberries are best eaten just as they are, with sugar and cream. They make a tasty addition to breakfast cereal or a fruit salad. Blackberries can be puréed and strained to make coulis, ice cream, sorbets and fools. They make delicious jam or jelly and in England are the classic partner for apples in a pie or crumble. There is no need to cook them before using them in a pie or a pudding.

Left: English Bramble liqueur

Above: Dewberry flowers, which appear before the fruits develop.

Blackberries go well with many other fruits besides apples, and can be used in savory game dishes. Use them to flavor spirits, such as vodka or eau-de-vie, or make a cordial to combat a cold. Commercially produced *crème de mûre* (blackberry liqueur) enhances the flavor of any dessert that incorporates fresh uncooked blackberries.

For a delicious variation on the classic Kir Royale, which is usually made with crème de cassis (black currant liqueur), pour a little crème de mûre into a champagne flute and top up with Champagne or sparkling white wine. Alternatively, to make an exceptionally luxurious cocktail, put some blackberries in a champagne flute, add a dash of orange liqueur, such as Cointreau, and top up with Champagne or sparkling white wine.

HYBRID BERRIES

There are a wide variety of raspberry/blackberry crossbreeds. Some of these occurred naturally, like the loganberry; others have been cultivated to produce a more robust or better-flavored fruit. All these hybrids can be cooked and frozen in the same way as raspberries or blackberries.

Loganberries The first loganberry appeared in 1881 at Santa Cruz in California in the garden of Judge J.H. Logan. It was a natural hybrid, probably derived from a cross between a native dewberry and a raspberry. Since then, loganberries have been

Right: Tayberries were bred in Scotland.

cultivated to produce very large, juicy, dark wine red berries with the consistency of blackberries, but with an intense raspberry flavor. Loganberries are very tart, so they need to be accompanied by plenty of sugar if they are to be eaten raw.

Youngberries These dewberry/loganberry hybrids resemble a dark red, elongated blackberry, but taste rather like a sweeter loganberry.

Boysenberries An even more elaborate hybrid—a cross between a youngberry and a raspberry, but resembling a large reddish purple blackberry.

Left: Large, sweet boysenberries are mostly used to make jam.

Boysenberries are sweeter than loganberries and can be eaten raw, although they are more often used to make jam.

Tayberries Tayberries are arguably the finest hybrids of all. Bred in Scotland, they are a cross between the American blackberry Aurora and a tetraploid raspberry. They grow on long, spiny canes. The bright red, elongated berries have a slightly tart, aromatic flavor and although they can be eaten raw, tayberries are better cooked.

Tummelberries are similar to tayberries, but fruit later in the season. Other, similar crossbreeds include **sunberries** and **wineberries.**

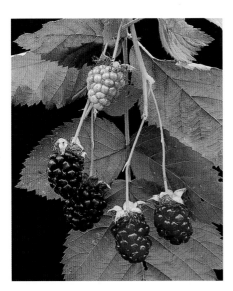

Above: Loganberries, which look more like reddish blackberries, have an intense raspberry flavor.

Left: Dark red youngberries are a hybrid of the dewberry and loganberry, but taste rather like a sweeter version of loganberry.

MULBERRIES

Mulberries grow on magnificent dome-headed trees, which can often be very ancient and grow up to 30 feet across, so they are rarely found in small modern yards! Silkworms feed on the leaves, but the berries are left to drop to the ground as they ripen and have a delicious, slightly musky flavor. Luscious black mulberries taste very good but beware—they stain everything with which they come into contact. Legend has it that rubbing a stain created by a ripe mulberry with an unripe mulberry (if you can reach one) will remove it.

Right: Mulberries taste very good, but the juice stains terribly.

dark wine red berries resemble loganberries.

History

Black mulberries are native to Western Asia. They were known to the ancient Greeks, but it was the Roman emperor Justinian who deliberately encouraged their propagation as part of an enterprise in silk production.

In the sixteenth century, it was discovered that silkworms preferred to feed on the white mulberry leaves, and many of these trees were planted in Europe in the vain hope of stimulating a silk trade. Some of these white mulberry trees still survive today.

Varieties

White mulberries are actually pinkish or pale red. There is also an American red mulberry, whose leaves turn beautifully yellow in autumn.

Black mulberries are considered finer than the white variety. The elongated,

Preparing and Serving

Ripe mulberries can be eaten just as they are, with or without the addition of cream, and are usually sweet enough not to need sugar. They also make a good addition to summer pudding.

Overripe fruit is best used for jams, jellies and sauces. Mulberries make excellent ice creams, fools and sorbets. Mulberry sauce goes well with richly flavored roast meats, such as game, duck and lamb.

HUCKLEBERRIES

These berries, which gave their name to Mark Twain's famous character Huckleberry Finn, are quite similar to blueberries, but have a tougher skin and hard internal seeds. They have a sharper flavor than blueberries, but can be eaten and cooked in exactly the same way.

Another variety of huckleberry is the **tangleberry**, which grows on the coast of North America. These purplish blue berries are sweeter than huckleberries and have a subtle tang of the sea.

Right: Huckleberries, which are similar to blueberries, have fairly tough skins and a sharp flavor.

BLUEBERRIES AND BILBERRIES

Blueberries and bilberries (also known as blaeberries, whortleberries or whinberries) are both small, round blue-black berries with a silvery bloom. They grow on shrubs on inhospitable, peaty moors and uplands. The flavor is mild and sweet and the texture firm.

American blueberries are generally larger and sweeter than bilberries. Today they are often cultivated, resulting in large, perfect berries that sometimes lack the distinctive flavor of the wild fruit.

Nutrition

Blueberries and bilberries are a source of vitamin C, iron and dietary fiber. They provide about 60 calories per 3¾ ounces.

Buying and Storing

The best blueberries and bilberries are those you pick yourself. If you buy them, look for plump berries of uniform size. Reject shriveled specimens, or those without the characteristic bloom. Unwashed berries will keep for up to a week in the bottom of the refrigerator.

Blueberries and bilberries can be frozen just as they are, provided they are in a sealed bag. Alternatively, poach them in a little lemon-flavored syrup and then freeze.

Right: Blueberries—mild and sweet-flavored.

Above: Dried blueberries are available in specialty food shops and greengrocers. They make a tasty addition to homemade fruit cakes and muesli, and are delicious scattered into fresh fruit salads or over breakfast cereal.

Above: Bilberries are smaller and less sweet than blueberries, but have a distinctive flavor.

Preparing and Cooking

Blueberries and bilberries have soft seeds, so they can be eaten raw. Simply rinse and drain them first. However, they are more usually baked in pies or muffins, or used as a jamlike topping for cheesecake. To cook, make a light sugar syrup and flavor it with lemon, orange and cinnamon or allspice, and poach the berries until tender.

Blueberry pie is a classic dessert, as is blueberry grunt, which consists of blueberries stewed with lemon and spice, baked with a dumpling-like topping. Blueberries can also be made into a sauce to serve with game.

ELDERBERRIES

Although you can seldom buy elderberries, you will find them growing all over the countryside in the summer. First come the creamy white flowerheads, whose flavor goes very well with gooseberries. These are followed by flat, wide clusters of small, sweet, almost black berries, which must be cooked before eating.

History

Elderberries have grown in Europe and Asia since prehistoric times. The bushes themselves were little loved, perhaps because of their unattractive smell, but the berries provided sustenance for the poor. People often used elderberries as a fabric dye and to make wine; later the berries were used to add color and extra flavor to thin, cheap wines.

Nutrition

Elderberries are an excellent source of vitamin C.

Choosing and Storing

Never pick elderberries growing close to a road, as they will be contaminated by dust and pollution. Good elderberries should be shiny and black. For elderflower syrup, choose creamy flowerheads that are fully open, but whose petals have not begun to drop. Use both flowers and berries as soon as possible after picking.

Below: Elderberries can be cooked with other fruits in pies and tarts or used to make jellies and sauces.

Preparing and Cooking

Use a fork to strip the berries from the stems. Elderberries can be cooked in the same way as red currants or other berries. Flowers should be shaken to dislodge any insects or loose petals and briefly rinsed in cold water.

Sprigs of elderflowers can be dipped in batter to make fritters, or made into an intensely flavored syrup. The berries can be made into jellies, or used to bulk out other berries in

pies, tarts and fools. Elderberries can be made into a savory sauce for pork and game. They are often used to make vinegar, and are excellent for making wine.

Elderflowers can be made into a refreshing summer drink. To make eight 1 1/4 pint bottles, you will need about 12 large elderflower heads. Choose blossoms that are fully open, but not shedding their petals, and wash thoroughly. Place in a large pan and pour 6 quarts boiling water over. Add a generous 1 cup sugar, 2 thinly sliced lemons and 1/2 cup white wine or cider vinegar. Stir and leave to macerate in a cool place for three days, stirring twice a day. Strain the liquid and pour into sterilized wine bottles. Cork very firmly and leave for at least a week before drinking.

Left: Elderflowers can be made into fritters and intensely flavored drinks.

Stripping elderberries

Hold the stem in one hand and run a fork through the berries.

ROWANBERRIES

These bright orangey red berries are the fruit of the mountain ash. They grow in large clusters and are a great favorite with wild birds. Rowanberries are not available commercially.

Nutrition

Rowanberries are very rich in vitamin C and pectin.

Preparing and Cooking

The best-known use for rowanberries is in a glorious deep orange jewellike jelly with a bittersweet flavor, which goes particularly well with rich meats and game. Rowanberries are also used to add color to sweet apple dishes, such as pies and crumbles, or they can be made into compotes and sauces. Cook them in the same way as other berries. They cannot be eaten raw.

Right: Rowanberries can be made into a vibrant jelly.

ROSE HIPS

These are the seed pods of roses, and appear after the plants have finished flowering. They vary in color from orange to deep red and make a beautiful sight in autumn in gardens and hedgerows. Hips contain extremely hairy seeds, which must be removed before they can be eaten.

Nutrition

Rose hips are so rich in vitamin C that in wartime Britain they were picked by both children and adult volunteers and used in vast quantities to make bright pink rose hip syrup for pregnant women and babies. A single rose hip typically contains twenty times more vitamin C than an orange.

Right: Rose hips are enormously rich in vitamin C.

Preparing and Cooking

Very ripe rose hips can be eaten raw, but they do not taste particularly pleasant. Plump rose hips can be made into a bittersweet jelly to serve with poultry or game, or sweetened with sugar or honey and boiled to a syrup. Rose hips can also be used to flavor vinegar, and make an attractive garnish for salads.

Before cooking rose hips, trim them, cut them in half and scoop out every trace of the seeds and prickly hairs. If making jelly or syrup, strain the liquid twice through a double layer of cheesecloth.

HAWS

The fruit of the hawthorn or May tree, the white spring blossom is followed by these small, wine red berries with a bitter, pungent taste.

Preparing and Cooking

Haws cannot be eaten raw, but make a delicious jelly when combined with crab apples. Elderberries can be added to the mixture to make a hedgerow jelly. Haws also make a good sauce for rich meats and game.

Right: Wine red haws are pretty to look at, but have a bitter, pungent taste.

GOOSEBERRIES

The gooseberry, a botanical cousin of the black currant, is native to Europe and North America. The fruits, which grow on dauntingly spiny bushes, come in many varieties—hard and sour, succulently soft and sweet, smooth and hairy—and in a range of colors, from vivid green to luscious purple.

History

Gooseberries were popular all over Britain well before Tudor times, when they grew wild in many kitchen gardens. The Tudors served them in savory sauces and in all manner of sweet dishes. They were first cultivated in the sixteenth century and became so popular that in the nineteenth century competitors formed gooseberry clubs to see who could grow the biggest berry (some are reputed to have been grown to the size of a bantam's egg).

For some reason, their popularity did not spread abroad; even today the French use them only in a sauce to cut the richness of oily fish. There is no specific French word for gooseberry; it shares its name with the red currant and is known as *groseille de maquereau* ("red currant for mackerel").

Varieties

Gooseberries have a very long season. Early gooseberries are usually bright green and rather hard. They cannot be eaten raw, but taste wonderful cooked. These are followed by the softer, mid-season fruits, which are not generally identified by variety when sold in supermarkets and greengrocers, but which you may find in gardens and farm stands.

Early Sulphur A very early variety with golden, almost transparent berries and a lovely sweet flavor.

Goldendrop As attractive as its name, this small, round yellow gooseberry has a fine rich flavor, which makes it ideal for eating raw as

a dessert fruit. Ready to pick in midsummer.

Langley's Industry A large, red, hairy berry with a lovely sweet flavor. Ideal for the less green-thumbed gardener, it will grow vigorously anywhere and can be picked early for cooking, or left to ripen fully on the bush to eat raw like grapes.

Above: Huge, deep red London berries are sweet enough to eat raw.

Leveller A mid-season yellowish green berry with a sweet flavor.

London This huge mid-season berry is deep red or purple. For thirty-seven years, between 1829 and 1867, it was the unbeaten British champion in major gooseberry competitions! These dessert gooseberries can be eaten fresh, just as they are.

Left: Green gooseberries—these early-cropping fruits cannot be eaten raw, but are delicious cooked.

Right: Fully ripe red gooseberries are sweet enough to be eaten just as they are.

Nutrition

Gooseberries are high in vitamin C and also contain vitamins A and D, potassium, calcium, phosphorus and niacin. They are rich in dietary fiber and provide only 17 calories per 3¾ ounces.

Buying and Storing

Choose slightly unripe green gooseberries for cooking. Check that they are not rock hard. Dessert varieties should be yielding and juicy (if possible, taste before you buy). Gooseberries will keep in the refrigerator for up to a week.

To freeze whole gooseberries, trim them and open-freeze on baking sheets. Pack the frozen berries in bags. Alternatively, purée and strain them, sweeten and freeze in rigid containers.

Below: You may find Leveller berries, which have a lovely sweet flavor, in garden centers, pick-your-own farms and farm stands.

Preparing

For recipes using whole gooseberries, wash, then trim them (this is not necessary if you are making jam or jelly, or are going to strain the cooked fruit).

Cooking

Gooseberries are rich in pectin, particularly when they are slightly unripe, which makes them ideal for jams and jellies. Their tartness makes an excellent foil for oily fish and rich poultry or meat.

Cook gooseberries very gently with a little water and sugar to taste until all the fruit has collapsed. If you like, flavor them with cinnamon, lemon or herbs. A few fennel or dill seeds will enhance a gooseberry sauce for fish.

In England, the first gooseberries of the season were traditionally used to make a Whitsun pie. They also make a good filling for suet pudding or crumble.

Worcestershire berries

A North American species of gooseberry that grows on a bush with wicked spines. The small purplish red berries are hardly much bigger than blackberries, but have the distinctive veining of gooseberries and a gooseberry flavor. Worcestershire berries can be eaten raw or cooked.

Trimming gooseberries

1 Hold the gooseberry between your forefinger and thumb.
2 Snip off the stem and flower end with sharp scissors or trim with a knife.

Puréed, strained and mixed with whipped cream, they make the perfect fruit fool. Gooseberries have an extraordinary affinity for elderflowers, which come into season at the same time as the early fruit and add a delicious muscat flavor to the berries.

Below: Sweet-tasting Early Sulphur are golden and almost translucent.

CRANBERRIES

These tart, bright red berries grow wild on evergreen shrubs in peaty marshland all over northern Europe and North America. They are closely related to blueberries and bilberries, but are much more sour and are always served cooked. **Cowberries** and **lingonberries** are very similar, but smaller.

Cranberries are sometimes known as "bounceberries," since they were traditionally tested for firmness by being bounced seven times. Any that failed the bounce test were too squashy and were therefore discarded. Because of their waxy skins, cranberries keep for much longer than other berries, which helps to explain their popularity.

Right: Bright red cranberries can be used in sweet and savory dishes.

History

For centuries before the first settlers arrived in America, the native American Indians prized wild cranberries for their nutritional and medicinal value, and used them to make a dye for fabric and for decorative feathers. Although cranberries were already known in Britain, the Pilgrims found that the American berries were larger and more succulent.

Below: Dried cranberries

Cranberry sauce

1 Thinly pare an orange with a swivel-bladed vegetable peeler, taking care to remove only the zest. Squeeze the juice and put it in a saucepan with the zest.

2 Add 3 cups cranberries and cook gently for a few minutes, until the cranberry skins pop.

3 Stir in sugar to taste and simmer for 5 minutes. Stir in 2 tablespoons port (optional). Pour the cranberry sauce into a bowl, then cool and chill before serving.

They called them "craneberries" because the pink blossoms resembled a crane's head, or possibly because the cranes, which lived in the marshlands, were partial to the berries.

Cranberries featured in the first-ever Thanksgiving feast in 1620 and have been a traditional part of the celebrations ever since. Commercial cultivation began in the nineteenth century, and today cranberries are available frozen, canned, dried, as juice and in jellies and relishes.

Nutrition

Cranberries contain vitamins C and D, potassium and iron. They were considered to be a good protection against scurvy. They are naturally very low in calories (but need sweetening to make them palatable).

Buying and Storing

Look for plump, firm, bright red berries and make sure that those at the bottom of the package are neither squashed nor shriveled. Fresh cranberries will keep in the refrigerator for four weeks, or they can be frozen in freezer bags and used without being thawed.

Preparing and Cooking

Cranberries can be used in sweet or savory dishes. Their most famous incarnation is as cranberry sauce, which is served with turkey or game. Their distinctive tartness even adds zest to firm-fleshed fish. The berries are high in pectin, so they make excellent jams and jellies. They combine well with oranges and apples, and can be mixed with blackberries and raspberries to make an autumnal variation on summer pudding.

Cranberries should be stewed slowly with sugar to taste and a little water or orange juice until the skins pop. Dried cranberries can be used in the same way as raisins. Cranberry juice can be mixed with soda water and white wine or grape juice to make a refreshing drink. It is also good with orange juice and vodka.

Cranberry and chestnut stuffing

The traditional Christmas accompaniments of cranberries and chestnuts can be combined to make the perfect stuffing for turkey or other poultry. To make about 1 pound (enough to stuff a 10–12-pound bird), soften 4 ounces (⅔ cup) finely chopped onion in 2 tablespoons butter in a saucepan. Stir in 6 ounces unsweetened chestnut purée and 2 tablespoons cooked cranberries or chunky cranberry sauce. Season to taste with salt and pepper and mix thoroughly. Take the pan off the heat and stir in 8 ounces fresh white bread crumbs. Coarsely crumble or chop 4 ounces cooked chestnuts (canned chestnuts are fine) and fold into the stuffing mixture. Let cool completely before stuffing the bird.

Below: Cranberry juice and soda water makes a refreshing drink.

BLACK CURRANTS, RED CURRANTS AND WHITE CURRANTS

These native European berries, with their glowing colors, make a beautiful sight in summer, hanging like tiny bunches of grapes on the bush. Each berry contains a mass of small seeds. Currants can be eaten whole, but because they are highly acidic, this is seldom the preferred option.

History

Currants grow wild all over Europe and even as far north as Siberia. For some inexplicable reason, they were not cultivated by the Romans, but became popular only in the sixteenth century, when they were prized for their health-giving properties.

Nutrition

All currants, particularly black currants, are very rich in vitamin C. Black currants are used in cordials, cough drops and other remedies designed to ward off colds; in the past, they were often used as a cure for quinsy. They are also high in pectin.

Buying and Storing

Choose plump, firm currants with shiny skins. They will keep in the refrigerator for several days. They can be frozen very successfully: Strip the currants

Below: Buffalo currants are a type of black currant with larger berries.

Right: Black currants grow wild all over Europe. The fruits have a tart flavor and are usually cooked.

from the stems, then rinse and drain them. Freeze in rigid containers. Sweetened or unsweetened black currant purée also freezes well.

Preparing

Strip the currants from the stems, unless this has already been done. If you wish, pick off the calyx tops before cooking the currants by pinching them between the nails of your forefinger and thumb. This is a tedious process and is seldom necessary.

BLACK CURRANTS

Although they are often combined with other currants in cooking (as in summer pudding), black currants are different from other types. They have tougher skins and, unlike other currants, which grow on old wood, they

fruit on new wood. Both the bushes and the currants themselves are highly aromatic and the fruits have a luscious, tart flavor.

Cooking

Black currants can be added raw to fruit salads if they are not too tart, but are usually cooked in a little water, with sugar to taste. Simmer until just tender—do not overcook them, or they will lose their fresh flavor. Black currants make wonderful jams and jellies and combine well with soft cheeses, rich meats and game. To serve black currants with meat, sauté them lightly

Stripping currants off the stem

Hold the bunch of currants by the stem and strip off the berries with the tines of a fork.

Right: White currants are less tart than other currants and can be eaten raw.

in butter, adding a pinch of sugar. They adapt well to other flavorings, such as mint and lemon, and are used to make the liqueur crème de cassis, which is the basis for Kir Royale and similar drinks.

RED CURRANTS

Red currants can be eaten raw. Small bunches look very decorative if frosted with egg white and sugar. They are an essential ingredient for summer pudding and make a good addition to creamy desserts, such as crème brûlée. For a refreshing summer drink, purée 4 cups red currants with 2 cups water and sugar to taste, then press the purée gently through a strainer placed over a pitcher. Serve with sparkling water or soda water, or add a dash of vodka or gin.

The most familiar use of red currants, however, is in the jewellike red currant jelly that goes so well with lamb and venison. Cumberland sauce (for game, ham and rich meats) is made by heating red currant jelly with lemon zest, port and sometimes mustard.

WHITE CURRANTS

These beautiful, translucent, silvery golden currants are an albino strain of red currants. They are less tart than other types and can be eaten raw. They look wonderfully decorative frosted with egg white and sugar. **Pink currants** are an even more attractive variety, with a beautiful pink flush.

Above: Red currant jelly

Left: Red currants are an essential ingredient for summer pudding.

Red currant jelly

1 Put the red currants (as many as you have) in a preserving pan with just enough water to cover. Simmer for 8–10 minutes, or until the currants are very soft.

2 Strain through a jelly bag, then measure the liquid. Pour it back into the pan and add 1½ cups sugar for every 2½ cups liquid. Stir over medium heat until dissolved.

3 Boil briskly for 10 minutes, or until setting point is reached, skimming off any scum as it rises to the surface. Pour the jelly into sterilized jars, seal and label.

CITRUS FRUITS

No family of fruits seems to store up sunshine more successfully
than citrus fruits. Golden oranges and tangerines, yellow
lemons, deep green limes—their glowing colors light up a room,
and the wonderful scent of their essential oils tempts the taste buds.
Wonderfully versatile, they can be juiced, enjoyed just as they
are or used in both sweet and savory dishes. All citrus fruits
have a tough, bitter peel that is highly scented and contains
aromatic essential oils. Inside, the fruit is segmented and
encloses juicy flesh, with a more or less acid flavor.
The fruits ripen on the tree and do not continue to develop after
picking, so they have excellent keeping qualities.

GRAPEFRUIT

One of the largest citrus fruits, grapefruit can vary in diameter from 4 to 7 inches. Most have deep yellow skins, but the flesh can range from very pale yellow (confusingly called "white") through rosy pink to deep pink (known as "ruby"). Generally speaking, the pinker the flesh, the sweeter the grapefruit will be.

History

Grapefruit are descended from the Malaysian **pomelo** or **shaddock**, a large, sour fruit (the pomelos sold today are a cross between a grapefruit and a shaddock). These fruits were brought to Europe from the West Indies in the seventeenth century and are now grown in every subtropical country of the world.

Varieties

The main varieties of grapefruit are white, pink or ruby, but you may also find the green-skinned **Sweetie,** whose flesh, as the name implies, is so sweet that it needs no sugar.

Nutrition

One of the most filling fruits, yet very low in calories (about 43 calories per 3¾ ounces), grapefruit are an excellent source of dietary fiber and vitamin C; one fruit provides one and a half times the adult daily requirement.

Above: Sweetie is a very sweet variety of grapefruit that needs no sugar.

Buying and Storing

Choose fruits that feel heavy for their size; they will be juicy. The skin can be thin or thick, depending on the variety, but it should be plump and firm; if it is puffy and coarse, the flesh will be dry. Avoid grapefruit with bruised or damaged skin. You cannot ripen grapefruit once they have been picked, but they can be kept in a cool place or in the refrigerator for a week or more.

Preparing and Serving

Grapefruit are best eaten raw and chilled, although in the 1960s it was fashionable to sprinkle them with brown sugar or brush with melted butter and caramelize them under the grill. They constitute the perfect breakfast food; perhaps the easiest way to enjoy them is freshly squeezed into a glass, but half a grapefruit on its own or with a little sugar is more satisfying. The fruits can also be used to make delicious marmalade to round off your breakfast.

Grapefruit can be used to start or finish a meal. The tart flavor goes well with seafood;

Above: White grapefruit have pale yellow flesh.

Segmenting grapefruit

1 Cut the grapefruit in half and remove the seeds.

2 Using a curved, serrated grapefruit knife, cut between the skin and flesh.

3 Using a small, sharp paring knife, cut carefully between the membrane that separates the segments. Start at the center, work out to the skin, then around the segment and back to the center again.

4 Finally, cut out the central core of the grapefruit with a sharp knife and remove the membrane.

grapefruit segments mixed with shrimp and avocado make a refreshing appetizer. They combine well with smoked fish and poultry, and segments are sometimes served as a garnish to cut the richness of liver or sweetbreads. The segments can also be used in fruit salads, mousses and sorbets. Grapefruit juice makes an unusual addition to salad dressings, and the peel can be candied to be used in cakes or coated with chocolate as a sweet with after-dinner coffee.

Left: The flesh of pink grapefruit can range from rosy pink to deep pink. As a rule of thumb, the pinker the color, the sweeter the grapefruit.

Below: Chocolate-coated grapefruit peel—a delectable sweet treat.

POMELOS

Although they resemble grapefruit, true pomelos are not a hybrid of the grapefruit, but a species in their own right. They are sometimes known as "shaddocks," after the sea captain who brought them from Malaysia to the West Indies. They are much larger than grapefruit, with thick, yellow, dimpled skin, pinkish yellow flesh and a sharp, refreshing flavor, which often needs a little sugar to make it palatable.

Below: Pomelos sold today are a smaller, rounder and smoother-skinned cross between the original pomelo or shaddock and grapefruit.

UGLI FRUIT

Despite its large size, baggy shape and mottled green skin, the Ugli is a hybrid of the grapefruit, orange and tangerine. It may not be the beauty of the citrus family, but the flavor is sweet and delicious—a cross between grapefruit and tangerine. The peel can be candied like grapefruit peel.

LEMONS

Arguably the most useful of all fruit, the distinctively shaped lemon can be very large or quite small, with thick or thin, smooth or knobbly skin. The skin contains aromatic essential oils, and a good lemon will perfume the air with its fragrance. The juicy, pale yellow, acid flesh enhances almost any other food and never fails to awaken and refresh the taste buds.

History

Originally from India or Malaysia, lemons were introduced into Assyria, where they were discovered by the soldiers serving Alexander the Great. They took them back to Greece, where lemons were used as a condiment and for medicinal and cosmetic purposes. The Crusaders brought lemons to the rest of Europe from Palestine, and their cultivation became widespread. Like limes, lemons became invaluable as a protection against scurvy and were carried by sailors on every sea voyage.

Nutrition

Rich in vitamin C and very low in calories, lemons provide only about 22 calories per 3¾ ounce.

Buying and Storing

Choose lemons that are firm and heavy for their size. Smooth-skinned lemons are best for juicing and cooking, while the knobbly-skinned varieties are easier to grate. Lemons become paler as they ripen and lose some juiciness and acidity, so avoid light yellow fruit; look instead for deep yellow specimens with glossy, unblemished skins. Do not buy lemons with patches of mold or those with hard, shriveled skins.

Lemons have often been treated with diphenyl, an ethylene gas that keeps the skins yellow and fresh-looking. If you are going to use the lemon rind, buy untreated or "unwaxed" fruit.

Lemons do not ripen once picked. They can be kept in a cool room or the refrigerator for at least a week.

Preparing and Cooking

Although few people would choose to eat a lemon raw, these citrus fruits are infinitely versatile. Their high ascorbic acid (vitamin C) content prevents oxidization, so lemon juice is often brushed over cut fruit or white vegetables, such as potatoes, celeriac or artichokes, to stop them from turning brown. Lemons can be distilled into alcoholic drinks, such as *limoncello,* a sweet *digestivo* that is served straight from the freezer.

Every part of the lemon can be used in sweet and savory cooking, from the juice to the zest. Lemon wedges are traditionally served as an accompaniment to fish dishes, particularly fried fish; their acidity counteracts the fattiness of all fried

Left: Smooth-skinned lemons are best for juicing and cooking.

Zesting or grating a lemon

1 Choose an unwaxed lemon. Hold it firmly in one hand.

2 Scrape a zester down the length of the lemon to pare off fine slivers of zest.

3 Chop the pared zest finely with a sharp knife if desired.

4 For grating, choose a knobbly-skinned lemon if possible. Grate it on the fine side of a grater, taking care to remove only the yellow zest. Work over a bowl, or, if you prefer, work over a piece of foil—this makes it easy to transfer the grated rind to a bowl or pan with the aid of a pastry brush.

foods. Lemon slices are a popular addition to tea and cold drinks, or can be used to garnish any number of sweet or savory dishes. Whole lemons can be preserved in salt and are widely used in North African dishes, such as Moroccan tagines.

Lemons give a wonderful flavor to sweet dishes. They can be used for jellies, jams and lemon curd or cheese and make refreshing mousses, sorbets and ice creams.

Lemon juice Lemon juice can be drunk on its own, with added sugar or as a refreshing tall drink, such as lemonade. It enhances the flavor of most other foods and can be used as a healthy substitute for salt. Use it in dressings, sauces and marinades; marinating fish for a long time in lemon juice will even "cook" the fish without heat, as in the Latin American dish seviche. Lemon

Above: Knobbly-skinned lemons are easy to grate.

Below: Lemon juice enhances the flavor of most other fruits.

juice will also tenderize meat. A few drops added to the cooking water helps poached eggs to coagulate, and a couple of spoonfuls will turn fresh cream into sour cream.

Lemon juice has nonculinary uses too. It acts as a bleach and can be used as a household cleaner or cosmetically, to whiten the skin or lighten blond hair.

Lemons yield more juice if they are warmed before squeezing; roll them between the palms of your hands for a minute or two, cover with boiling water or microwave on High for 30 seconds before squeezing. Do not squeeze lemons too hard, or the juice will become bitter.

Lemon zest and peel
The essential oils in lemon zest have an aromatic flavor that enhances many dishes. The zest can be obtained by grating or peeling it into strips with a zester or channel knife. Use it as a flavoring for butter, sauces, custards, mousses, cakes, cookies and tarts. For a milder lemon flavor, rub a lump of sugar over the surface of a lemon so that it absorbs the oils, then add the sugar cube to a sauce or dessert.

Lemon peel (including the white pith) contains pectin, which helps to set jams and jellies. Strips of peel (minus pith) can be added to casseroles, or candied to serve with coffee or to add to cakes and puddings.

CITRON

A lemon or pear-shaped citrus fruit originally from China, citrons are large fruit, sometimes up to 8 inches long, with thick, knobbly, greenish skin. They give very little juice, but this can be used like lemon juice. Citron flesh is very bitter and unpalatable, but the attractive green peel can be candied and used like candied lemon peel; it develops a lovely translucency. The peel can also be used for marmalade and jams. In Corsica, citrons are used to make a liqueur called Cédratine.

Right: Citrons are large fruit with bitter, unpalatable flesh.

LIMES

Limes are the smallest members of the true citrus family. They have thin, fairly smooth, green skins and a highly aromatic, acid flavor. Unlike lemons, limes will grow in tropical regions and are an essential ingredient of Southeast Asian, Mexican, Latin American and Caribbean cooking.

History

Limes originated in India. Attempts were made to grow them in Mediterranean countries, but they proved insufficiently hardy. They do very well in Egypt, however, where they are more plentiful than lemons. They are widely grown in the West Indies, and it was from these islands that supplies came for the British navy, to supplement the sailors' rations and help to prevent scurvy. Limehouse, in London's docklands, takes its name from the warehouses where the fruit was stored.

Varieties

There are two or perhaps three types of true limes:
Persian or Tahitian Large limes, with pale fine-grained pulp and a very acidic flavor.
Bearss are seedless but otherwise almost identical, and are regarded by some as a variety of the Persian or Tahitian lime and not a separate type.
Mexican, Key and West Indian limes are small and oval, with a strong, sharp flavor.

Nutrition

High in vitamin C, limes contain some potassium, calcium and phosphorus, and provide about 20 calories per 3¾ ounces.

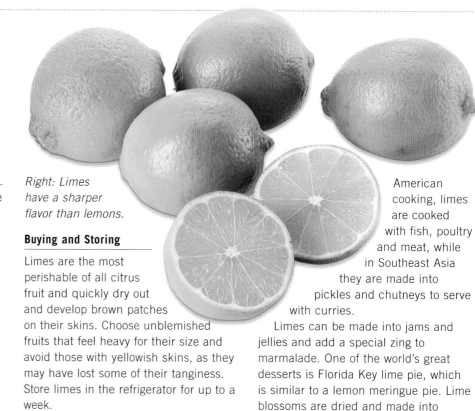

Right: Limes have a sharper flavor than lemons.

Buying and Storing

Limes are the most perishable of all citrus fruit and quickly dry out and develop brown patches on their skins. Choose unblemished fruits that feel heavy for their size and avoid those with yellowish skins, as they may have lost some of their tanginess. Store limes in the refrigerator for up to a week.

Preparing and Serving

Limes can be used in the same way as lemons, but will add a sharper flavor, so use fewer of them. Classic seviche is made by marinating chunks of white fish in lime juice until they turn opaque. Freshly squeezed juice is used in rum punches, margaritas and daiquiris, or commercially made into a cordial.

Strips of lime zest can be buried in sugar to add a delicious fragrance. A few drops of lime juice squeezed over tropical fruit, such as papayas, melons and prickly pears, will do wonders for the flavor. In Caribbean and Latin American cooking, limes are cooked with fish, poultry and meat, while in Southeast Asia they are made into pickles and chutneys to serve with curries.

Limes can be made into jams and jellies and add a special zing to marmalade. One of the world's great desserts is Florida Key lime pie, which is similar to a lemon meringue pie. Lime blossoms are dried and made into infusions or used to flavor ice creams and mousses.

Paring and cutting julienne strips of citrus zest
1 Wash and dry the lime, lemon or orange. Using a swivel-blade vegetable peeler, peel downward to remove long strips of zest. Do not include the bitter white pith.
2 With a small sharp knife, square off the strips.
3 Cut them lengthwise into fine julienne strips.

KAFFIR LIMES

These are not true limes, but belong to a subspecies of the citrus family. Pale green and gnarled, the fruits have a haunting, scented citrus bouquet, but unfortunately the flesh is inedible. In Thailand and Indonesia, the finely grated rind is sometimes used in cooking, but it is the leaves that are most useful in culinary terms. When torn or shredded, they impart a distinctive flavor to soups, fish and chicken dishes, and curries.

Right: Kaffir limes are not eaten, but the finely grated rind is used in Southeast Asian cooking.

KUMQUATS

Kumquats are not true citrus fruits, but belong to a similar species, *Fortunella.* Their name comes from the Cantonese *kam kwat,* meaning "golden orange." The small, elongated fruits are about the size and shape of a large olive, with a thin orange rind that is edible. The rind is sweeter than the sour pulp and the two parts eaten together provide a delicious sour-sweet sensation.

Nutrition

Kumquats are a source of vitamins C and A and have some calcium, phosphorus and riboflavin. They provide about 65 calories per 3¾ ounces.

Buying and Storing

Look for unblemished fruit with taut orange rind. Kumquats can be kept in the refrigerator for up to a week.

Preparing and Cooking

Kumquats can be eaten whole, just as they are, or sliced into miniature rings and used in winter salads and fruit salads. They taste superb poached in syrup, and can also be canned with sugar and alcohol and served whole or chopped with ice cream, duck, red meats or cheese. They make delicious marmalade and jam and can be used in cake and cookie mixes. For unusual petits fours, dip whole kumquats into melted bittersweet chocolate.

Kumquats combine well with bitter salad greens like chicory and frisée and make excellent stuffings for poultry.

Limequats

These are, as the name suggests, a cross between limes and kumquats. Limequats are bright green with thin, edible skins, but they are extremely sour, so cannot be eaten raw. They should be cooked or preserved like kumquats and can be served in the same way.

Whole kumquats can be cooked with fish, poultry and white meats, and spiced kumquat preserve is a Christmas treat.

Left: Not true citrus fruits, kumquats can be eaten whole—skin and all.

BERGAMOTS

These small, yellow citrus fruit are seldom found in their natural state. They are best known for the essential oil contained in the rind, which is used in confectionery and perfumery, but most famously as a highly distinctive flavoring for Earl Grey tea. Bergamot oil is used in the barley sugar made in the French town of Nancy. The fruit can also be made into delicious and unusual marmalade.

Right: Seldom used for cooking, bergamots are best known for their essential oil, which gives Earl Grey tea its unusual, aromatic aroma and flavor.

TANGERINES <u>OR</u> MANDARINS

Sometimes known as "easy peelers," tangerines or mandarins are part of a large family of small citrus fruit. They resemble slightly flattened oranges with loose orange skin and have a fragrant aroma, which in Great Britain is inextricably bound up with Christmas. The tangerine family all have aromatic skins, which can easily be detached from the segments (unlike oranges and lemons), and segments that separate easily. The flesh is sweet and perfumed, but often contains a large number of seeds.

History

As the name suggests, tangerines or mandarins almost certainly originated in China and were brought to Italy in Roman times by Arab traders. Like oranges, they were regarded as a symbol of luxury and prosperity. They

Right: Easy to peel, satsumas have a refreshing tart flavor.

are now grown throughout North Africa and the Mediterranean.

Varieties

The names of many types of tangerine are commonly interchanged, so you may find a bewildering variety of fruits that are essentially the same.

Clementine The smallest of the tangerines, with bright orange skin and no seeds. This, and their sweet, aromatic flesh, make clementines the most popular tangerine variety. They are sometimes sold with the leaves still attached, which makes them particularly attractive.

Mandarin Most commonly sold canned, tiny peeled tangerine segments are sold as mandarin oranges, although they are usually satsumas. The deliciously sweet, vibrant segments make an attractive decoration for a dessert.

Satsuma These largish tangerines from Japan have loose skin and a refreshing, rather tart flavor. Satsumas contain very few seeds.

Right: These tangerines, grown in Italy, have sweet flesh but often contain a large number of seeds.

Making tangerine shells

1 Choose attractive, well-shaped fruit. Cut off the top of each to make a lid.

2 Carefully scoop out the segments with a teaspoon, a few at a time. Scrape out any pith or membrane, taking care to avoid breaking the skin. Fill the shells with iced tangerine pulp.

Right: The clementine is the smallest and most popular variety of tangerine.

Ortanique Also known as "honey tangerines" because of their delicious sweetness, ortaniques are a hybrid, which can be found growing on the same trees as tangerines or oranges.
Tangelo These are a cross between a tangerine and a grapefruit, and have the easy-peeling qualities of the former. Tangelos are irregularly shaped and have a refreshing, tart flavor, rather like an orange.
Mineola Another tangerine–grapefruit hybrid, mineolas can be recognized by the distinctive bulge at their stem end. They have bright orange skin and are very easy to peel. The sweet, juicy flesh has no seeds.

Nutrition

All tangerines and their hybrids are extremely good sources of vitamin C and beta-carotene. They provide about 40 calories per 3¾ ounces.

Buying and Storing

Many varieties of tangerine have loose, puffy skins, which are no indication of quality. Choose fruits that feel heavy for their size; they will contain more juice. Avoid fruits with damaged skins and, if you are buying prepacked fruits, check that none is moldy—it will quickly taint all the others.

Tangerines do not keep as long as other citrus fruit, but can be stored in the refrigerator for up to a week.
Canned mandarin oranges are a very useful pantry item. Use them in trifles, chocolate desserts and on cheesecakes. Children love them set in orange or mandarin jelly.

It is also possible to buy canned peeled whole mandarins in syrup—the lazy cook's answer for a simply sensational dessert. Just make a caramel sauce, add the drained fruit and decorate with some fresh orange or mandarin zest. A dash of orange liqueur gilds the lily.

Preparing and Serving

All varieties of tangerine can be used in the same way as oranges. The peel is as useful as the flesh, and the zest can be candied or used to flavor sweet liqueurs. Strips of peel can be dried and used in savory stews or included with herbs to make a bouquet garni.

Tangerine segments can be eaten on their own. Dipped in melted chocolate or crystallized, they make a delicious after-dinner sweet. Tangerine juice adds a distinctive flavor to marinades for pork and poultry; combine it with Asian aromatics like five-spice powder, ginger and soy sauce.

ORANGES

Below: Navel oranges contain a tiny embryonic fruit.

Despite their name, oranges are not always orange; they can also be green, yellow or mottled with red. The size can vary too—an orange can be as large as a football or as small as a cherry—and the flavor can range from sweet to intensely sour. Orange trees are beautiful all year round. Their dark, glossy evergreen leaves give off a wonderful citrus scent. The beautiful, waxy white, star-shaped flowers also have an intense aroma, which is captured in orange-flower water. The fruits turn from green to bright orange or yellow, making a striking contrast with the leaves.

Like other citrus peel, orange rind contains essential oils that are used in cooking and perfumery.

History

Oranges originated in China. They were probably known to the ancient Greeks and may have been the mythical Golden Apples of the Hesperides. If so, they would have been bitter oranges, which were the only variety

Right: Cointreau—flavored with the peel of bitter oranges.

known at the time. Over the centuries, traders took oranges to India and Arabia and thence to the Mediterranean region. When the first oranges reached Europe, they were so rare that they became a symbol of opulence, to be offered as luxury gifts; the Medici family adopted five oranges as their coat of arms. The oranges were too precious to be eaten raw (in any case, they would have been too sour), but were made into preserves. The first sweet oranges to arrive in Europe were brought from India by traders in the seventeenth century. They became popular throughout Europe and were served in theaters as refreshments—hence Nell Gwynn's appearance in the history books.

Varieties

Oranges fall into two groups: sweet oranges, which can be eaten raw, and bitter oranges, which cannot.

Sweet oranges

Sweet oranges can be divided into four main categories, which are available at different times of the year.

Navel These seedless oranges take their name from the navellike protuberance at the end, which contains a tiny embryonic fruit. They have thick, pebbly skins and very sweet, juicy flesh. The skin is particularly good for making candied peel.

Blond These pale-skinned winter oranges include **Jaffa** and **Shamouti**. The large fruit have thick skins that are easy to peel. The flesh is crisp and juicy. If you are lucky, you may find **Salustianas oranges**, which are full of juice and contain no seeds.

Blood oranges These small oranges have red-flushed skins and jewellike flesh, which can range from golden to deep ruby red. These are the best oranges to use for sorbets and desserts, where color is important. They are an essential ingredient of *sauce Maltaise*,

Peeling and segmenting oranges

1 Using a serrated knife, cut a thin slice from each end of the orange to expose the flesh.

2 Cut off the peel in a circular motion, removing the white pith.

3 Hold the fruit over a bowl to catch the juice. Cut each segment between the membranes.

4 Squeeze out all the juice.

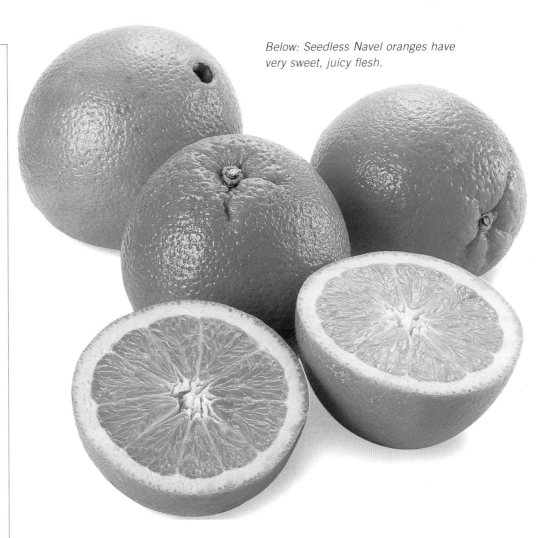

Below: Seedless Navel oranges have very sweet, juicy flesh.

an orange-flavored hollandaise that takes its name from the sour but juicy Maltese blood orange.

Late oranges These include **Valencia** oranges, which have smooth, thin skins and contain few or no seeds; they are the world's most popular variety. They have pale flesh and are very juicy, with a sharp flavor. Valencia are the best oranges for juicing.

Bitter oranges

As well as the sweet oranges, there are bitter, or sour oranges.

Seville or **Bigarade** cannot be eaten raw, but are used for making marmalade, jams and jellies. Vast numbers are grown in Seville, but surprisingly, the Spaniards never make marmalade; almost all their oranges are exported to Britain. Seville oranges are used in the classic *sauce bigarade*, which is traditionally served with roast duck. In the south of France, these oranges are crystallized and the blossoms are distilled to make aromatic orange-flower water. The aromatic oils from the peel are used to flavor such liqueurs as Grand Marnier and Cointreau. Bitter oranges have a very short season and are available only in late winter and early spring.

Nutrition

An orange provides twice the adult daily requirement of vitamin C and is high in dietary fiber. The average fruit provides about 50 calories.

Buying and Storing

Choose firm oranges that feel heavy for their size—these will be juicy. Never buy oranges with damaged, shriveled or moldy skin. Oranges keep well; they can be stored at room temperature or in the refrigerator for up to two weeks. The juice and grated zest can be frozen.

Right: Bitter Seville oranges have a very short season—they are available only in January.

Right: Valencia oranges are the world's most popular variety of orange and are the best type for juicing.

Candied orange peel

1 Choose thick-skinned oranges. Wash and dry well. Peel the oranges with a swivel vegetable peeler.

2 Using a sharp knife, cut the peel into thin julienne strips.

3 For each orange, bring to a boil 1 cup water with ½ cup granulated sugar. Add the strips of orange peel, half-cover the pan and simmer until the syrup has reduced by three-quarters. Let cool completely.

4 Sift confectioners' sugar in a thick, even layer over a baking sheet. Roll the candied peel in the sugar. Dry in a cool oven. Store the peel in a jar; it will keep for 2–3 months.

Preparing and Serving

Oranges are best eaten in their natural state, but can be used in an almost infinite variety of desserts, pastries and sweetmeats: fruit salads, mousses, soufflés, ice creams, sorbets and granitas and, perhaps most famous of all, crêpes suzette. They can be squeezed for juice, in which case keep the rind to use in other ways (grated zest can be ground with sugar for sprinkling on breakfast cereals or for use in cakes or custards, for example). The juice can be drunk or used in a marinade for poultry or fish. Fresh sliced oranges combine well with spices like cinnamon, ginger and cardamom, and a sprinkling of distilled orange-flower water enhances their flavor dramatically. Candied orange peel is good in cakes, cookies and Christmas pudding. Crystallized quartered orange slices make an attractive decoration for desserts and cakes.

Oranges go well in savory dishes. Combine them with watercress, beet or chicory and thinly sliced raw red onion for a refreshing salad, or glaze carrots in orange juice and butter. Add orange juice and zest to tomato sauces and soups, or add strips of pared rind to hearty fish soups and

Right: Blood oranges

Duck in bitter orange sauce

The acidity of bitter oranges is the perfect foil for the richness of duck. For *caneton à la bigarade*, pare the rind of a Seville orange, removing only the zest. Cut this into julienne strips. Squeeze the orange and set the juice aside. Roast a duck, then keep it hot. Drain off the fat from the roasting tin, then deglaze the pan with a little white wine. Add 1¼ cups rich chicken stock and the orange juice, reduce until syrupy, then add the orange zest, season and simmer for about 5 minutes. Beat in 2 tablespoons cubed chilled butter. Carve the duck and pour the sauce over. Garnish with peeled orange segments.

meat or poultry casseroles. Peeled orange slices are also good with liver and fish (especially trout and salmon).

EXOTIC
FRUITS

*Thanks to modern transportation methods, tropical fruits are no
longer merely the stuff of travelers' tales. Rambutans,
carambolas, guavas, passion fruit and pomegranates are stocked
on greengrocers' shelves, alongside recent rarities, which have
now become commonplace, such as mangoes, fresh dates and kiwi
fruit. Most supermarkets now label tropical fruits with
preparation and serving suggestions, so it is easy to venture
into the realms of the exotic.*

BANANAS

Bananas are surely the best-known tropical fruit and one of the most healthy and versatile. Neatly packaged in their attractive easy-to-peel skins, hygienically enclosing the sweet, creamy white flesh, bananas are the perfect convenience food.

The banana plant, whose elongated, fanlike leaves can grow to over 4 yards long, is actually an enormous herb. "Hands" of up to 200 bananas point upward through the leaves like fingers.

Above: Bananas, shown here in their unripe state, grow upward in bunches on a huge plant that is actually a giant herb.

History

Bananas originated in Southeast Asia and have grown in the tropics since ancient times. There is a theory that the fruit of the Tree of Knowledge in the Garden of Eden was actually a banana; certainly, a banana leaf would have protected Adam's modesty more effectively than a fig leaf. Before man began to cultivate bananas, the fruits contained so many bitter black seeds that they were almost inedible.

Varieties

Hundreds of different varieties of banana flourish in the tropics, from sweet yellow pygmy fruit to large, fibrous plantains and green bananas, which can only be used for cooking.

The most common varieties of sweet banana are the long, curved yellow

Left: Finger or Sugar bananas are tiny— often no more than the length of a lady's finger!

dessert fruit, which develop a speckled brown skin as they ripen. The most widely available of these is Cavendish, but unless you are an expert it is practically impossible to differentiate between individual varieties.

Finger or **Sugar** These are tiny bananas, often no more than 3 inches long. They have creamy flesh and a very sweet flavor.

Apple These yellow bananas are also very small. They have golden flesh and when very ripe have a faint taste and aroma of apple.

Right: Perhaps the best-known tropical fruit, easy-to-peel yellow bananas, which come in a variety of sizes, are the perfect convenience food.

Right: When very ripe, small Apple bananas have a faint taste and aroma of apple.

Red bananas These bananas from Ecuador have brownish red skins and smooth, yellowish pink, sweet flesh with a creamy texture. Their color makes it hard to assess the exact degree of ripeness, so they can sometimes prove rather disappointing. Allow a few blackish patches to develop on the skin before eating.

Green bananas Large green bananas are suitable only for cooking. They have crisp flesh and are often used as a substitute for potatoes, although they have a blander flavor. Fried green banana rings are good in curries.

Plantain These fruits resemble large bananas, but are flatter in shape. They have firm, pinkish flesh, which is less sweet than that of dessert bananas but contains more starch. They are almost always used in savory dishes and can be cooked like potatoes. Very firm plantains can be peeled, then sliced wafer-thin and deep-fried like potato chips. As plantains ripen, their flesh becomes darker and sweeter, and the fruit can be used in desserts.

Right: Small (as here) or large, red bananas have the same sweet, creamy flesh.

Nutrition

Bananas are extremely nutritious, being rich in potassium, riboflavin, niacin and dietary fiber. Bananas also contain vitamins A and C and some calcium and iron. They have a high energy value (99 calories per 3¾ ounces) and are good for growing children and athletes. They are also excellent for low-salt, low-fat and cholesterol-free diets.

Buying and Storing

Bananas are harvested unripe and stored in a humid atmosphere to ripen slowly. Unripe bananas are green all over; these are inedible. Fruit with green-tinged ends are slightly underripe, with a crisp texture and refreshing taste. Perfectly ripe bananas are uniformly yellow; as the fruit continues to ripen, brown speckles appear on the skin until it is covered with brown mottling. By this stage, the flesh is soft and sweet and is best for mashing. Once the skin has become brown all over, the banana is too ripe to eat; the flesh will have collapsed, but it can still be used for cooking.

Do not buy bananas with damaged skins, or those that are too ripe. Unlike other fruit, they will continue to ripen rapidly at home. Never store them in the refrigerator, as the skins will blacken. Kept in a fruit bowl, bananas will hasten the ripening of other fruit.

Dried bananas Drying intensifies the sweetness of bananas. Dried bananas are dark brown, sticky and extremely sweet. They are usually eaten as a highly nutritious but calorific snack, but can also be added to winter fruit salads or savory stews.

Canned bananas Asian food stores sell whole baby bananas, sometimes complete with blossom, canned in heavy syrup. Only for those with a very sweet tooth!

Peeling plantains

1 Using a sharp knife, trim the fruit. Cut in half horizontally.

2 Slit the plantain skin along the natural ridge with a sharp knife. Take care not to cut through the flesh.

3 Ease up the edge of the skin and run your thumb tip underneath to lift up the skin. Lift off and discard the skin.

Right: Plantains are almost always used in savory dishes and can be cooked like potatoes.

Preparing and Cooking

Peel bananas just before using, removing the white threads from the flesh. Slice the bananas and, if not serving immediately, brush with lemon juice to prevent discoloration.

Dessert bananas are delicious eaten raw, but cooking brings out the sweetness and enhances the flavor. Raw bananas can be made into ice cream, milk shakes and trifles. Sliced bananas can be added to fruit salads or used to garnish sweet and savory dishes. In Indonesia and the Far East, they are served as an accompaniment to rice dishes such as *nasi goreng* and curries. They combine well with other tropical ingredients, especially brown sugar, coconut, exotic fruits like pineapple, passion fruit and mango, and rum.

Bananas can be baked in their skins, then split and served with melted butter and lemon juice. Alternatively, cook them over the dying embers of a grill until the skins turn black. Split them, sprinkle with rum and serve with heavy cream. Another rich dessert is banoffi pie, a very sweet concoction of bananas and toffee. A less sweet but equally delicious combination is broiled bananas wrapped in bacon. Banana fritters are always popular; cut the fruit into chunks, coat in batter and deep-fry, or wrap in phyllo pastry, brush with melted butter and

Above: Dried bananas are dark brown, sticky and very sweet.

deep-fry. Mashed bananas make deliciously moist cakes and tea breads.

Green bananas and plantains are starchier than sweet bananas and contain less sugar, so they are served as a vegetable. They can be boiled, baked, mashed, fried or broiled, and are an essential ingredient of many African and West Indian dishes. Banana leaves are often used as a wrapping for savory fillings and add a pleasant aromatic flavor to both chicken and fish.

BABACOS

The babaco is a hybrid of the papaya. Pointed at the stem end and blunt at the other, this large five-sided fruit reveals a soft white core when halved. When unripe, the waxy skin is pale green, maturing to yellow. When ripe, the pale orangey pink flesh is succulent and juicy, with a faint aroma of fresh strawberries, and the flavor resembles that of a rather bland papaya.

History

The babaco is native to Ecuador. European botanists discovered it about seventy years ago, and it is now widely grown in New Zealand and in the Channel Islands.

Nutrition

The fruit contains valuable enzymes that help to digest fat and proteins and can be used to tenderize meat. It is a good source of vitamin C.

Buying and Storing

Babacos keep well. Yellow fruit are ready to eat right away and should be stored in the refrigerator, where they will keep for about five days. Pale green babacos can be kept for a few days at room temperature, until yellow and ripe.

Preparing and Cooking

Babacos can be sliced, skin and all, and eaten raw. The delicate flavor can be livened up with lemon or lime juice and sugar. The flesh can be diced and used raw in salads, or squeezed to make a refreshing juice. Babacos can also be poached in syrup and served as a dessert with cream, custard or vanilla or ginger ice cream, but you will need to flavor the syrup with lime juice and

aromatics. On a savory note, the fruit makes excellent sauces, chutneys and relishes. Stewed babaco can be served as an accompaniment to roast chicken, pork and ham.

Babaco for breakfast
For a deliciously different breakfast experience, try serving your favorite cereal with chilled cooked babaco. Make a syrup by boiling equal quantities of water and sugar with the juice of a lemon or lime and a split vanilla bean, a cinnamon stick or a grating of nutmeg. Dice the babaco (there is no need to peel it) and poach gently in the syrup for about 10 minutes, until tender. Chill well before using.

*Right:
Babacos are ripe when yellow all over—keep fruits that are still mottled green (as here) at room temperature for a few days, until they are completely yellow.*

BREADFRUIT

The fruit of a very tall tree, these large round- to egg-shaped fruits weigh from 11 ounces to 6½ pounds. They have thick, warty, greenish skin and white starchy flesh with a breadlike texture, which sometimes contains up to 200 edible seeds and sometimes none at all. Breadfruit form part of the staple diet in the tropics.

History

Native to the Pacific and East Indies, breadfruit came to fame in the famous 1787 mutiny on the *Bounty*, when, during the voyage to the West Indies, Captain William Bligh gave the last remaining fresh water to his precious cargo of breadfruit in preference to the crew. After being cast adrift, and enduring immense hardship, the overbearing captain arrived in Timor and was again sent out to collect breadfruit, earning himself the name "Breadfruit Bligh."

Nutrition

Breadfruit is very starchy. It is high in fiber and contains small amounts of vitamin C and folic acid.

Below: Breadfruit

Preparing and Cooking

Breadfruit are normally eaten as a vegetable. When really ripe, they can be eaten raw, but they are more usually cooked. They can be peeled and boiled, roasted or fried like potatoes, or baked whole in the oven.

CARAMBOLAS

Native to Indonesia and the Moluccas, carambolas, or star fruit, are now widely available in supermarkets. The uncut yellow or pale amber fruit has a waxy skin and is cylindrical in shape, with concave sides and five ridged edges; it resembles an elongated Chinese lantern. When the fruit is sliced crosswise, the slices are perfect star shapes, which are wonderful for decorative purposes. Although the fruit often tastes less exciting than it looks, it is refreshing and juicy to eat.

History

Carambolas originated in the Malay Archipelago, between Southeast Asia and Australia, but they are now also grown in Africa, Brazil, the West Indies and the United States.

Nutrition

Carambolas are a good source of vitamin C, and contain some potassium, niacin and phosphorus. They provide about 50 calories per 3¾ ounces.

Buying and Storing

Some carambolas have more flavor than others; there is no way of telling before you taste, so they are best used as an attractive decoration or in conjunction with other exotic fruits. Choose firm, undamaged fruits and hope for the best. They will keep in the refrigerator for up to a week.

Preparing and Serving

A good carambola will be sweet and tangy enough to eat on its own, complete with skin. Slice the fruit crosswise and, if you wish, cut out the flat central seeds with a sharp knife. The fruits are generally eaten raw as part of a fruit salad or made into jams, but they can also be poached in a syrup enlivened with lime juice.

Left: Carambolas make a wonderful garnish. When cut crosswise, the slices are perfect star shapes, hence the carambola's other name—star fruit.

CHERIMOYAS, CUSTARD APPLES AND SOURSOPS

Native to South America and the West Indies, cherimoyas are the fruit of shrubs belonging to the annona species. The large heart-shaped or oval fruit is made up of many corpels, or concave sections, with scaly yellowish green or tan skin, rather like a pinecone or a half-prepared globe artichoke. Inside, the fruit has creamy white, custardlike flesh with a sweet-sour flavor (hence its name) reminiscent of pineapples and bananas, and large black seeds.

Varieties

There are many different varieties of cherimoya, of which custard apples and soursops are the most widely available.
Custard apples These are heart-shaped or oval and can weigh up to 1 pound.

Below: Heart-shaped soursops have a tangy, acidic flavor.

They have light tan or greenish quilted skin, which develops brown patches as the fruit ripens; the flesh is particularly mellow and custardlike.
Soursop Also called prickly custard apples or bullock's hearts, soursops are the largest of this group of fruits. They have dark green skins covered in numerous short spines. The white juicy flesh has a tangy, acidic flavor, which gives the fruit its descriptive name. Once ripe, soursops rapidly ferment and become inedible.

Nutrition

Cherimoyas are high in vitamin C and iron, and provide 92 calories per 3¾ ounces.

Buying and Storing

Cherimoyas are fragile, so choose compact fruit with unblemished skin and tightly packed corpels; once these have separated, the fruit is past its best. Press gently to check that the fruit has a slight "give." Cherimoyas should be eaten as soon as possible after buying, but can be kept in the bottom of the refrigerator for a day or two. Unripe fruit should be kept in a brown paper bag at room temperature until they are ready to eat.

Preparation and Serving

All types of cherimoya can be eaten fresh. Simply cut the fruit in half

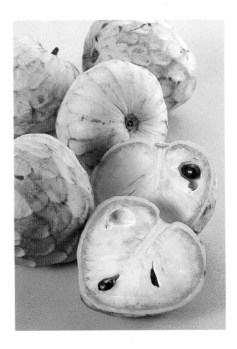

Above: Custard apples have delicious mellow flesh that is soft, almost like custard (hence their name).

lengthwise and scoop the flesh straight from the shell with a spoon, discarding the inedible seeds. For a special treat, add a dollop of cream.

Cherimoya flesh makes a delicious fruit sauce when blended with bananas and cream, or it can be blended with four times its volume of water to make a refreshing drink; stir in sugar to taste. The fruits can also be made into jams, jellies and sorbets.

CURUBA

Also known as the "banana passion fruit," the curuba is like an elongated passion fruit, with soft yellowish skin. The orange pulp has a sharp flavor and needs a little sugar to make it palatable. The skin can be peeled off in the same way as a banana. Curubas marry well with other tropical fruits and can be used in the same way as you would passion fruit.

Right: Curuba have a sharp flavor and can be used like passion fruit.

DATES

Dates are the fruit of the date palm, which grows in subtropical and desert areas throughout North Africa, the Arab States, California and Australia. The finger-shaped fruit grows in clusters of several dozen at the top of the tall trees, ripening from green to burnished brown. Date palms are prolific; the average annual yield of a single palm is 110 pounds.

Until a few years ago, only dried dates were available outside their native lands, but now fresh dates are exported, although only a few of the many varieties reach the stores.

History

Dates are one of the world's oldest cultivated fruits. It is probable that the Babylonians grew them as long as 8,000 years ago; certainly records show that they have been cultivated for over 5,000 years. In early times, the date palm was regarded as the "tree of life." Every part of it was used; the buds and fruit were eaten or dried and ground into flour, the sap was drunk, the fibers were woven and the date pits were used as fuel or fodder for donkeys and camels. Even today, dates are still known as the "bread of the desert."

Left: Boxed halawi dates.

Above: Date palms grow throughout North Africa, the Arab States, California and Australia.

The ancient Greeks and Romans were also fond of dates and often combined them with meat in their cooking.

Varieties

Of the many varieties of date, only a few are exported, and these are seldom sold by name. The most popular variety is the golden brown *deglet noor* ("date of the light") from North Africa and Israel; you may also find the very sweet *halawi* or the fragrant *khaleseh,* which can be recognized by its orange-brown skin. The finest dates are the large crinkly-skinned *medjool* from Egypt and California, whose flesh is intensely mellow and sweet.

Nutrition

Dates are extremely nutritious. They contain more natural sugar than any other fruit and deliver a substantial amount of dietary fiber and potassium, as well as providing many vitamins and mineral salts. They provide 144 calories per 3¾ ounces.

Buying and Storing

Fresh dates These should be plump and moist, with a smooth skin and a slightly crunchy texture. They are sold loose or in baskets. Dates are ripe when they are burnished brown. Unripe dates are more golden; they can be eaten in this state, but the flesh will be crisp and less honeyed than that of ripe dates. To ripen, keep the dates at room temperature. Fresh dates can be frozen whole, but check that they have not been previously frozen (they almost always have been).

Semi-dried dates These are sold in a cluster on the stem. They have wrinkled skins and a chewy texture.

Dried dates These are the old familiar Christmas favorites, sticky and intensely sweet, and are often sold sitting on a frilly doily inside a long box decorated with palm trees and camels. Since the advent of fresh dates, their popularity has declined. Dried dates are also sold pressed into blocks for use in cooking. Some Asian markets stock tiny, wrinkled red dates and smoky black dates with the flavor of a bonfire, which are only suitable for cooking. Semi-dried and dried dates will keep for months, but do not store them near strong-smelling foods like onions, as they absorb odors.

Below: Dried deglet noor dates in their familiar long box.

Stuffed dates

1 Cut the dates in half and pick out the pits.

2 Fill the cavities of the dates with cream cheese and sandwich the halves together.

3 Alternatively, mold a little marzipan to fill the cavities, roll the date halves in sugar and top each with a walnut half.

Right: Dried dates pressed into a block. For cooking, this type of date may need to be softened in hot water before using.

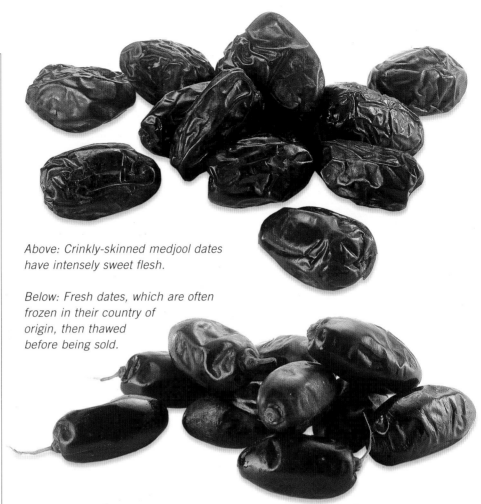

Above: Crinkly-skinned medjool dates have intensely sweet flesh.

Below: Fresh dates, which are often frozen in their country of origin, then thawed before being sold.

Preparation and Cooking

Fresh dates can be eaten just as they are. If you prefer to peel them, gently pinch the skin at the stem end until the fruit pops out. They can be pitted and filled with plain or colored marzipan or nuts, or rolled in sugar to serve as decorative petits fours.

Fresh dates also make good additions to fruit salads and winter compotes. Surprisingly, they are also good in savory dishes; in North Africa, they are used in tagines (fragrant stews) and curries, or as a sauce or stuffing for fish, meat or poultry.

Above: Dried Chinese dates are only suitable for cooking.

Dates have a particular affinity with cheese. Serve them on a cheese board, or halve and pit them and sandwich together with cream cheese.

Dried dates are good in moist cakes and hot sticky puddings, and combine very well with nuts, particularly walnuts and almonds. For cooking, dried dates should be pitted and chopped, using scissors dipped in hot water.

DRAGON FRUIT

Dragon fruit, or pitihayas, come in both yellow and pink versions. Pink dragon fruit are large, fuschia-pink fruit about 4 inches long, covered with pointed green-tipped scales, rather like the leaves of a globe artichoke. Inside, they are spectacularly beautiful, with translucent pearly white flesh dotted with a mass of edible black seeds, which add an appealing crunch. The flesh is sweet and refreshing, with a slightly acidic melonlike flavor. It has the texture of kiwi fruit.

Yellow dragon fruit look more like prickly pears or mini-pineapples. They taste exactly like the pink variety.

Nutrition

Dragon fruit are rich in vitamin C and dietary fiber.

Buying and Storing

Yellow dragon fruit are ripe when golden all over. Both pink and yellow varieties should yield when gently squeezed in the hand. Best eaten as soon as they are ripe, but the fruits can be kept in the refrigerator for up to three days.

Preparing and Serving

Dragon fruit are best eaten on their own, sprinkled with lemon or lime juice to enhance the flavor. They should be served chilled. Cut them in half lengthwise, then scoop out the flesh from the shell. The shells can be used as unusual serving dishes.

Above: Brightly colored dragon fruit have sweet, refreshing flesh.

DURIANS

The disgusting, all-pervading, sewagelike smell is legendary and has given rise to the alternative name: civet fruit. When ripe, the flavor of the flesh, however, is delicious.

Durians are large fruit that can weigh up to 10 pounds. Round or oval, they have a woody, olive green outer layer covered with stubby, sharp spikes, which turns yellow as they ripen. They consist of three to five segments containing aromatic creamy white flesh with the texture of rich custard; the flavor is sweet, a little like that of strawberries, with a creamy aftertaste. The large brown seeds are edible if cooked.

History

Durians originated in Malaysia or Borneo and from there spread to Southeast Asia in prehistoric times. Despite their unspeakable smell, they have always been considered an aphrodisiac.

Nutrition

Durians are starchy fruits. They contain a small amount of fat and are a good source of potassium and vitamin C.

Buying and Storing

It is essential to eat durians very fresh; don't attempt to store them, however briefly, or your house will smell of blocked sewers. Never buy fruit with damaged skin, or the smell will be

unbearable. Do not buy durians abroad and attempt to bring them home, as they are banned by most airlines! Take care not to drip juice onto clothing or table linen, as it stains indelibly. Despite all these dire warnings, don't be put off from trying this exotic fruit; it really does taste wonderful.

Preparing and Serving

Durians are best eaten raw. Use a large sharp knife to slit the skin at the segment joints, press out the segments and scoop out the flesh and seeds with a spoon. The rich, custardy flesh can be eaten just as it is, or puréed to make ice cream or milk shakes. Durian flesh is also used for making jam and cakes, and is available canned. The richness of the pulp also makes an excellent foil to hot, spicy foods like curries and chile dishes. Durian seeds can be roasted or boiled and eaten like nuts.

Left: The horrible, all-pervading sewage-like smell of durians is legendary. However, when they are ripe, the flavor of the flesh is delicious.

FEIJOAS

Although a distant member of the guava family, feijoas resemble small, slightly pear-shaped passion fruit, with a dark green skin that yellows as the fruit ripens. The thin, tough skin protects a soft jellylike pulp containing tiny, hard seeds, which are edible. Despite its alternative name of "pineapple guava," the feijoa tastes more like an aromatic strawberry. Treat it like guava.

History

Originally from South America, the feijoa takes its name from the Portuguese botanist Dom da Silva Feijoa, who discovered it in Brazil. It is also cultivated in New Zealand.

Nutrition

Feijoas are an excellent source of vitamin C and are rich in iodine. They provide 20 calories per 3¾ ounces.

Right: Feijoas taste a little like aromatic fresh strawberries.

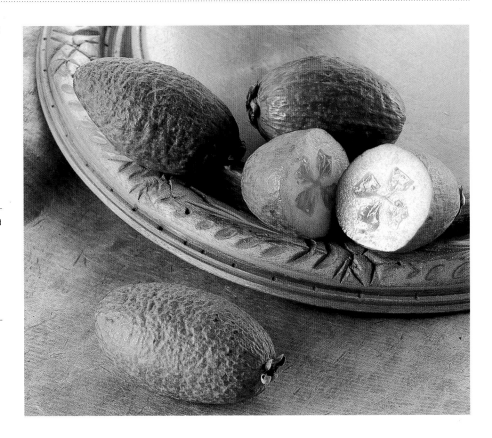

GENIP

The bright green dimpled skin of the genip, or mamoncilla, gives rise to its alternative name of "Spanish lime," but it is related to neither the lime nor the lychee, which it resembles in flavor.

Genips are small, round tropical fruits, about 1¼ inches in diameter, that grow on trees in bunches like grapes. The tough green skin protects a jellylike pink pulp containing a large central seed.

The flesh is juicy and sweet, with a slightly acidic note. Despite its pale color, genip juice stains horribly and if you get it on your clothes or table linen, it will never come out.

GRANADILLAS

Granadillas, or grenadillas, are the largest members of the passion fruit family and can weigh several pounds. In their unripe state, these large specimens are used as vegetables, but they are seldom exported. The granadillas you will find in stores are smooth, round, orange-skinned fruits, with grayish pulp containing small, hard seeds. They look more attractive than passion fruit, but taste less fragrant. Granadillas can be eaten and used in exactly the same way as passion fruit.

Right: Granadillas

GUAVAS

Similar in shape to pears or plums, guavas can be as small as 1 inch or as large as 4 inches in diameter. They have thin, pale green skins, which turn light yellow as they ripen; the flesh varies from white to deep pink or salmon red. It contains a number of flattish, hard but edible seeds. Guavas are highly scented with an aromatic sweet-acid flavor, not unlike that of quinces.

Above: Guavas are delicious eaten raw.

Guavas are available canned in syrup and made into sweet fruit drinks.

Varieties

There are several varieties of guava, the most common being the familiar yellow fruit. Strawberry or cherry guavas are smaller, with reddish purple skins.

Nutrition

Guavas are exceptionally rich in vitamin C and are a good source of niacin, potassium and dietary fiber. They provide 62 calories per 3¾ ounces.

Preparing and Cooking

Ripe guavas are delicious eaten raw. They can be poached in syrup, but must be simmered gently, as the flesh easily disintegrates. The flesh can be puréed to use in ice creams and sorbets, or made into jams and jellies (alone, or with other fruits) or sweet drinks. Like quinces, they have an affinity for apples; a few slices of peeled guava added

Preparing guavas

To eat guavas raw, cut in half and squeeze over a little lime juice. Scoop out the flesh from the skin.

to an apple pie or applesauce impart a special fragrance.

Guavas can also be used in savory dishes and are particularly good in a sauce for duck or game birds. They make an interesting addition to salads, and can be stuffed with cream cheese and served as an appetizer.

JACKFRUIT

Jackfruit are related to breadfruit. The large, irregularly shaped oval fruits can weigh as much as 44 pounds. They have a rough, spiny skin, which ripens from green to brown, and each fruit contains large, white edible seeds. Ripe jackfruit have a pungent, musty odor.

History

Jackfruit come originally from the rain forests of India and Malaysia, and are now grown in Asia, Africa, South America and Australia.

Preparing and Cooking

Ripe jackfruit can be peeled and eaten raw; the pulp is sweet and rather bland. They are better boiled,

roasted or fried, to be served as a vegetable or in a curry. The seeds can be eaten boiled, fried or roasted like chestnuts. Jackfruit is only available canned, in syrup, in the United States.

Below: Jackfruit are huge—they can weigh up to 44 pounds.

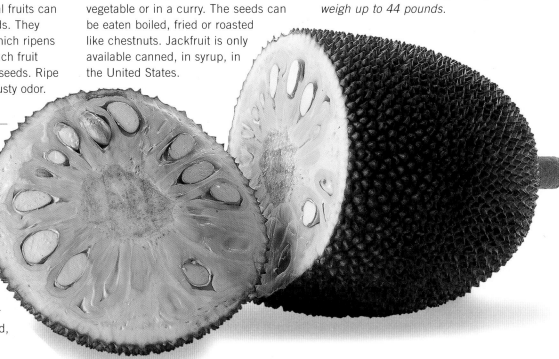

JAMAICAN PLUMS

Also known as "hoy" or "hog" plums, golden apple, limbu and mombin, this fruit belongs to the same family as the mango and is grown in the West Indies, Central and South America, Southeast Asia and India. The golden yellow to deep red and purple fruits are small, about 1½ inches long and 1 inch in diameter. They grow several to a branch and, like mangoes, have soft skin and contain a large central pit. The firm, yellow flesh, which is juicy, deliciously fragrant and sweet, is more akin to pineapple or apple than mango. The distinctive flavor has a slightly acidic tang. Unfortunately, these fruits are fragile and do not travel well, but you may find them in Indian markets. Jamaican plums can be eaten raw, sweetened with a little brown sugar or sprinkled with rum or liqueur and served with cream. They combine well with other fruits in a fruit salad, and can also be poached, pickled or made into jams, jellies and sorbets. They make a good addition to curries.

Right: Unripe Jamaican plums

JUJUBES

Also known as Chinese jujubes, apples or dates, these small greeny brown fruits have been cultivated in Northern China for more than 4,000 years and are now grown extensively in India (where they are known as *bec* or *bor*), Asia, Southern Europe and more recently on the West Coast of the U.S. and in Australia. Jujubes, which ripen in the autumn, can be oblong, egg-shaped or round. They have crisp pearly white flesh enclosing a single pit, with the sweet flavor and texture of an unripe pear. Most fruits are deep brown when ripe, but can be bought while still firm but orange-red with just a hint of brown and left at room temperature for a day or two to ripen.They can be eaten raw, stewed with orange juice, candied or made into jams and jellies.

Left: Jujubes

KIWANOS

This strange-looking fruit is also known as horned melon, horned cucumber and jelly melon. The oval fruits have thick, bright golden orange skin covered in sharp spikes. The skin conceals a bright green, jellylike flesh encasing edible seeds, rather like a passion fruit, with a subtle taste of cucumber, banana and lime.

History

Originally from Africa, kiwanos are now grown commercially in New Zealand, Portugal and the United States.

Preparing and Cooking

Cut the fruit in half, then spoon the pulp straight from the shell. It makes a refreshing drink or it can be added to fruit salads or cocktails. The shells can be used as serving dishes. Blend the pulp with plain yogurt, honey and vanilla ice cream to make an unusual milk shake.

Right: With their spiky skin, kiwanos resemble strange miniature prehistoric monsters.

KIWI FRUIT

These cylindrical fruit, 3–4 inches in length, are covered with a light brown fuzzy skin that looks very dull in comparison with the beautiful bright green interior, with its crown of tiny, edible black seeds arranged around a white core. The flavor is delicate, yet refreshing and tangy.

History

Kiwi fruit were formerly known as Chinese gooseberries, in recognition of the fact that they originated in the Yangtze Valley. They are now extensively grown in New Zealand, Australia, South America and even Italy and France.

Nutrition

A single kiwi fruit contains more than a day's vitamin C requirement for an adult, plus vitamin E, and provides only 50 calories per 3¾ ounces.

Buying and Storing

Choose plump, unwrinkled fruit with unblemished skins. Kiwis are ripe when they yield to gentle pressure like a ripe pear; however, hard, unripe fruit can easily be ripened at home. Store at room temperature, but not in a bowl with other fruits, since the enzymes

Right: Kiwi fruit are delicious eaten raw—scoop out the flesh with a teaspoon.

in kiwi fruit cause them to ripen very quickly. Firm, unripe kiwis will keep for several weeks if stored in a cool place.

Preparing and Serving

The skin of a kiwi fruit is edible but the fuzzy texture is not particularly pleasant, so it is best to peel the fruit with a small sharp knife. For the most attractive effect, slice kiwis horizontally.

When nouvelle cuisine was in its heyday, slices of kiwi fruit appeared as a garnish for almost every dish, however inappropriate. Kiwis are certainly decorative, but they are good eaten as a fruit in their own right. They make an attractive addition to fruit salads, open fruit tarts and meringues, or can be puréed to make a sorbet or coulis. They go well with

white meats, prosciutto, poultry and fish, especially salmon and shellfish.

Kiwi fruit contain enzymes that make an excellent meat tenderizer. Rub the peeled skin or slices of kiwi into both sides of a cheaper cut of meat and leave for 20 minutes; the meat will become tender enough to broil.

The same enzymes, however, will prevent gelatin from setting and will curdle milk products, so do not attempt to make ice cream with raw kiwi. Cooking destroys the enzymes, but also the delicate flavor and texture.

KUBOS

Looking rather like wine red guavas, kubos are pear-shaped fruit with thick bitter skin and refreshingly sweet, slightly tangy, creamy white flesh

spattered with tiny, edible, crunchy black seeds. The texture is a little like that of an unripe pear. To eat, cut the fruit in half lengthwise and scoop out

the pulp with a spoon, or spoon the pulp over ice cream. The flesh can be combined with other fruits and makes a good addition to fruit salads.

LONGANS

Distant relatives of the lychee, longans are small, round, undistinguished-looking fruit. The brittle light brown skin encloses translucent, jellylike flesh around a single large inedible pit. They

taste similar to lychees but have a pleasant peppery tang. Longans are grown throughout Southeast Asia and China, where they are particularly popular; the Chinese name means

"dragon's eye." Fresh longans can be peeled and eaten like lychees, on their own or in fruit salads, sweet-and-sour dishes and stir-fries. Asian food stores sell longans canned in syrup.

LOQUATS

Native to China and South Japan, the loquat is one of the few subtropical fruits that belongs to the apple and pear family; it is sometimes known as a Japanese medlar. The name comes from the Cantonese *luk-kwyit*, meaning "rush orange," which describes the color of the loquat's flesh. The fruits are small and plum-shaped, with apricot-colored skin and white or yellowy orange flesh surrounding inedible brown pits. They have a sweet scent and a delicate mangolike flavor that is greatly enhanced by a squeeze of lime or lemon juice.

Buying and Storing

Ripe loquats are speckled with brown patches; perfect, apricotlike fruit are

Right: Loquats are one of the few subtropical fruits that belong to the apple and pear family.

still unripe. These can be ripened at home by being kept in a fruit bowl for a few days.

Preparing and Serving

Loquats can be eaten raw, complete with skin, or poached in a light syrup. They go well with other fruits, like

apples, pears and peaches, and make a wonderful ice cream to accompany these fruits. Loquats make good jams, jellies and chutneys (leave in a few of the seeds to impart a bitter almond flavor); they can also be cooked with brown sugar and wine vinegar to make a sauce for poultry.

LYCHEES

The leathery, scaly, reddish skin or "shell" of the lychee encloses pearly white translucent flesh that is firm and jellylike. This sweet, fragrant flesh is wrapped around a large, shiny, inedible brown seed. Canned lychees are

available in stores—and are often served as a dessert in Chinese restaurants—but they have none of the fragrance and subtlety of the fresh fruit.

History

Lychees have been cultivated in China for thousands of years. They have been considered a symbol of romance ever since a concubine of one of the Chinese emperors insisted on having teams of horses carry lychees hundreds of miles across country for her pleasure.

Nutrition

Lychees are rich in vitamin C. They provide about 65 calories per 3¾ ounces.

Buying and Storing

Choose lychees whose shells are as pink or red as possible. Greenish fruits are underripe, while brown fruit are past

Left: Lychees

their prime. Although the shells act as protection, lychees quickly dry out, so do not buy too many at a time, and eat them as soon as possible after purchase. They will keep in the refrigerator for up to a week.

Preparing and Serving

Fresh lychees are best eaten raw as a refreshing end to a meal. Diners simply remove the shells, then nibble or suck the flesh off the pits.

Lychees can also be pitted and added to fruit salads, or poached in lemon-scented syrup and served chilled, alone or with ice cream or other poached fruits. For an unusual appetizer, serve pitted fresh lychees stuffed with cream cheese and nuts.

Use these succulent fruits in savory dishes too—they are good in Chinese sweet-and-sour dishes and also in salads (particularly when combined with avocado). They also make an interesting accompaniment to cold meats like pork and duck.

MANGOES

Among the most delicious and luxurious of all tropical fruits, different varieties of mangoes are grown throughout the tropics, from the Caribbean to Africa, Southeast Asia, Australia and India. Although they come in many different shapes, sizes and colors, mangoes are typically curved oblong fruits with green, pinkish gold or red skin and glorious orange, highly perfumed flesh surrounding a very large, hairy, inedible flat pit. The meltingly soft flesh is always juicy and sweet, although it sometimes has an acid overtone. Some mangoes have fibrous flesh; others are succulent and buttery. Certain varieties are said to have a flavor of mint, lemon, banana or pineapple, but in reality mangoes have their own distinctive taste, unlike any other fruit.

Below: Mangoes have meltingly soft flesh that is juicy and sweet.

History

The history of the mango goes back over 6,000 years and is closely connected with Hinduism. Buddha was said to have been presented with a mango grove so that he could rest in its shade. Mangoes are native to Malaysia and India, and they form part of the local legend and folklore. The name comes from the Tamil *man-key* ("fruit of the tree"). Nineteenth-century traders introduced the fruit to the West Indies, Africa and South America.

Varieties

There are over 2,500 varieties of mango. They can be round-, oval-, heart- or kidney-shaped and can weigh between 5 ounces and 1½ pounds. All mangoes are green when unripe, but some remain green when they ripen, while others turn golden or bright red, or a combination of these colors.

Popular varieties include the **Alphonso** or **Alphonsine** from India, which has supple, buttery flesh and a heady, sweet flavor. West Indian varieties include the small **Julie** and the round, juicy **Bombay**. Cultivated varieties like **Parvin, Kent** and **Tommy Atkins** have thinner skins than wild mangoes and are less fibrous. **Ruby mangoes**, from the Gambia, have an excellent flavor but are rather fibrous. To eat one of these glowing red fruit, squeeze it gently between your hands, then pierce the skin and suck out the juice.

Nutrition

Ripe mangoes are rich in vitamins, especially A and C, and are a good source of beta-carotene. They provide about 59 calories per 3¾ ounces.

Buying and Storing

Color is not necessarily an indication of ripeness in a mango; some remain solidly green when ripe. Buy unblemished fruit with no black blotches on the skin, as these indicate that the fruit is overripe and will have mushy flesh. The best test of a mango is its aroma, which should be highly perfumed. The fruit should be just yielding when gently pressed.

Mangoes will ripen at home if left in a warm place. To hasten ripening, place them in a brown paper bag with a banana or kiwi fruit. Eat the mangoes as soon as they are ripe.

Canned mangoes Mango slices are available canned in syrup. These are extremely sweet and are best drained before eating. They can be puréed to make a coulis or ice cream.

Above: Parvin

Preparing a mango

1 Place the mango narrow side down on a chopping board. Cut off a thick lengthwise slice, keeping the knife as close to the pit as possible. Turn the mango around and repeat on the other side. Cut off the flesh adhering to the pit and scoop out the flesh from the mango slices.

2 To make a "hedgehog," prepare the mango as above and score the flesh on each thick slice with crisscross lines at 1/2-inch intervals, taking care not to cut through the skin.

3 Fold the mango halves inside out and serve.

Right: Thin-skinned Tommy Atkins mangoes.

Dried mangoes

These can be added to chutneys and relishes, or mixed with other dried fruits in cake and tea bread recipes.

Preparing and Serving

Mangoes are so delicious that they are best savored in their raw state, perhaps with a squeeze of lime or lemon. The main disadvantage of this is that they are extremely difficult to eat elegantly. Indeed, it is said that the only way to eat them is in the bath. The secret of retaining a modicum of dignity is to remove the pit before attempting to eat the juicy flesh.

Whichever way you cut a mango, some flesh will always be left clinging to the pit. On no account waste this—wait until no one can see you, then cut off the skin and suck the aromatic pulp off the pit for a real treat!

Mangoes make an exotic addition to fruit salads and can be puréed to make sorbets and ice creams. They go well with other tropical flavors, like passion fruit and rum. They are excellent served with cured meats like prosciutto or smoked chicken, and make a refreshing accompaniment to spicy dishes and curries. Shrimp or other shellfish combine well with mango.

Ripe mangoes can be mixed with chiles to make a delicious salsa, while unripe green fruit are traditionally used to make mango chutney and pickles, which go well with cold meats and curries. In the West Indies and Asia, unripe mangoes are used as a vegetable and are baked or stewed with chicken and meat dishes.

Right: Kent, another of the 2,500 varieties of mango.

MANGOSTEENS

Despite their name, mangosteens have nothing to do with mangoes. Nor are they related to lychees, although their pearly white flesh looks very similar.

Mangosteens are apple-shaped with rather leathery, reddish brown skin that is deep purple when ripe. The flesh is divided into five segments, each containing a large seed. The segments are enclosed in dark pink pith, which should be removed before eating. Mangosteens have a sweet, refreshing flavor, rather like that of a plum, but more highly perfumed.

History

Mangosteens are indigenous to Southeast Asia. The trees are slow to grow; it is fifteen years before they bear fruit. They are now grown commercially in parts of Thailand, Central America and Australia.

Preparing and Serving

The flavor of mangosteens is too fragrant and delicate to be impaired by cooking. Eat them just as they are, or add to fruit salad. Peeled mangosteens look spectacular surrounded by a ribbon of strawberry or raspberry coulis.

Serving a mangosteen

1 Using a small, sharp knife, cut the skin around the equator of the shell, then lift off the top half of the shell and spoon out the flesh.

2 Alternatively, cut the mangosteens in half and scoop out the flesh with a spoon.

Above: Mangosteens have a highly perfumed flavor. Eat the pearly white fruit segments just as they are, or add them to fruit salad.

MARACOYAS

Also known as yellow passion fruit, maracoya is a largish fruit with vibrant green, thick, shiny skin that turns yellow as it ripens. Inside is a mass of translucent orange pulp enclosing hard gray seeds, just like a passion fruit, but sharper and less aromatic. Use in exactly the same way as passion fruit, adding plenty of sugar.

Right: Maracoyas

PASSION FRUIT

Passion fruit takes its name from its exotic flower, which is said to symbolize the Passion of Christ. Native to the Americas, these round or oval fruits have a leathery purplish brown skin (some, like those from Brazil, are yellow in color), which wrinkles when the fruits are fully ripe. Inside, the edible seeds are surrounded by intensely fragrant, translucent greenish orange pulp with a distinctive sour-sweet flavor and a wonderful scent. The fruits can be as small as a cherry or as large as an orange, but the ones most commonly available in stores are about 3 inches long.

Left: Passion fruit

Nutrition

The fruits contain vitamins A and C and are a good source of dietary fiber. They contain 34 calories per 3¾ ounces.

Buying and Storing

Choose fruit that feel heavy for their size, with firm, slightly wrinkled skins. Very wrinkly passion fruit with extremely dark skins will have dried out. Passion fruit can be ripened at room temperature; do not keep them in the refrigerator. The pulp can be frozen in ice cube trays, then packed into plastic bags. The juice is sold in cartons.

Preparing and Serving

The simplest way to eat passion fruit is on its own; cut the fruit in half and scoop out the pulp and seeds with a spoon. Both are edible, but the pulp can be strained to make a smooth coulis or refreshing drink. Passion fruit enhances the flavor of all other fruits and makes a delicious topping for a meringue or cheesecake.

Strained pulp can be made into ice creams and sorbets, or added to yogurt. Passion fruit jelly goes well with roast meats, or it can be spread on bread or toast. The juice makes an excellent marinade for rich meats like venison and game birds.

PAPAYAS

The papaya is native to North America, but it is now grown in most tropical or subtropical regions of the world. The large, pear-shaped fruits grow to about 8 inches in length. Some varieties remain green when ripe, but most turn deep yellow or orange. Papayas have beautiful, deep salmon pink flesh, with an abundance of edible gray-black seeds in the central cavity. The soft, juicy, sweet flesh tastes like a cross between melons and peaches.

Right: Papayas

Nutrition

Papayas are rich in vitamin A and calcium and contain large quantities of the enzyme papain, which breaks down protein and can be used to tenderize meat. Papain also makes papayas very easy to digest. They provide about 45 calories per 3¾ ounces.

Buying and Storing

Choose uniformly yellow fruit. Sniff them; they should have a delicate scent. Papayas bruise easily, so do not buy any with damaged or shriveled skins. If the fruit is not ripe, check the skin around the stem end; it should be yellow, otherwise the papaya will never ripen. Ripe papayas should be eaten immediately. Fruit that is not quite ripe should be left at room temperature until soft and yellow. The flesh can be cubed or puréed and frozen.

Preparing and Serving

Simply cut the papaya in half lengthwise and scoop out the seeds from the cavity. You can eat them (they have a peppery flavor), but they are not particularly pleasant. Squeeze a little lime or lemon juice on the flesh before serving.

Papayas can be used in the same way as melons, served solo with a good squeeze of lime, or sprinkled with ground ginger and served with cured meats like prosciutto or smoked chicken. The cubed flesh can be added to fruit salads, piled on top of meringues, made into ice creams and sorbets, or served with yogurt and preserved ginger. It also goes well with savory dishes like seafood and chicken curries. Finely chopped papaya is perfect with chiles in a fresh salsa. The skins can be used to tenderize cheaper cuts of meat. The papain, however, prevents gelatin from setting, so do not attempt to make a fruit jelly, cold soufflé or mousse with papaya.

Slightly unripe papayas can be used in salads, while fruit that is still hard is ideal for relishes and chutneys. Large fruit can be stuffed like zucchini and baked as a vegetable dish.

PERSIMMONS

Persimmons, also known as "kaki" or "date" plums, arouse strong feelings. People either love them or loathe them. When fully ripe these fruits, which originated in Japan, are exceptionally beautiful; the name means "food of the gods." They resemble large orange tomatoes, but have a wide, pale brown calyx and translucent, inedible skin. At their best, they have very sweet, honeyed flesh; unripe persimmons, however, are almost inedible, horribly sour and astringent.

Nutrition

Persimmons, rich in vitamin A, yield potassium, calcium and iron. They contain about 30 calories per 3¾ ounces.

To dry persimmons

Peel the fruit, leaving the calyxes and stems intact. Arrange on a rack over a baking sheet and dry in a very low oven. The sugar that is naturally present in the persimmons will crystallize on the outside. Dried persimmons taste like a mixture of dried figs, prunes and dates. They can be used in place of these fruits and added to cakes and puddings.

Above: Persimmon

Buying and Storing

Persimmons should be plump and extremely soft and pulpy, with undamaged skins. A perfect specimen will look as though it is about to burst, but this is exactly as it should be. Handle with great care and eat immediately, or store briefly in the bottom of the refrigerator. To ripen, place in a brown paper bag with a banana.

Preparing and Cooking

The fruit are best eaten raw; slice off the top and spoon out the flesh. Serve with cream or yogurt, use to make mousses, custards and ice creams or purée the flesh to make a sauce for ham, pork and game. Slightly unripe fruit can be poached in syrup or peeled and cooked like applesauce.

Sharon fruit

Developed in the Sharon Valley in Israel, this nonastringent variety of persimmon can be eaten while still firm and does not require peeling. Sharon fruit are less highly flavored than persimmons, and benefit from a squeeze of lemon or lime juice, but are treated in much the same way. They can be added to salads and make an attractive garnish for avocado vinaigrette.

PEPINOS

This beautiful fruit, with its smooth golden skin heavily streaked with purple, is sometimes called a "tree melon." Native to Peru, the pepino is a relative of the tomato, potato and eggplant family (*Solanacae*), but looks rather like a melon. The pale yellow flesh is quite tart, with a flavor suggestive of lemon, pineapple and melon. The sweet seeds of this fruit are edible.

Nutrition

Pepino fruits are rich in vitamin C, and also yield some vitamin A. They contain about 25 calories per 3¾ ounces.

Preparing and Serving

Pepinos can be peeled and eaten raw, but they are best poached with sugar or honey to counteract their acidity. Serve the fruit like melon, add pepino cubes to fruit salad or serve with vanilla ice cream.

Right: Pepinos

PHYSALIS

Also known as "cape gooseberries," "ground cherries," and "golden berries," physalis are distantly related to tomatoes, peppers, eggplant and potatoes, although you would never guess this by looking at them. The small, orange-gold berries are encased in a papery beige husk, similar to a Chinese lantern. They have a rather tart, mildly scented flavor reminiscent of a ripe dessert gooseberry with a hint of strawberry.

History

Although physalis are native to South America, the fruits seem to have been known to the Greeks as early as the third century AD. Physalis were introduced to England in the eighteenth century, but did not become popular until two centuries later. The early settlers in South Africa cultivated physalis in the Cape of Good Hope, which gave rise to their common name, cape gooseberries.

Preparing and Serving

Physalis are delicious eaten raw; the inedible papery husk is simply peeled back and used as a "handle," leaving the luscious berries free to be devoured as they are or dipped in fondant icing or melted chocolate. As such, they are very popular as petits fours and make attractive decorations for cheesecakes, meringues and pastries.

Physalis can also be cooked—they make the most delicious jams and jellies.

Above: Physalis

Dipping physalis in fondant icing

1 Peel back the papery husk like petals and fold into "wings."

2 Holding each physalis by the husk, dip into warm fondant icing.

3 Transfer to a plate lined with baking parchment and let cool.

PINEAPPLES

Pineapples are probably the most recognizable of all fruit. In fact, they are multiple fruits consisting of dozens of lozenge-shaped protuberances, each one being the fruit of a single flower, which together make up a single pineapple. Resembling a large pinecone topped with a spiky gray-green plume of leaves, a whole pineapple makes a spectacular addition to a fruit platter.

Above: Crystallized pineapple

The warm, distinctive aroma of the fruit is also very pleasing.

Pineapples are very versatile fruit, their sweet, acidic taste lending itself to sweet and savory dishes.

History

Native to South and Central America, pineapples had been cultivated for centuries before Christopher Columbus discovered them on his voyage to the West Indies in 1493. Astonished by the extraordinary appearance and flavor of the fruit, he brought some back to Europe, where they were regarded with wonder and awe. Due to their rarity and high cost, they became a symbol of hospitality, and stone pineapples often featured on the gateposts of houses to welcome guests.

The first pineapples, ripened in greenhouses, were presented to Louis XV of France, whose passion for the fruit made them even more highly prized. Pineapples are now grown in every tropical region of the world.

Varieties

There are hundreds of pineapple varieties, ranging from very large to miniature fruits. They are seldom sold by name, although **Golden Pineapple** is becoming familiar in some stores and markets. The color of the skin varies from orange to greenish yellow, while the degree of juiciness and sweetness depends upon the season.

Nutrition

Pineapples, rich in vitamin C and dietary fiber, provide about 46 calories per 3¾ ounces. They contain bromelain, an enzyme that aids digestion, so are the perfect

Left: Large, small and baby pineapples

Making pineapple wedges with plumes

1 Place the fruit upright, hold it firmly and slice it in half vertically with a sharp serrated knife, cutting down through the plume into the flesh. Cut each piece in half again to make four wedges.
2 Run a small, sharp knife between the rind and flesh. Slice off the core on each wedge, then slice the fruit into neat pieces, leaving these in place.

fruit to finish a rich meal. The enzyme breaks down protein, and so can be used to tenderize meat, but it will prevent gelatin from setting.

Buying and Storing

Choose a plump pineapple that feels heavy for its size, with a fresh, stiff plume. To test for ripeness, gently pull out one of the bottom leaves; it should come out easily. Avoid lifeless-looking, bruised or withered fruit with browning leaves. Use the fruit as soon as possible after purchase. Do not store whole pineapples in the refrigerator, although peeled, sliced or cubed pineapple can be chilled in an airtight container for up to three days. Fresh, peeled and sliced pineapple is available and should also be kept chilled.
Dried and crystallized pineapple Both can be eaten as a snack or used to make cakes and desserts.
Canned pineapple Chunks and rings are available in syrup or juice. They are useful pantry items, but lack the aromatic flavor of fresh pineapple. Crushed pineapple is also available.

Preparing and Cooking

Pineapples are delicious on their own, served in wedges or rings. Some people like to add a splash of kirsch, but a good pineapple should need no enhancement (although, surprisingly, a grinding of black pepper does wonders for the flavor). They go very well with other fruits; a hollowed-out pineapple shell complete with plume makes a spectacular container for fruit salad or tropical fruit sorbets.

Sliced pineapple can be made into a variety of hot desserts. Sauté in butter and brown sugar, make crisp fritters or combine with other fruits on skewers to make grilled fruit kebabs.

Tropical flavors, such as ginger, vanilla, cinnamon, allspice, coconut and rum, go extremely well with pineapple. Perhaps the most famous combination of pineapple, coconut and rum is the piña colada cocktail.

Pineapples' refreshing sweet-sour flavor makes them perfect for savory dishes, and they are often used in Chinese cooking. Traditionally, pineapple is cooked with ham and pork, but it also goes well with lamb, poultry and fish, particularly in spicy dishes and curries.

Below: Dried pineapple can be eaten as a snack or chopped to use in cake and other dessert recipes.

Peeling a pineapple

1 Cut the pineapple across into slices of the desired width.

2 Use a small, sharp knife to cut off the rind.

3 Hold each slice upright and cut out the "eyes."

4 Remove the central core of each slice with an apple corer.

POMEGRANATES

This attractive, apple-shaped fruit has leathery reddish gold skin and a large calyx or crown. Inside is a mass of creamy white edible seeds, each encased in a translucent sac of deep pink or crimson pulp and held together by segments of bitter, inedible yellow membrane that extend outward to the skin. These seeds gave the fruit its name, which means "grain apple." Eating a pomegranate is hard work, as each fleshy seed must be picked out individually, but their delicate, slightly tart flavor and refreshing, juicy texture make the effort worthwhile. Be warned, however, that pomegranate juice stains indelibly.

History

Originally from Persia, pomegranates have been linked with many cultures and religions for centuries and have been a symbol of fertility since ancient times because of their numerous seeds. Venus, the goddess of love, was said to have given pomegranates as presents to her favorites.

Until the Renaissance, pomegranates were used mainly for medicinal purposes in Europe, although they have always featured in the cooking of Middle Eastern countries. Nowadays, they are widely cultivated, from France, Spain and Israel to America and all over Asia.

Nutrition

Pomegranate seeds are rich in vitamin C and are a good source of dietary fiber. They provide about 72 calories per 3¾ ounces.

Buying and Storing

A pomegranate that feels heavy for its size is likely to be full of juice. Choose glossy fruit and avoid those whose skin looks hard and dry. They will keep in the refrigerator for up to a week. Dried pomegranate seeds are used in Middle Eastern cooking.

Preparing and Serving

If you have the patience, pomegranates are fun to eat raw; cut them open and pick out the seeds with a pin. Either suck out the juice and discard the

Below: Inside pomegranates is a mass of seeds, each encased in deep pink pulp.

Preparing a pomegranate

1 Cut off a thin slice from one end.

2 Stand the fruit upright. Cut downward through the skin at intervals, using a small, sharp knife.

3 Bend back the segments and use your fingers to push the seeds into a bowl.

4 Remove all the bitter pith and membrane.

seeds or eat the jellylike cells, seeds and all. The seeds make a decorative addition to fruit salads and can be used as a pretty topping for creamy desserts, ice cream or cheesecake. They have a particular affinity with almonds and make a jewellike garnish for couscous. In India and Pakistan, the seeds are used in meat dishes.

Pomegranate juice Extract the juice very gently, using a handheld lemon squeezer; electric or mechanical juicers will crush the seeds and make the juice bitter. The juice is delicious in refreshing tall drinks, such as pomegranate-flavored lemonade, or it can be used to make a syrup to color and flavor alcoholic drinks and cocktails. Commercially produced pomegranate syrup is called grenadine.

The juice can also be used for sorbets and sauces, and makes a delicious pink jelly for savory dishes, particularly those from the Middle East. Use it to marinate pheasant, turkey or chicken, or to make a sauce for chicken or turkey, which can then be garnished with pomegranate seeds.

PRICKLY PEARS

Also known as "cactus pears" and "Indian figs," prickly pears are the fruit of a cactus. They certainly live up to their name, the skin being covered in tiny, painful prickles. Prickly pears are generally 3 inches long, with greenish orange skin and orangey pink flesh with a melonlike texture. The flavor is sweet and aromatic. The small seeds can be eaten raw, but become hard when they are cooked.

Buying and Storing

Prickly pears are orangey yellow when ripe. Choose unblemished fruit and ripen it at room temperature if necessary.

Preparing and Cooking

Prickly pears are usually peeled and eaten raw with a squeeze of lime or lemon and perhaps a little cream.

Prickly pears go well with other fruit and are good in fruit salads. They can be made into jams or mixed with oranges to make an unusual marmalade. Mix raw strained pulp with ginger to make a sauce for cooked ham, or serve slices of prickly pear instead of melon with cured meats like prosciutto. Try adding stewed prickly pear segments to a fruit compote, or make a sauce or ice cream with the strained purée. Candied or crystallized slices of prickly pear can be used to decorate cakes and desserts.

Right: Prickly pears have a sweet and aromatic flavor.

RAMBUTANS

Rambutans are related to lychees and are sometimes known as "hairy lychees." Originally from Malaysia but now grown in tropical Central America and Southeast Asia, they are larger than lychees (about 2 inches in diameter) and look quite different, but have a similar texture. The taste is similar too, but slightly sharper. Rambutans resemble small, hairy animals, their reddish brown leathery skins being covered with soft, curly spines or hairs.

Preparing and Serving

Rambutans can be used in exactly the same way as lychees. To prepare, cut around the equator of the rambutan with a sharp knife, penetrating the skin only. Lift off the top half of the skin, leaving the fruit on the half shell, like an egg in a (rather hairy) egg cup. They can be added to fruit salads, served with ice cream (coffee ice cream is particularly compatible) or made into jams or jellies, but are best eaten on their own. For an unusual appetizer, wrap peeled and pitted rambutans in prosciutto and serve speared on

Above: Rambutans

toothpicks. Rambutans are also available canned in syrup.

SAPODILLAS

The unprepossessing appearance of this drab oval fruit from Central America belies its delicious taste, which resembles that of vanilla-flavored banana custard. Inside the rough, light brown skin of the ripe fruit, the honey-colored flesh is sweet and luscious, with a core containing inedible, hard black seeds.

Right: Sapodillas are sweet and luscious—like vanilla-flavored banana custard.

Buying and Storing

Ripe sapodillas should have wrinkled brown skins and "give" slightly when pressed. Unripe fruit has smooth skin with a greenish tinge. Avoid this—unripe fruit is full of tannin and the flesh is unpleasantly grainy and mouth-puckeringly unpalatable. Instead, let the fruit ripen for up to a week in a fruit bowl. Ripe sapodillas can be kept in the refrigerator for up to a month.

Preparing and Serving

Sapodillas can be eaten just as they are—simply cut them in half, scoop out the flesh and discard the seeds. A squeeze of lime or lemon enhances the flavor. The flesh can be mashed and stirred into cream or custard, or made into ice creams, fools and mousses. It can be added to cakes and tea breads and makes an unusual pancake filling. Mix puréed sapodilla flesh with homemade mayonnaise or lime vinaigrette to make a sauce or dressing to be served with cold fish or chicken.

The milky sap of the sapodilla tree is used to make chicle gum, the main component of chewing gum.

SNAKE FRUIT

Also known as salak, this large member of the lychee family acquired its nickname from its beautifully patterned scaly brown snakelike skin. The creamy flesh is divided into four segments, each enclosing a very large inedible brown pit. The flesh is denser and less juicy than a lychee's and has a distinctive apple flavor. Although the hard shells protect the fruit, the flesh quickly dries out, so eat them as soon as possible after purchase.

Snake fruit can be peeled and eaten just as they are, or added to fruit salads. They are delicious poached in a light lemon- or vanilla-scented syrup and served chilled, alone or with vanilla ice cream or sorbet as a refreshing end to a meal.

Right: Snake fruit—so named because the patterned, scaly brown shell resembles snake skin.

TAMARILLOS

Also known as "tree tomatoes," tamarillos look like large egg-shaped tomatoes with thick, smooth, wine red skins. Each fruit has two lobes containing a multitude of black seeds.

Buying and Storing

Tamarillos with a greenish tinge will be unripe. Ripe fruit is bright purplish or orangey red and is soft to the touch. The fruit will keep in the refrigerator for several days.

Preparing and Cooking

Tamarillos can only be eaten raw when they are completely ripe. At this stage the flavor is tangy, sweet and sour, while unripe fruit has a quite unpleasant tannin taste.

To enjoy tamarillos at their best, cut them in half, sprinkle with a little sugar and leave overnight in the refrigerator. The next day, scoop out the chilled pulp with a spoon. Do not attempt to eat the skin, which is horribly bitter. Remove it by plunging the fruit into boiling water for about a minute, then slipping it off, or peel the fruit with a sharp vegetable peeler or knife.

Raw tamarillos can be used in fruit salads or puréed and made into jam and ice cream. They can be stewed or dredged in brown sugar and broiled. They make excellent chutney and a delicious sweet-sour sauce to go with fish or poultry.

Above: Tamarillos are members of the same family as tomatoes, eggplant and potatoes.

MELONS, GRAPES, FIGS AND RHUBARB

Some fruits are in a class of their own. Melons, grapes and figs

have little in common, apart from the fact that they are all

fruits, and rhubarb cannot even lay claim to that characteristic:

It is technically a vegetable. Without these treasures, however, the

food world would be a poorer place. Melons are the cool fruits,

grapes the sybarites' choice, figs the sweetest treats and rhubarb

the perfect springtime treat!

MELONS

Sweet melons are members of a large family of fruits and vegetables that grow on trailing vines and include cucumbers, and squashes. They come in a huge number of varieties (possibly thousands) and range in size from a single portion to melons that are large enough to provide a dozen servings. They have a hard, often beautifully patterned rind and very juicy, refreshing flesh enclosing a central cavity filled with a large number of pale, pointed, edible seeds.

History

Melons originated in Africa or Asia and have been known in China for at least 3,000 years. These early melons were bitter, rather like cucumbers, and could not be eaten raw. Hybridization resulted in sweeter fruits, which the Moors brought to Spain from Persia or Africa. They were taken to Italy, and by the fifteenth century reached France, where they were propagated enthusiastically by the Avignon popes. Christopher Columbus took melons to the New World; when his men had eaten the fruit, they discarded the seeds, which produced large melon crops. These popular fruits are now grown in most warm parts of the world.

Varieties

Melons fall into two main categories—summer fruit, which includes all those varieties with crosshatched skin that looks like brown netting, and winter melons, which have smooth or finely ridged pale or bright yellow rind and delicate, pale flesh, which can be rather lacking in taste.

Summer melons

Cantaloupe This summer melon takes its name from the Italian town of Cantalupo near Rome, where the fruits were grown in profusion on the papal estate. Most cantaloupes are slightly elongated, with craggy pale green or golden rinds, marked into segments, and have aromatic orangey yellow flesh.

Charentais Charentais have smooth, gray-green rinds and very fragrant orange flesh. A ripe Charentais gives off a heady, delicious aroma. Most Charentais melons are grown around Cavaillon in France, and are sometimes sold under this name. The French writer Alexandre Dumas so loved these melons that he offered the municipality of Cavaillon all his published and future works in exchange for a lifetime annuity of twelve melons a year.

Galia A relative of the Ogen, Galia is a round melon with a raised pattern of fine netting on the skin. The skin turns from green to golden as it ripens, and the fragrant flesh is green and juicy.

Muskmelons These summer melons, also known as "nutmeg" melons, are round or oval, with a raised pattern of lacy netting on the rind. The skins can be green or orange, and the sweet, highly aromatic flesh ranges from orangey pink to pale green. They take their name from the Romans' habit of sprinkling the fruit with powdered musk to accentuate the flavor. Muskmelons are often hothouse-grown.

Ogen A hybrid developed in Israel, this cantaloupe melon has a smooth, pale green skin, marked with green or orange lines, which turns golden when the fruit is ripe. The juicy flesh is sweet and aromatic.

Pineapple or **khoob melons** These large oval melons have orangey yellow netted skin and beautiful, juicy orange flesh, which has the aroma and faint flavor of pineapple.

Above: Ein d'Or, one of the winter melons, has golden skin and delicately flavored flesh.

Winter melons

In addition to the winter melons listed below, there are the golden **Ein d'Or** and the **Piel de Sapo,** with rough-ridged, dark green skin and green-to-orange flesh. Its name means "toad's skin."

Casaba is a walnut-shaped melon with ridged, deep yellow skin and pale creamy flesh.

Crenshaws are pointed at the stem end and have smooth golden skins. They have the best flavor of all winter melons, with sweet juicy salmon pink flesh and a pleasant aroma.

Honeydew is the most common winter melon. Sadly, its name is often more flavorful than its taste.

Watermelons *See separate entry below.*

Nutrition

Melons have a very high water content, so are low in calories (30 calories per 3¾ ounces). The more orange the flesh, the more beneficial carotenes it contains.

Left: The aromatic orangey yellow flesh of cantaloupes is delicious served with cured meats.

Buying and Storing

Melons should feel heavy for their size and give off a pleasant, sweet aroma; they should not smell too musky, as this is a sign that they are overripe. Gently press the stalk end with your thumb; it should "give" slightly, but check that the fruit has not started to rot. The rind should be thick and unblemished with a good color for its type.

To ripen a melon, keep it at room temperature. Ripe melons are best kept in a cool, airy place. The refrigerator is fine, but wrap the melon in plastic wrap or a plastic bag first, or the smell will permeate other foods. Melon balls or cubes can be frozen in rigid containers for up to three months, either as they are or in a light syrup.

Preparing and Serving

Aromatic ripe melons are best eaten raw, on their own, in a fruit salad (use the melon shell as a container) or as an hors d'oeuvre with prosciutto or salami. Melons can be served in long slices, balls or cubes. They should always be chilled. A sprinkling of salt and pepper or ground ginger enhances the flavor. Small, round varieties can be halved horizontally, seeded and served as they are or with a filling such as raspberry coulis or ice cream. They can also be filled with port, although purists frown on this practice. For single-portion melons, cut off a lid and scoop out the seeds. Always scoop out melons into a strainer set over a bowl to catch all the juice. The seeds can be dried and roasted in the oven to make a delicious snack.

Melon goes well with sweet or savory ingredients. It makes a refreshing salad if mixed with cucumber and tossed in lemon juice, a light cream cheese or yogurt dressing, or a vinaigrette made

Above: Piel de Sapo—its name means "toad's skin."

Left: Galia melons are fragrant and juicy.

with lemon juice. Add cubes of blue cheese, such as Cambozola or Gorgonzola dolce. Melon cubes also enhance cold chicken, shrimp and other seafood bound in a light mayonnaise.

For the simplest and prettiest of desserts, scoop out balls of different-colored melon flesh (white, yellow, orange—perhaps even red watermelon), pile into a glass bowl and serve chilled, with a sprinkling of sugar if needed, and

a decoration of mint sprigs or nasturtium flowers. Melons make very refreshing sorbets, fools, mousses and ice creams. Spiced with pieces of preserved ginger, they also make excellent jams.

Chunks of melon can be made into a cool pickle that goes well with hot and cold meats or cold ham and poultry. The rind can also be pickled; remove the hard, colored, outer layer of rind, leaving the white inner rind.

Preparing melons for serving

1 If the melons are small, either cut off the lids or cut the melons in half, then scoop out the seeds into a strainer set over a bowl. Pour any juice from the bowl back into the melons; serve them plain or with a filling of other fruit like strawberries and raspberries.

2 For a prettier effect, "vandyke" the melon. Make a 1-inch diagonal cut where you want the lid to be. Turn the knife and cut down on the opposite diagonal to make an inverted V. Continue to cut zigzags all around the fruit in this way, then lift off the lid. Remove the seeds.

3 For melon slices, cut a large melon in half lengthwise. Scoop out the seeds and cut the melon into long wedges.

4 To make melon "boats," slice the melon as in step 3. Run a flexible knife between the melon rind and flesh to release the flesh. Slice the flesh on the rind into 3/4-inch chunks. Push alternate chunks in opposite directions to give a staggered effect.

Above:
Honeydew melons

WATERMELONS

Watermelons are huge round or oval fruits that weigh up to 26½ pounds—much larger than sweet melons. They have solid dark green or paler striped skins, and vibrant pink or red flesh studded with large, flat, black, edible seeds. The flesh is very watery, and can taste rather insipid, but a slice of chilled watermelon is one of the most refreshing experiences imaginable.

History

Watermelons are thought to have originated in India, but may have come from tropical Africa. They were enjoyed by the ancient Egyptians, but were unknown in Europe until the thirteenth century. They became a symbol of the martyrdom of San Lorenzo in Italy; every year on August 10 in Florence, the patron saint of cooks is celebrated with an orgy of watermelon eating.

Varieties

Smaller varieties of watermelon are now available, weighing from 5½–10 pounds. These include **Sugar Baby,** a particularly sweet, round variety with very dark green skin and red flesh. **Tiger** has a paler green skin, striped with yellow or green, as its name suggests. **Golden watermelons** have bright yellow flesh and a more delicate (or dull) flavor than the red-fleshed varieties. They do, however, look very pretty when mixed with red watermelons.

Nutrition

The high water content of watermelons means that they are low in calories; only 30 calories per 3¾ ounces. They contain some vitamins B and C.

Buying and Storing

Watermelons should be firm and evenly colored and feel heavy. Tap them with your knuckles; they should not sound hollow. The side where the melon has rested should be yellowish, not white or green. Watermelons are usually sold cut into wedges. Do not buy those with faded flesh, or with white seeds; these are unripe. Whole and cut watermelons can be wrapped in plastic wrap and kept in the refrigerator for at least a week.

Preparing and Serving

Watermelons are generally cut into wedges and eaten on their own as a thirst quencher. Cubes or balls make an attractive addition to fruit salads and melon medleys, and they can be made into sorbets (add plenty of lemon for flavor). In some African countries, unripe watermelons are prepared like squashes as a vegetable dish. The rind can be pickled, and is sometimes candied. The seeds can be toasted and eaten (discard the outer shell).

Left: Tiger watermelons are—as the name suggests—striped.

GRAPES

These best known of all vine fruits grow in pendulous bunches on a stalk. The skins can be green, pale yellow, purple, bluish or red; in England, green grapes are known as "white" and purple as "black." Some grapes have a bloom; others have almost waxy skins. Inside, the pulp is translucent and usually contains a few seeds, although there are several varieties of seedless grapes.

Some varieties are grown as dessert or table grapes; others are cultivated exclusively for wine making. Some varieties are also grown for drying into raisins, golden raisins (sultanas) and currants. Generally speaking, table grapes are not used for wine making and vice versa, but there are one or two dual-purpose varieties.

History

Grapes are among the oldest cultivated fruits and were known to man long before Noah planted his vineyard on Mount Ararat. Wild grapes were already established in the Caucasus in the Stone Age, and it was not long before man discovered

Right: Alphonse Lavalle grapes are firm and crisp to eat.

how to ferment them into wine. It is certain that the ancient Egyptians made wine, although they used it for temple rituals rather than social drinking. The ancient Greeks and Romans, however, were enthusiastic consumers of wine and grapes and planted a huge number of vineyards. They also learned the technique of drying the fruit.

It was the Gauls who first put wine into wooden casks, and later, medieval monks became expert wine makers. They also pressed grapes into *verjus,* a sour liquid resembling vinegar. In nineteenth-century England, the Victorians were hugely enthusiastic about grapes and cultivated magnificent specimens in hothouses. At the same time, in France, a *uvarium,* or grape spa, offered medicinal and weight loss cures consisting entirely of grapes.

Varieties

A wide variety of table grapes is available, both seedless and seeded,

Left: Red and white grape juice is refreshing to drink on its own or mixed with sparkling mineral water.

the finest by far being **Muscat.** Seedless grapes contain less tannin than the seeded fruit and are easier to eat. The main varieties are listed below.

GREEN GRAPES

Italia The nearest inexpensive alternative to Muscat grapes, Italia are very large, roundish, seeded fruit with greenish yellow skins and a luscious, musky flavor.

Perlette Small, seedless, thin-skinned grapes with a rather tart flavor.

Sultana These small, elongated grapes with thin, greenish gold, bloomy skins and sweet, juicy pulp grow in compact, conical bunches. The varieties Perlette and Thompson are both hybrids of Sultana.

Thompson Seedless Medium-size elongated fruit with thin, bloomy skins and very sweet, juicy pulp.

RED GRAPES

Alphonse Lavalle These large, round, seeded grapes grow in a compact bunch. They have thick, purplish black skin, with firm, crisp pulp.

Cardinal Large oval fruit with reddish purple skin and firm, fleshy pulp, which can sometimes lack flavor. They grow in large, unevenly shaped bunches.

Flame Seedless A smallish grape with thin, wine red skin and very sweet, juicy pulp. These are mostly grown in Chile.

Napoleon The thick, dark purple skin on these large grapes has a heavy white bloom. The flesh is particularly sweet, although not very juicy.

MUSCAT GRAPES

Without doubt, these are the king of grapes, with a wonderful perfumed flavor almost like nectar. The very best are hothouse-grown and are displayed in shops cocooned in padded paper to preserve their beautiful bloom. All Muscats are large; the green varieties are pale green or golden, while red Muscats can be either red or black. The best Muscat grape of all is the **Chasselas,** whose skin turns almost bronze when ripe.

Muscat grapes are used for making sweet Muscat dessert wines, which encapsulate the honeyed flavor of the grapes.

Nutrition

Grapes are highly nutritious, containing natural sugars, potassium, iron and dietary fiber. They provide about 80 calories per 3¾ ounces.

Buying and Storing

Now that grapes are available all year round, many are sold underripe. The best way to judge a bunch of grapes is to taste a stray fruit; there is nearly always one that has fallen off the bunch. A perfect bunch of grapes should be of equal size and shape, with the bloom still on. Green grapes should have a golden or amber tinge; avoid any

Right: Red Muscat grapes can either be black (as here) or red.

Below: Wonderfully perfumed, Green Muscat are the king of grapes.

Left: Italia grapes, which can be green (as here) or black, have a luscious musky flavor and are the closest inexpensive alternative to Muscat grapes.

Peeling and seeding grapes

1 Put the grapes in a heatproof bowl and pour enough boiling water over to cover. Leave for about 20 seconds.

2 Drain off the hot water, rinse the grapes in cold water, then peel off the skins with your fingers.

3 Cut each grape in half and pick out the seeds with the tip of a sharp knife.

Right: Grown mostly in Chile, rich-colored Flame seedless grapes are sweet and juicy, with thin, easy-to-eat skins.

Above: Immensely popular, Thompson seedless grapes are very sweet, with thin bloomy skins.

that are uniformly vivid green. Red varieties should not be tinged with green. It is easier to spot overripe grapes, as they will fall off the bunch and often show traces of browning or mold. Do not buy wrinkled grapes, or bunches with tiny specimens attached; these will be very sour.

Store grapes in a bowl in a cool, dry place; they will keep for at least a week. To store them for longer, place in a sealed plastic bag and keep in the salad drawer of the fridge for up to two weeks. Remove the grapes from the refrigerator and keep at room temperature for at least an hour before serving so that the flavor can develop fully.

Grape juice Naturally sweet, clear red and white grape juice, from crushed grapes, is delicious served chilled on its own or mixed with sparkling mineral water.

Grapeseed oil Grape seeds are pressed into a very pale oil with a delicate, almost neutral flavor. This healthy oil is extremely rich in polyunsaturated fats. It can be used for cooking, but is best used in its natural state, in salad dressings, for example. It is the perfect oil to choose for making mayonnaise because it has such a mild flavor and it never separates.

Above: Large, golden muscatel raisins from Muscat grapes are often dried and sold on their stems.

DRIED GRAPES

The best of these are sun-dried, without undergoing any chemical processes. Dried grapes—raisins, currants and sultanas—sometimes contain bits of stem and the occasional seed, so pick them over carefully before using.

Artificially dried grapes are usually cleaner, but may need to be plumped up in boiling water for a few seconds before being added to cake mixtures.

Raisins The best raisins are made from Muscat grapes and come from California and Spain. These large, deep amber fruit are tender and sweet and can be eaten on their own, with cheese and nuts, or used in rice and couscous dishes. Smaller, black raisins are used for making cakes and puddings, muesli and mincemeat. All raisins benefit from being plumped up in brandy before cooking.

Golden Raisins or Sultanas These small, golden, dried fruits are made from seedless white grapes. They are deliciously moist, with a tender texture and delicate flavor.

Currants These small dried fruits are made from Turkish and Greek seedless red grapes.

Serving and Cooking

Grapes are best eaten on their own as a snack or dessert, or at the end of a meal with cheese or nuts. For an unusual sandwich, try Brie with halved grapes. They make a good addition to fruit salad and savory salads, combined with crunchy vegetables and walnuts. Green and red grapes make attractive garnishes, particularly in small clusters frosted with egg white and sugar. They can be used to make jams and jellies; a few small grapes look beautiful suspended in a clear jelly.

Their slight acidity makes grapes a good foil for rich meats like foie gras and calf's liver. They can also be used to stuff quail, chicken or guinea fowl, or to make a sauce for

Above: Clockwise from top left, golden raisins (sultanas), currants and raisins.

poultry or ham. A classic French dish is sole Véronique: rolled fillets of sole poached in white wine and garnished with green grapes. It is best to peel and seed grapes before cooking and to poach them lightly in wine or syrup so that they keep their shape. For savory dishes, they can be sautéed in butter.

Caramelizing grapes

1 Combine scant 1 cup sugar and ¼ cup water in a small, heavy saucepan. Stir over low heat until the sugar has dissolved. Bring to a boil, add 1 teaspoon lemon juice and boil until the syrup turns a deep golden brown.

2 Carefully add 1 tablespoon hot water (protecting your hand with an oven mitt, as the mixture will "spit") and shake the pan to mix. Spear a pair of grapes on a fork by the stem and dip them into the caramel to coat. Slide the caramelized grapes off the fork and leave on an oiled baking sheet for about 10 minutes, until the caramel cools and hardens.

FIGS

These oval or pear-shaped fruits are among the most luscious of all and can be eaten fresh or dried. They are not juicy in the conventional sense, nor do they have a particularly strong flavor, but they are succulent and sweet, conjuring up images of sunny Mediterranean gardens.

Figs come in three main varieties—green, black and red—and range in color from palest green to dark gold, burnished brown or deep purple. The entire fig is edible (although some people prefer to peel them), from the soft, thin skin to the sweet, succulent red or purplish flesh and the myriad tiny seeds. Skin color makes little difference to the taste of a fig. Their high natural sugar content makes them the sweetest of all fruits. The flavor varies, depending on where they were grown and how ripe they are.

History

Figs were said to grow in the Garden of Eden and their leaves, it is alleged, were used to cover the nakedness of Adam and Eve. Over the centuries, prudes have delighted in defacing works of art depicting naked bodies with carefully placed fig leaves.

Below: Although green in color, in England these figs are classified as white.

Figs probably originated in Asia Minor and were one of the first fruits to be cultivated. They were known to the ancient Egyptians at the time of the pharaohs and were brought to the Mediterranean long before the arrival of the ancient Greeks and Romans, rapidly becoming an important part of the Mediterranean diet. The world's oldest known living fig tree is said to be growing in a Sicilian garden.

Figs are now widely cultivated and exported from France, Greece, Turkey, Brazil and the United States.

Above: Turkish purple figs

Varieties

You will seldom find figs in stores or markets labeled according to their variety; instead, they are classified by color—green, black and red. In reality, they range from palest green to dark gold, burnished brown or deep purple. In Italy, you are most likely to find the green **Kadota,** while in France you may come across **Buissone, Barbillone** and **Dauphine Violette.** Imported figs from Turkey are generally purple with deep red flesh.

Nutrition

Figs consist of 83 percent natural sugars. They are a good source of calcium, are high in fibre and contain vitamins A, B and C. They are well known for their laxative and digestive properties. A single fig provides about 30 calories.

Buying and Storing

Ripe figs are very delicate and do not travel well, so it is often difficult to find imported fruit at a perfect stage of maturity. Look for unblemished fruit that is soft and yielding when gently squeezed but still holds its shape. Figs should have a faint, delicate aroma; if they smell sour, they are overripe and will taste sour too. If you are buying figs in their country of origin, you may find some with split skins. Provided you are going to eat them immediately, this does not matter. Be careful not to squash the figs on the way home, or you will end up with a squishy inedible pulp.

Ripe figs should ideally be eaten on the day they are bought, but can be stored in the salad drawer of the refrigerator for up to three days. Remove them well before serving, as chilling spoils the delicate flavor. Underripe fruit can be kept at room temperature for a day or two until the skin softens, but they will never develop the wonderful flavor of figs that have ripened in the sun naturally on the tree.

Right: Dried figs are sometimes sold strung together in a ring.

DRIED FIGS

Dried figs are made from very ripe autumn fruits, usually golden Smyrna figs from Turkey or deep purple Mission figs from California. They are spread out to dry in the sun and must be turned several times before they are dried completely. This process flattens the figs into the familiar cushion shape. Dried figs contain large amounts of sugar and are highly nutritious. The best have a soft texture and are sold loosely packed so that they remain plump. Less high quality figs are commonly sold in blocks or strung together like a necklace. Store them in a cool, dry place.

Eat dried figs

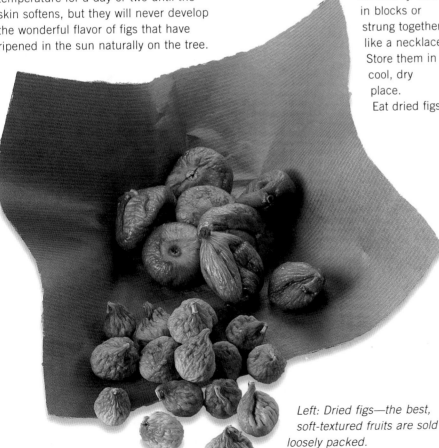

Left: Dried figs—the best, soft-textured fruits are sold loosely packed.

as they are, or stuff them with marzipan, nuts or cream cheese. They are used in compotes, poached in wine or served with creamy custard puddings. They can be baked in cakes, steamed puddings and tea breads. They are extensively used in Middle Eastern cooking and go especially well with poultry and game. Dried figs can be substituted for prunes in chicken, pork and rabbit recipes, such as terrines, stews and casseroles. Soak them— preferably in red wine—for several hours before cooking.

Dried figs are also used to make popular, delicious bar cookies, sold commercially and in old-fashioned bake shops.

CANNED OR PRESERVED FIGS

These are usually green Kadota figs preserved in heavy syrup. Canned figs are very sweet and are best served in a fruit compote. A dollop of whipped cream or strained, plain (Mediterranean-style or Greek) yogurt will temper the sweetness.

Preparing and Cooking

The best way to enjoy a fig is to pick a perfectly sun-ripened fruit straight off the tree. Wash it briefly and pat it dry very gently. Serve it whole. Always serve figs at room temperature, never chilled. They look particularly attractive on a bed of fig leaves, especially if each fruit is slit into four pieces and opened out to resemble a flower. The centers can be

Above: Dried figs dusted with cornstarch to keep the fruits separate.

Above: Almost too sweet on their own, green preserved figs are best served with cream or plain yogurt.

or ice cream. They also go well with savory dishes like duck and lamb. To poach figs, put them in a saucepan and cover with syrup, red or white wine or port. Add your chosen flavorings—honey, cinnamon, vanilla and lemon are all suitable. Bring to a boil, lower the heat, cover and simmer gently for about 15 minutes, until the figs are tender. Using a slotted spoon, transfer the figs to a serving dish, then boil the poaching liquid until it is thick and syrupy before pouring it over the fruit.

To cook figs in butter, cut them in half vertically, then arrange them cut side up in a heatproof dish. Put a pat of butter on each fig half. Sprinkle with port or Marsala and a pinch of cinnamon or nutmeg, and broil until lightly browned. Serve with meat or poultry, or brush with honey before broiling and serve as a dessert.

To caramelize figs, dip the fruit in water, then roll in granulated or vanilla sugar until completely coated. Place in a shallow baking dish and bake in a preheated oven at 425°F for about 15 minutes, or until the sugar has caramelized. Let cool, then chill before serving.

stuffed, if you like. Cream cheese mixed with honey and chopped nuts, fresh raspberries or raspberry mousse make delicious fillings.

Fresh figs are usually eaten raw as a dessert fruit, or as an hors d'oeuvre with prosciutto or salami. They have an affinity for nuts such as walnuts, pistachios and almonds and make an excellent addition to a cheese platter with grapes and nuts.

They can be stuffed with sweet or savory fillings like cream or blue cheese, celery and walnuts or marzipan, and are especially delicious filled with mascarpone and berries. Figs can also be successfully cooked in compotes, preserves and jams. For desserts, they can be poached in wine, honey or syrup; they can also be caramelized or made into tarts

Making fig flowers

Cut each fig downward into quarters, starting from the stem end and leaving the quarters attached at the base. Gently pull the sections apart to open them out like the petals of a flower. Serve the figs plain or with your chosen creamy filling.

RHUBARB

Strictly speaking, rhubarb is not a fruit, but a vegetable; it is the fleshy stalk of the rhubarb plant, a relative of sorrel and dock. The stems are succulent, but too sour to eat raw, and the leaves contain oxalic acid, which makes them highly poisonous. The normal growing season is late spring to late summer, but early forced rhubarb, grown under covered pots, is available throughout the spring months. Main crop rhubarb stalks vary from green to purplish pink; the forced variety has spindly, tender bright pink or red stems, crowned with yellow leaves, and tastes much better.

History

Rhubarb originated in Northern Asia and Siberia. It has been cultivated for centuries, but was originally used as a medicinal and ornamental plant. It was not until the eighteenth century that British gardeners began to grow rhubarb for cooking.

Preparing rhubarb

1 Using a large knife, cut off and discard the leaves and the root end of the stalk. Peel off any stringy fibers with a swivel-blade vegetable peeler.

2 Cut the rhubarb into pieces.

Nutrition

Rhubarb is one of the lowest calorie foods, providing only 7 calories per 3¾ ounces. It contains significant amounts of calcium, potassium and thiamine (vitamin B1) and has natural laxative properties.

Buying and Storing

Choose crisp, firm stalks that look bright and release sap when you snap them. Rhubarb can be stored for a few days in the bottom of the refrigerator, but wilts quickly. It freezes well: Cut the stalks into short lengths, blanch briefly in boiling water, refresh in ice water and freeze in freezer bags.

Preparing and Cooking

All rhubarb needs to be sweetened when it is cooked, usually with sugar. This can be added at the outset, or when it has been cooked until tender. Use a stainless steel pan and only a spoonful or two of water. Poach gently until the fruit is tender. Rhubarb makes a wonderful pie or tart filling, and a delicious crumble, especially when mixed with banana.

Puréed rhubarb can be made into ice cream, sorbets, mousses and fools. Citrus fruits and spices, particularly ginger, vanilla and cinnamon, complement the flavor of rhubarb. Rhubarb can be combined with any of these to make excellent jams and chutneys. Because it is a vegetable, rhubarb goes well with savory dishes like scrambled eggs, but you will still need to add sugar. It adds piquancy to rich casseroles, particularly pork, lamb and duck. Its sharp acidity makes it a good substitute for sorrel in sauces, especially to serve with oily fish, such as mackerel.

Above: Early forced rhubarb, grown under covered pots, is pink and tender.

Below: Tougher, main-crop rhubarb is grown outdoors.

COOKING
WITH
FRUIT

APPLE, PEAR AND QUINCE RECIPES

Apples, pears and quinces are wonderfully versatile. Dutch Apple Cake and Chocolate Pear and Pecan Pie are just two of the tempting treats in store, while Hot Quince Soufflés and Iced Pear Terrine make memorable desserts.

ICED PEAR TERRINE WITH CALVADOS AND CHOCOLATE SAUCE

THIS TERRINE, BASED ON A CLASSIC FRENCH DESSERT, MAKES A REFRESHING AND IMPRESSIVE END TO ANY MEAL. FOR FLAVOR, BE SURE THE PEARS ARE RIPE AND JUICY.

<u>SERVES EIGHT</u>

INGREDIENTS
   3–3½ pounds ripe Bartlett pears
   juice of 1 lemon
   ½ cup sugar
   10 whole cloves
   6 tablespoons water
   julienne strips of orange zest,
     to decorate
For the sauce
   7 ounces semisweet chocolate
   ¼ cup hot strong black coffee
   1 cup heavy cream
   2 tablespoons Calvados or brandy

1 Peel, core and slice the pears. Place them in a saucepan with the lemon juice, sugar, cloves and water. Cover and simmer for 10 minutes. Remove the cloves. Allow the pears to cool.

2 Process the pears with their juice in a food processor or blender until smooth. Pour the purée into a freezerproof bowl, cover and freeze until firm.

3 Meanwhile, line a 9 x 5 x 3 inch loaf pan with plastic wrap. Allow the wrap to overhang the sides of the pan. Remove the frozen pear purée from the freezer and spoon it into a food processor or blender. Process until smooth. Pour into the prepared pan, cover and freeze until firm.

4 Make the sauce. Break the chocolate into a large heatproof bowl. Place the bowl over a saucepan of hot water. When the chocolate has melted, stir in the coffee until smooth. Gradually stir in the cream and then the Calvados or brandy. Set the sauce aside.

5 About 20 minutes before serving, remove the pan from the freezer. Invert the terrine onto a plate, lift off the plastic wrap and place the terrine in the refrigerator to soften slightly. Warm the sauce over hot water. Place a slice of terrine on each dessert plate and spoon some of the sauce over. Decorate with julienne strips of orange zest and serve at once.

QUINCE <u>AND</u> GINGER MOUSSE <u>WITH</u> ALMOND COOKIES

QUINCES AND GINGER ARE PERFECTLY MATCHED FLAVOR PARTNERS. AS WITH ANY QUINCE RECIPE, YOU CAN SUBSTITUTE PEARS OR APPLES WITH EQUALLY DELICIOUS RESULTS.

SERVES FOUR

INGREDIENTS

1 pound quinces
⅓ cup sugar
grated zest of ½ lemon
6 tablespoons water
2 pieces preserved ginger in syrup,
  finely chopped, plus 1 tablespoon
  syrup from the jar
1 tablespoon powdered gelatin
⅔ cup heavy cream
2 egg whites
mint leaves and blackberries dusted
  with sugar, to decorate

For the cookies

4 tablespoons butter
2 tablespoons sugar
½ cup all-purpose flour
½ cup ground almonds
a few drops of pure almond extract

1 Grease four ⅔-cup ramekins and line the bottoms with baking parchment. Peel the quinces, core and put in a saucepan with the sugar, lemon zest and ¼ cup of the water. Bring to a boil, lower the heat, cover and simmer for 10 minutes, or until softened. Remove the lid; continue cooking until the liquid has almost evaporated.

2 Cool the quince mixture slightly, then purée in a food processor or blender. Press the purée through a strainer into a large bowl, then stir in the ginger and ginger syrup and set aside.

3 Pour the remaining 2 tablespoons water into a small heatproof bowl and sprinkle the gelatin on top. Let soak for 5 minutes. Stand the bowl in a pan of hot water, stirring occasionally, until the gelatin has dissolved.

4 Lightly whip the cream. Stir the gelatin into the quince purée, then fold in the whipped cream. In a greasefree bowl, beat the egg whites to stiff peaks; fold into the quince mixture. Divide among the prepared ramekins, level the tops and chill until firm. Preheat the oven to 375°F.

5 Make the cookies. Line a baking sheet with baking parchment. Cream the butter and sugar until smooth. Add the flour, almonds and almond extract and mix to a dough with a knife. Roll out thinly on a lightly floured surface; cut into rounds with a 3-inch cutter. Transfer to the baking sheet. Chill for 10 minutes, then bake for 10–12 minutes.

6 Cool slightly on the paper, then lift onto a wire rack to cool. Run a knife around each mousse; turn out onto dessert plates. Discard the paper. Decorate and serve with cookies.

SPICED APPLE CRUMBLE

ANY FRUIT CAN BE USED IN THIS POPULAR DESSERT, BUT YOU CAN'T BEAT THE COMBINATION OF BLACKBERRY AND APPLE. HAZELNUTS AND CARDAMOM SEEDS GIVE THE TOPPING EXTRA FLAVOR.

SERVES FOUR TO SIX

INGREDIENTS
    butter, for greasing
    1 pound cooking apples
    1 cup blackberries
    grated zest and juice of 1 orange
    ⅓ cup light brown sugar
    custard, to serve
For the topping
    1½ cups all-purpose flour
    ⅓ cup butter
    ⅓ cup sugar
    ¼ cup chopped hazelnuts
    ½ teaspoon crushed cardamom seeds

VARIATIONS
This wonderfully good-natured dessert can be made with all sorts of fruit. Try plums, apricots, peaches or pears, alone or in combination with apples. Rhubarb makes a delectable crumble, especially when mixed with bananas.

1 Preheat the oven to 400°F. Generously butter a 5-cup baking dish. Peel and core the apples, then slice them into the prepared baking dish. Level the surface, then scatter the blackberries over. Sprinkle the orange zest and light brown sugar evenly over the top, then pour the orange juice over. Set the fruit mixture aside while you make the crumble topping.

2 Make the topping. Sift the flour into a bowl and rub in the butter until the mixture resembles coarse bread crumbs. Stir in the sugar, hazelnuts and cardamom seeds. Scatter the topping over the top of the fruit.

3 Press the topping around the edges of the dish to seal in the juices. Bake for 30–35 minutes, or until the crumble is golden. Serve hot, with custard.

BAKED STUFFED APPLES

THIS TRADITIONAL APPLE DESSERT IS EXCEPTIONALLY SIMPLE AND SPEEDY. BAKE THE APPLES IN THE OVEN ON THE SHELF UNDER THE SUNDAY ROAST FOR A DELICIOUS END TO THE MEAL.

SERVES FOUR

INGREDIENTS
    4 large cooking apples
    ½ cup light brown sugar
    6 tablespoons butter, softened
    grated zest and juice of ½ orange
    ¼ teaspoon ground cinnamon
    2 tablespoons crushed ratafia biscuits
        (almond-paste cookies) or other
        dessert cookies
    ½ cup pecans, chopped
    ½ cup deluxe mixed glacé fruit, chopped

COOK'S TIP
Use a little butter or oil to grease the baking dish, if you like, or pour a small amount of water around the stuffed apples to keep them from sticking to the dish during baking.

1 Preheat the oven to 350°F. Wash and dry the apples. Remove the cores with an apple corer, then carefully enlarge each core cavity to twice its size by shaving off more flesh with the corer. Score each apple around its equator, using a sharp knife. Stand the apples in a baking dish.

2 Mix the brown sugar, butter, orange zest and juice, cinnamon and ratafia crumbs. Beat well, then stir in the nuts and glacé fruit. Divide the filling among the apples, piling it high. Shield the filling in each apple with a small piece of foil. Bake for 45–60 minutes, until each apple is tender.

APPLE CREPES WITH BUTTERSCOTCH SAUCE

THESE WONDERFUL DESSERT CREPES ARE FLAVORED WITH SWEET CIDER, FILLED WITH CARAMELIZED APPLES AND DRIZZLED WITH A RICH, SMOOTH BUTTERSCOTCH SAUCE.

3 Make the filling. Core the apples and cut them into thick slices. Heat 1 tablespoon of the butter in a large frying pan. Add the apples to the pan. Cook until golden on both sides, then transfer the slices to a bowl with a slotted spoon and set them aside.

4 Add the rest of the butter to the pan. As soon as it has melted, add the brown sugar. When the sugar has dissolved and the mixture is bubbling, stir in the cream. Continue cooking until it forms a smooth sauce.

SERVES FOUR

INGREDIENTS
   1 cup all-purpose flour
   pinch of salt
   2 eggs
   ¾ cup whole milk or half-and-half
   ½ cup apple cider
   butter, for greasing pan
For the filling and sauce
   4 crisp eating apples
   7 tablespoons butter
   1⅓ cups light brown sugar
   ⅔ cup heavy cream

1 Make the crêpe batter. Sift the flour and salt into a large bowl. Add the eggs and milk and beat until smooth. Stir in the cider; set aside for 30 minutes.

2 Heat a small, heavy nonstick frying pan. Add a pat of butter and ladle in enough batter to coat the pan thinly. Cook until the crêpe is golden underneath, then flip it over and cook the other side until golden. Slide the crêpe onto a plate. Repeat with the remaining mixture to make seven more.

5 Fold each pancake in half, then fold in half again to form a cone; fill each with some of the fried apples. Place two filled pancakes on each dessert plate, drizzle some of the butterscotch sauce over and serve at once.

VARIATIONS
You could just as easily use plums, pears, strawberries or bananas to fill the crêpes. If you like, add a touch of Grand Marnier to the apples toward the end of cooking.

PEAR AND CINNAMON FRITTERS

IF YOU DON'T LIKE DEEP-FRYING AS A RULE, MAKE AN EXCEPTION FOR THIS DISH. FRITTERS ARE IRRESISTIBLE, AND A WONDERFUL WAY OF PERSUADING CHILDREN TO EAT MORE FRUIT.

SERVES FOUR

INGREDIENTS
  3 ripe, firm pears
  2 tablespoons sugar
  2 tablespoons kirsch
  peanut oil, for frying
  1 cup finely crushed amaretti cookies
For the batter
  ¾ cup all-purpose flour
  ¼ teaspoon salt
  ¼ teaspoon ground cinnamon
  ¼ cup milk
  2 eggs, separated
  3 tablespoons water
To serve
  2 tablespoons sugar
  ¼ teaspoon ground cinnamon
  clotted cream or crème fraîche

1 Peel the pears, cut them into quarters and remove the cores. Toss the wedges in the sugar and kirsch. Set aside for 15 minutes.

2 Make the batter. Sift the flour, salt and cinnamon into a large bowl. Beat in the milk, egg yolks and water until smooth. Set aside for 10 minutes.

3 Beat the egg whites in a greasefree bowl until they form stiff peaks; lightly fold them into the batter. Preheat the oven to 300°F.

4 Pour oil into a deep, heavy saucepan to a depth of 3 inches. Heat to 360°F, or until a bread cube added to the oil browns in 45 seconds.

5 Toss a pear wedge in the amaretti crumbs, then spear it on a fork and dip it into the batter until evenly coated. Lower it gently into the hot oil and use a knife to push it off the fork. Add more wedges in the same way, but do not overcrowd the pan. Cook the fritters for 3–4 minutes, or until golden. Drain on paper towels. Keep hot in the oven while cooking successive batches.

6 Mix the sugar and cinnamon and sprinkle some over the fritters. Sprinkle a little cinnamon sugar over the cream or crème fraîche; serve with the hot fritters.

VARIATIONS
Also try apples, apricots and bananas.

POACHED PEARS IN PORT SYRUP

THE PERFECT CHOICE FOR AUTUMN ENTERTAINING, THIS SIMPLE DESSERT HAS A BEAUTIFUL, RICH COLOR AND FANTASTIC FLAVOR THANKS TO THE PORT AND LEMON.

SERVES FOUR

INGREDIENTS
 2 ripe, firm pears, such as Bartlett or
  Comice
 pared zest of 1 lemon
 ¾ cup ruby port
 ¼ cup sugar
 1 cinnamon stick
 ¼ cup cold water
 whipped cream, to serve
To decorate
 2 tablespoons sliced hazelnuts, toasted
 fresh mint, pear or rose leaves

COOK'S TIP
Choose pears of similar size, with the stems intact, for the most attractive effect when fanned on the plate.

1 Peel the pears, cut them in half and remove the cores. Place the lemon zest, port, sugar, cinnamon stick and water in a shallow pan. Bring to a boil over low heat. Add the pears, lower the heat, cover and poach for 5 minutes. Let the pears cool in the syrup.

2 When the pears are cool, transfer them to a bowl with a slotted spoon. Return the syrup to the heat. Boil rapidly until it has reduced enough to lightly coat the back of a spoon. Remove the cinnamon stick and lemon zest and let the syrup cool.

3 To serve, place each pear in turn on a board, cut side down. Keeping it intact at the stem end, slice it lengthwise, then, using a metal spatula, carefully lift it off and place on a dessert plate. Press gently so that the pear fans out. When all the pears have been fanned, spoon the port syrup over them. Top each portion with a few hazelnuts and decorate with fresh mint, pear or rose leaves. Serve with whipped cream.

APPLE CHARLOTTES

THESE TEMPTING LITTLE FRUIT CHARLOTTES ARE A WONDERFUL WAY TO USE WINDFALLS.

SERVES FOUR

INGREDIENTS

12 tablespoons (1½ sticks) butter
1 pound cooking apples
8 ounces eating apples
¼ cup water
scant ⅔ cup sugar
2 egg yolks
pinch of grated nutmeg
9 thin slices white bread,
  crusts removed
whipped cream or custard, to serve

COOK'S TIP
A mixture of cooking and eating apples
gives the best flavor, but there's no
reason why you can't use only cooking
apples; just sweeten the pulp to taste.

1 Preheat the oven to 375°F. Put a pat of the butter in a saucepan. Peel and core the apples, dice them finely and put them in the pan with the water. Cover and cook for 10 minutes, or until the cooking apples have pulped down. Stir in ½ cup of the sugar. Boil, uncovered, until any liquid has evaporated and what remains is a thick pulp. Remove from the heat, beat in the egg yolks and nutmeg and set aside.

2 Melt the remaining butter in a separate saucepan over low heat until the white milk solids start to separate from the clear yellow liquid. Remove from the heat. Let stand for a few minutes, then strain the clear, clarified butter through a cheesecloth-lined sieve.

3 Brush four ⅔-cup individual charlotte or pudding molds with a little of the clarified butter; sprinkle with the remaining sugar. Cut the bread slices into 1-inch-wide strips. Dip the strips into the remaining clarified butter; use to line the molds. Overlap the strips on the bottom to give the effect of a swirl and let the excess bread overhang the tops of the molds.

4 Fill each lined mold with apple pulp. Fold the excess bread over the top of each mold to make a lid; press down lightly. Bake for 45–50 minutes, or until golden. Run a knife between each charlotte and its mold, then turn out onto dessert plates. Serve with whipped cream or custard.

HOT QUINCE SOUFFLES

THESE DELICIOUS FRUITS ARE BEGINNING TO BE MORE WIDELY AVAILABLE IN SHOPS AND MARKETS.
YOU CAN USE PEARS INSTEAD, BUT THE FLAVOR WILL NOT BE AS INTENSE.

SERVES SIX

INGREDIENTS

   2 quinces, peeled and cored
   ¼ cup water
   ½ cup granulated sugar,
    plus extra for sprinkling
   5 egg whites
   melted butter, for greasing
   confectioners' sugar, for dusting
For the pastry cream
   1 cup milk
   1 vanilla bean
   3 egg yolks
   ⅓ cup granulated sugar
   ¼ cup all-purpose flour
   1 tablespoon Poire William liqueur

1 Cut the quinces into cubes. Place in a saucepan with the water. Stir in half the granulated sugar. Bring to a boil, lower the heat, cover and simmer for 10 minutes, or until tender. Remove the lid; boil until most of the liquid has evaporated.

2 Cool slightly, then purée the fruit in a blender or food processor. Press through a strainer into a bowl; set aside.

3 Make the pastry cream. Pour the milk into a small saucepan. Add the vanilla bean and bring to a boil over low heat. Meanwhile, beat the egg yolks, granulated sugar and flour in a bowl until smooth.

4 Gradually strain the hot milk onto the yolks, whisking frequently until the mixture is smooth.

5 Discard the vanilla bean. Return the mixture to the clean pan and heat gently, stirring, until thickened. Cook, for another 2 minutes, whisking constantly, to ensure that the sauce is smooth and the flour is cooked.

6 Remove the pan from the heat and stir in the quince purée and liqueur. Cover the surface of the pastry cream with plastic wrap to prevent it from forming a skin. Allow to cool slightly while you prepare the ramekins.

7 Preheat the oven to 425°F. Place a baking sheet in the oven to heat up. Butter six ⅔-cup ramekins and sprinkle the inside of each with granulated sugar. In a greasefree bowl, beat the egg whites to stiff peaks. Gradually beat in the remaining granulated sugar, then fold the egg whites into the pastry cream.

8 Divide the mixture among the prepared ramekins and level the surface of each. Carefully run a sharp knife between the side of each ramekin and the mixture, then place the ramekins on the hot baking sheet and bake for 8–10 minutes, until the tops of the soufflés are well risen and golden. Generously dust the tops with confectioners' sugar and serve the soufflés at once.

COOK'S TIP
Poire William is a clear, colorless pear eau-de-vie, which sometimes is sold with a ripe pear in the bottle. Kirsch, made from cherries, also works well in this recipe to complement the flavor of the quinces.

TARTE TATIN

IF YOU USE FROZEN PUFF PASTRY, THIS TASTY TART CAN BE MADE VERY EASILY.

SERVES SIX TO EIGHT

INGREDIENTS
  3 crisp eating apples
  juice of ½ lemon
  4 tablespoons butter, softened
  ⅓ cup sugar
  9 ounces frozen puff pastry, thawed
  whipped cream or créme fraîche,
    to serve

1 Preheat the oven to 425°F. Cut the apples into quarters and remove the cores. Toss the apple quarters in the lemon juice to prevent them from discoloring.

2 Spread the butter over the bottom of a heavy 8-inch omelet pan that can safely be used in the oven. Sprinkle the sugar over the bottom of the pan and add the apple wedges, rounded side down.

3 Cook over medium heat for 15–20 minutes, or until the sugar and butter have melted and the apples are golden. Cut the pastry into a 10-inch round and place on top of the apples; tuck the edges in with a knife. Place the pan in the oven and bake for 15–20 minutes, or until the pastry is golden. Carefully invert the tart onto a plate. Cool slightly before serving with cream.

COOK'S TIP
To turn out the Tarte Tatin, place the serving plate upside down on top of it, then, protecting your arms with oven mitts, hold both pan and plate firmly together and carefully turn them over. Lift off the pan.

PHYLLO-TOPPED APPLE PIE

WITH ITS CRUNCHY PHYLLO TOPPING AND MINIMAL BUTTER, THIS MAKES A LIGHT DESSERT, A GOOD CHOICE FOR AN APPLE PIE ADDICT WATCHING HIS OR HER FAT INTAKE.

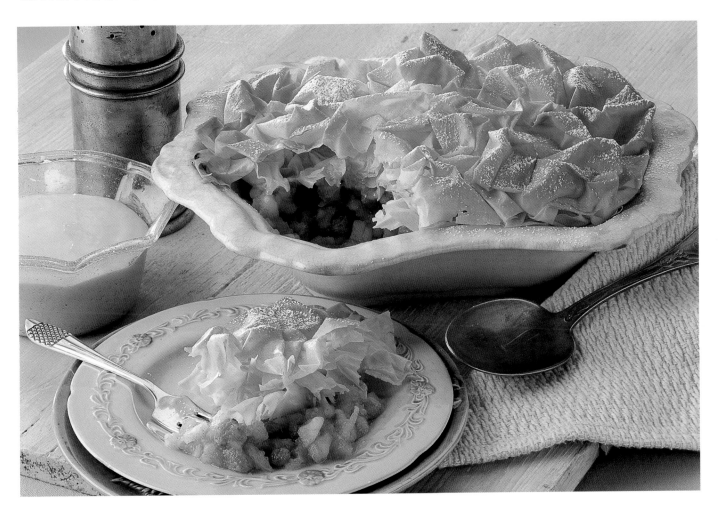

SERVES SIX

INGREDIENTS

2 pounds cooking apples
⅓ cup granulated sugar
grated zest of 1 lemon
1 tablespoon lemon juice
½ cup golden raisins
½ teaspoon ground cinnamon
4 large sheets phyllo pastry, thawed if frozen
2 tablespoons butter, melted
confectioners' sugar, for dusting

VARIATION

To make phyllo "Christmas crackers," cut the buttered phyllo into 8-inch-wide strips. Spoon a little of the filling along one end of each strip, leaving the sides clear. Roll up and twist the ends. Brush with more butter; bake for 20 minutes.

1 Peel, core and dice the apples. Place them in a saucepan with the granulated sugar and lemon zest. Drizzle the lemon juice over. Bring to a boil, stir well, then cook for 5 minutes, or until the apples have softened. Stir in the golden raisins and cinnamon. Spoon the mixture into a 5-cup pie dish and level the top. Let cool.

2 Preheat the oven to 350°F. Place a pie funnel in the center of the fruit. Brush each sheet of phyllo with melted butter. Crunch up loosely and place on the fruit to cover it completely.

3 Bake for 20–30 minutes, until the phyllo is golden. Dust with confectioners' sugar before serving with custard or cream.

CHOCOLATE, PEAR AND PECAN PIE

THE RICHNESS OF DEEP, DARK CHOCOLATE COUPLED WITH JUICY PEARS GIVES A CLASSIC PECAN PIE AN OUT-OF-THE-ORDINARY TWIST. THE RESULT IS UTTERLY DELICIOUS—AND UTTERLY IRRESISTIBLE.

2 Peel the pears, cut them in half and remove the cores with a small spoon. Place ¼ cup of the sugar in a pan with the water. Add the lemon zest and bring to a boil. Add the pears. Cover, lower the heat and simmer for 10 minutes. Remove the pears from the pan with a slotted spoon and set aside to cool. Discard the cooking liquid.

3 Break the chocolate into a large heatproof bowl. Melt over a pan of barely simmering water. Beat in the butter until combined. Set aside. In a saucepan, heat the remaining sugar and golden or corn syrup together over low heat until most of the sugar has dissolved. Bring to a boil, lower the heat and simmer for 2 minutes.

4 Whisk the eggs into the chocolate mixture until combined, then whisk in the syrup mixture. Stir in the vanilla extract and pecans.

SERVES EIGHT TO TEN

INGREDIENTS
11 ounces shortcrust pastry, thawed
   if frozen
3 small pears
scant ¾ cup sugar
⅔ cup water
pared zest of 1 lemon
2 ounces good-quality semisweet
   chocolate
4 tablespoons unsalted butter, diced
¾ cup golden syrup or light corn syrup
3 eggs, beaten
1 teaspoon pure vanilla extract
1¼ cups pecans, chopped
1 tablespoon maple syrup (optional)
ice cream, to serve

1 Preheat the oven to 400°F. Roll out the pastry on a lightly floured surface and line a deep 9-inch fluted tart pan. Chill the pastry shell for 20 minutes, then line it with baking parchment and baking beans. Bake for 10 minutes. Lift out the paper and beans and return the pastry shell to the oven for 5 minutes. Set aside to cool.

5 Place the pear halves flat side down on a board. Using a fine, sharp knife, make lengthwise cuts all along each pear, taking care not to cut all the way through. Using a spatula, lift the pear halves and arrange in the pastry shell. Pour the pecan mixture over the top, so the pears are visible through the mixture.

6 Bake for 25–30 minutes, or until the filling is set, then let cool on a wire rack. If you like, glaze the surface of the pie with maple syrup before serving with ice cream.

FRENCH APPLE TART

THIS GLORIOUS TART MAKES A TRULY INDULGENT DESSERT. FOR AN EARLY MORNING TREAT, TRY A SLICE FOR BREAKFAST WITH A CUP OF STRONG BLACK COFFEE.

SERVES EIGHT

INGREDIENTS
    12 ounces sweet shortcrust pastry,
      thawed if frozen
    whipped cream, to serve
For the filling
    8 tablespoons (1 stick) butter, softened
    ½ cup sugar
    2 large eggs, beaten
    1 cup ground almonds
    ¼ cup all-purpose flour
For the topping
    3 eating apples
    ¼ cup apricot jam
    1 tablespoon water

1 Preheat the oven to 375°F. Place a baking sheet in the oven to heat up. Roll out the pastry on a lightly floured surface and use it to line a 9-inch fluted tart pan.

4 Using a spatula, carefully transfer each row of apple slices to the tart, arranging them on the filling so they resemble the spokes of a wheel. You may need to overlap the slices slightly in the middle to fit. Press the slices down well into the filling. Warm the apricot jam with the water, then press the mixture through a strainer into a small bowl.

5 Using a pastry brush, brush half this apricot glaze over the apples. Place the pan on the hot baking sheet and bake the tart for 45 minutes, or until the pastry is golden and the apples have started to singe slightly.

6 Warm the remaining apricot glaze and brush it over the apples. Let the tart cool slightly before serving with cream.

2 Beat all the ingredients for the filling together until light and fluffy. Spoon into the pastry shell and level the surface.

3 Make the topping. Peel the apples, remove the cores, and cut the apples in half. Place each half, cut side down, on a board. Using a fine, sharp knife, slice the apples thinly, keeping the shape, then press down lightly to fan each apple half in a row.

VARIATION
A red currant glaze would also look good on this tart. Warm red currant jelly with a little lemon juice and brush it over the apples. Straining is not needed.

DUTCH APPLE CAKE

THE APPLE TOPPING MAKES THIS CAKE REALLY MOIST. IT IS JUST AS GOOD HOT AS IT IS COLD.

MAKES EIGHT TO TEN SLICES

INGREDIENTS

2¼ cups self-rising flour
2 teaspoons baking powder
1 teaspoon ground cinnamon
generous ½ cup sugar
4 tablespoons butter, melted
2 eggs, beaten
⅔ cup milk
For the topping
2 crisp, juicy eating apples
1 tablespoon butter, melted
¼ cup demerara sugar
¼ teaspoon ground cinnamon

VARIATION
Add a few golden raisins or raisins to the apples if you like.

1 Preheat the oven to 400°F. Grease and line an 8-inch round cake pan. Sift the flour, baking powder and cinnamon into a large mixing bowl. Stir in the sugar. In a separate bowl, whisk the melted butter, eggs and milk together, then stir the mixture into the dry ingredients.

2 Pour the cake mixture into the prepared pan, smooth the surface, then make a shallow hollow in a ring around the edge of the mixture.

3 Make the topping. Peel and core the apples, slice them into wedges and slice the wedges thinly. Arrange the slices around the hollow in the cake mixture. Brush with the melted butter, then scatter the demerara sugar and ground cinnamon over the top.

4 Bake for 45–50 minutes, or until the cake has risen well, is golden and a skewer inserted into the center comes out clean. Serve immediately with cream, or remove from the pan, peel off the lining paper and cool on a wire rack before slicing.

PEAR AND POLENTA CAKE

POLENTA GIVES THE LIGHT SPONGE THAT TOPS THE SLICED PEARS A NUTTY CORN FLAVOR THAT COMPLEMENTS THE FRUIT PERFECTLY. SERVE WITH CUSTARD OR CREAM.

MAKES TEN SLICES

INGREDIENTS

¾ cup turbinado sugar
4 ripe pears
juice of ½ lemon
2 tablespoons honey
3 eggs
seeds from 1 vanilla bean
½ cup sunflower oil
1 cup self-rising flour
⅓ cup instant polenta

1 Preheat the oven to 350°F. Generously grease and line an 8½-inch round cake pan. Scatter 2 tablespoons of the turbinado sugar over the bottom of the prepared pan.

COOK'S TIP
Use the tip of a small, sharp knife to scrape out the vanilla bean seeds. If you do not have a vanilla bean, use 1 teaspoon pure vanilla extract instead.

2 Peel and core the pears. Cut them into chunky slices and toss in the lemon juice. Arrange them on the bottom of the prepared cake pan. Drizzle the honey over the pears and set aside.

3 Mix together the eggs, seeds from the vanilla bean and the remaining turbinado sugar in a bowl.

4 Beat the egg mixture until thick and creamy, then gradually beat in the oil. Sift together the flour and polenta and fold into the egg mixture.

5 Pour the mixture carefully into the pan over the pears. Bake for about 50 minutes, or until a skewer inserted into the center comes out clean. Cool in the pan for 10 minutes, then turn the cake out onto a plate, peel off the lining paper, invert and slice.

APPLE AND CIDER SAUCE

THIS SAUCE COULDN'T BE SIMPLER TO MAKE. IT TASTES GREAT WITH ROAST PORK, DUCK OR GOOSE.

<u>MAKES 1 POUND</u>

INGREDIENTS
  1 pound cooking apples
  ⅔ cup apple cider
  ½ teaspoon cider vinegar
  2 tablespoons butter
  2 whole cloves
  a few sprigs of fresh thyme
  1 tablespoon honey
  2 teaspoons Dijon mustard

1 Peel, core and slice the apples. Place them in a saucepan with the cider, cider vinegar, butter, cloves and thyme. Simmer over low heat, stirring occasionally, for 10 minutes, or until the apples are soft and pulpy, then raise the heat and cook until most of the liquid has evaporated.

2 Remove the cloves and thyme sprigs and beat in the honey and mustard. Taste and add more honey if necessary, but the sauce is best when slightly tart.

COOK'S TIP
Press the sauce through a strainer if you prefer it to be perfectly smooth.

APPLE AND RED ONION MARMALADE

THIS MARMALADE CHUTNEY IS GOOD ENOUGH TO EAT ON ITS OWN. SERVE IT WITH PORK SAUSAGES OR IN A HAM SANDWICH INSTEAD OF MUSTARD.

<u>MAKES 1 POUND</u>

INGREDIENTS
  ¼ cup extra virgin olive oil
  2 pounds red onions, thinly sliced
  ½ cup demerara sugar
  2 crisp, juicy eating apples
  6 tablespoons cider vinegar

1 Heat the oil in a large, heavy saucepan and add the onions.

2 Stir in the sugar and cook, uncovered, over medium heat, stirring occasionally, for about 40 minutes, or until the onions have softened and become a rich golden color.

3 Peel, core and grate the apples. Add them to the pan with the vinegar and continue to cook for 20 minutes, until the chutney is thick and sticky. Spoon into a sterilized jar and cover.

4 When cool, label and store in the refrigerator for up to 1 month.

STONE FRUIT RECIPES

Juicy and full of flavor, peaches, plums, apricots, cherries and nectarines make perfect partners for crisp pastry. Try the irresistible Baked Peaches with a Lattice Crust or Plum and Marzipan Pastries. For simpler but equally delicious desserts, choose Peach Melba Syllabub or Plum and Custard Creams.

PLUM AND CUSTARD CREAMS

THIS SOPHISTICATED VERSION OF STEWED PLUMS AND CUSTARD, A STANDARD ENGLISH NURSERY DESSERT, IS PRETTILY LAYERED IN A PARFAIT GLASS AND TASTES AS GOOD AS IT LOOKS.

SERVES SIX

INGREDIENTS

1½ pounds red plums, pitted
  and sliced
grated zest and juice of 1 orange
¼ cup sugar
about 2 cups custard sauce (créme
  anglaise), prepared in advance
1¼ cups heavy cream
2 tablespoons water
1 tablespoon powdered gelatin
1 egg white
plum slices and fresh mint sprigs,
  to decorate

COOK'S TIP
Use a long metal skewer or thin metal spoon handle to marble the custard and plum purée mixtures together.

1 Put the plums in a saucepan with the orange zest and juice. Add the sugar and heat, stirring constantly, until the sugar has dissolved. Cook the plums for 5 minutes, until tender. Cool slightly, then purée in a food processor until smooth. Press through a strainer into a bowl and set aside to cool.

2 Put the custard in a saucepan, add half the cream and heat until boiling. Meanwhile, pour the water into a heatproof bowl and sprinkle the gelatin on top; set aside for 5 minutes, until softened. Whisk the soaked gelatin into the hot custard until it has dissolved. Allow the mixture to cool.

3 Whip the remaining cream to soft peaks, then fold it into the custard mixture. In a grease-free bowl, beat the egg white to soft peaks, then fold it into the custard too. Set aside, stirring occasionally, until just starting to set.

4 Quickly spoon alternate spoonfuls of the custard and the plum purée into six tall parfait glasses. Marble the mixtures together. Chill for 2–3 hours, or until the custard has set. Decorate each dessert with plum slices and fresh mint sprigs just before serving.

SPICED FRUITS JUBILEE

BASED ON THE CLASSIC CHERRIES JUBILEE, THIS IS A GREAT WAY TO USE A GLUT OF ANY STONE FRUIT. THE SPICED SYRUP IS A DELICIOUS BONUS. SERVE WITH THE BEST VANILLA ICE CREAM YOU CAN FIND.

SERVES SIX

INGREDIENTS
   ½ cup sugar
   thinly pared zest of 1 unwaxed lemon
   1 cinnamon stick
   4 whole cloves
   1¼ cups water
   8 ounces tart red plums, pitted
    and sliced
   8 ounces nectarines, pitted
    and chopped
   1½ cups cherries, pitted
   1 teaspoon arrowroot
   5 tablespoons brandy
   vanilla ice cream, to serve

1 Put the sugar, lemon zest, cinnamon stick, cloves and water in a pan. Bring to a boil, stirring. Lower the heat and simmer for 5 minutes, then lift out the spices with a slotted spoon and discard.

2 Add the fruit, cover the pan and simmer for 5 minutes. Drain the fruit, reserving the syrup, and set it aside; return the syrup to the pan. Boil it, uncovered, for 2 minutes, or until thick.

3 Put the arrowroot in a small bowl and stir in 2 tablespoons of the brandy. Stir the mixture into the syrup. Continue cooking and stirring until the sauce thickens. Return the fruit to the pan.

4 Place scoops of ice cream in serving bowls and spoon the hot fruit on top. Warm the remaining brandy in a small pan, then set it alight. Ladle it over the fruit at the table for maximum effect.

PEACH MELBA SYLLABUB

IF YOU ARE MAKING THIS SOPHISTICATED DESSERT FOR A DINNER PARTY, COOK THE PEACHES AND RASPBERRIES THE DAY BEFORE TO ALLOW THE FRUIT TO CHILL. WHIP UP THE SYLLABUB AT THE VERY LAST MINUTE TO MAKE A DELICIOUS, LIGHT-AS-A-CLOUD TOPPING.

SERVES SIX

INGREDIENTS
    4 peaches, peeled, pitted and sliced
    1¼ cups blush or red grape juice
    ⅔ cup raspberries
    raspberry or mint leaves, to decorate
    ratafia biscuits or other dessert
        cookies, to serve
For the syllabub
    ¼ cup peach schnapps
    2 tablespoons blush or red grape
        juice
    1¼ cups heavy cream

VARIATIONS
Use dessert pears and sliced kiwi fruit instead of peaches and raspberries. Instead of the syllabub, top the fruit with whipped cream flavored with Advocaat and finely chopped preserved ginger.

1 Place the peach slices in a large saucepan. Add the grape juice. bring to a boil, then cover, lower the heat and simmer for 5–7 minutes, or until tender.

2 Add the raspberries and remove from the heat. Set aside in the refrigerator until cold. Divide the peach and raspberry mixture among six dessert glasses.

3 For the syllabub, place the peach schnapps and grape juice in a large bowl and beat in the cream until it forms soft peaks.

4 Spoon the syllabub on top of the fruit and decorate each portion with a fresh raspberry or mint leaf. Serve with dessert cookies.

NECTARINE AND HAZELNUT MERINGUES

IF IT'S INDULGENCE YOU'RE SEEKING, LOOK NO FURTHER. SWEET NECTARINES AND CREAM SYLLABUB PAIRED WITH CRISP HAZELNUT MERINGUES MAKE A SUPERB DESSERT.

SERVES FIVE

INGREDIENTS
    3 egg whites
    ¾ cup superfine sugar
    ½ cup chopped
        hazelnuts, toasted
    1¼ cups heavy cream
    ¼ cup sweet dessert wine
    2 nectarines, pitted and sliced
    fresh mint sprigs, to decorate

VARIATIONS
Use apricots instead of nectarines if you prefer, or try this with a raspberry filling.

1 Preheat the oven to 275°F. Line two large baking sheets with baking parchment. Beat the egg whites in a greasefree bowl until they form stiff peaks when the whisk or beaters are lifted. Gradually beat in the superfine sugar, a spoonful at a time, until the mixture forms a stiff, glossy meringue.

2 Fold in two-thirds of the chopped toasted hazelnuts, then spoon five large ovals onto each lined baking sheet. Scatter the remaining hazelnuts over five of the meringue ovals. Flatten the tops of the remaining five ovals.

3 Bake the meringues for 1–1¼ hours, until crisp and dry, then carefully lift them off the baking parchment and cool completely on a wire rack.

4 Whip the cream with the dessert wine until the mixture forms soft peaks. Spoon some of the cream syllabub onto each of the plain meringues. Arrange a few nectarine slices on each. Put each meringue on a dessert plate with a hazelnut-topped meringue. Decorate each portion with mint sprigs and serve the meringues immediately.

BLACK CHERRY CLAFOUTI

THIS FAVORITE RECIPE HAS BEEN REPRODUCED WITH ALL MANNER OF FRUIT, BUT YOU SIMPLY CAN'T BEAT THE CLASSIC VERSION USING SLIGHTLY TART BLACK CHERRIES.

SERVES SIX

INGREDIENTS

   2 tablespoons butter, for greasing
   2 cups black cherries, pitted
   ¼ cup all-purpose flour
   ½ cup confectioners' sugar, plus
     extra for dusting
   4 eggs, beaten
   1 cup whole milk or half-and-half
   2 tablespoons kirsch

1 Preheat the oven to 350°F. Use the butter to grease a 5-cup gratin dish thickly. Scatter the cherries over the bottom.

2 Sift the flour and confectioners' sugar together into a large mixing bowl and gradually beat in the eggs until the mixture is smooth. Beat in the milk until blended, then stir in the kirsch.

3 Pour the batter carefully over the cherries, then bake for 35–45 minutes, or until just set and lightly golden.

4 Allow the clafouti to cool for about 15 minutes. Dust liberally with confectioners' sugar just before serving.

VARIATIONS
Try other liqueurs in this dessert. Almond-flavored liqueur is delicious teamed with cherries. Hazelnut, raspberry or orange liqueur would also work nicely.

ICED GIN AND DAMSON SOUFFLES

FOR AN UNFORGETTABLE TASTE SENSATION, USE SLOE GIN FOR THESE DELICIOUS INDIVIDUAL FROZEN SOUFFLES. THEY ARE PERFECT FOR A PARTY AND CAN BE MADE AHEAD.

MAKES SIX

INGREDIENTS
- 1¼ pounds damsons
- 1 cup water
- 1¼ cups sugar
- 2 tablespoons gin or sloe gin
- 4 large egg whites
- 1¼ cups heavy cream, whipped
- fresh mint leaves, to decorate

4 Meanwhile, beat the egg whites in a grease-free bowl until they form stiff peaks. Still beating, slowly pour in the hot syrup until the meringue mixture is stiff and glossy. Fold in the whipped cream and fruit purée until combined.

5 Spoon into the dishes to come 1 inch above the rim of each. Freeze until firm. Remove from the freezer 10 minutes before serving. Remove the collars, then decorate each with damson slices and mint leaves.

1 You will need six ⅔-cup ramekins. Fit each with a collar of greased baking parchment that extends about 2 inches above the rim.

2 Slice two damsons and set aside for the decoration. Put the rest of the damsons in a pan with half the water and ¼ cup of the sugar. Cover and simmer the mixture for about 7 minutes, or until the damsons are tender. Press the pulp through a strainer placed over a bowl to remove all the pits and skin, then stir in the gin and set aside.

3 Combine the remaining sugar and water in the clean pan and heat gently until the sugar has dissolved. Bring to a boil and cook the syrup until it registers 238°F on a sugar thermometer, or until a small amount of the mixture dropped into a cup of cold water can be molded to a soft ball.

CARAMELIZED APRICOTS <u>WITH</u> FRENCH TOAST

PAIN PERDU IS THE FRENCH NAME FOR FRENCH TOAST WHICH LITERALLY TRANSLATES AS "LOST BREAD." A BRITISH VERSION IS KNOWN AS POOR KNIGHTS.

SERVES FOUR

INGREDIENTS
   6 tablespoons unsalted butter, clarified
   1 pound apricots, pitted and
      thickly sliced
   ½ cup sugar
   ⅔ cup heavy cream
   2 tablespoons apricot brandy or brandy
For the French toast
   2½ cups milk
   1 vanilla bean
   ¼ cup sugar
   4 large eggs, beaten
   8 tablespoons (1 stick) unsalted
      butter, clarified
   6 brioche or challah slices,
      diagonally halved
   ½ teaspoon ground cinnamon

1 Heat a heavy frying pan, then melt 1½ tablespoons of the butter in it. Add the apricots and cook for 2–3 minutes, until golden. Using a slotted spoon, transfer to a bowl. Add the rest of the butter to the pan with the sugar and heat gently, stirring, until golden.

2 Pour in the cream and brandy and cook gently until the mixture forms a smooth sauce. Boil for 2–3 minutes, until thickened, then pour the sauce over the apricots and set aside.

3 To make the French toast, pour the milk into a saucepan and add the vanilla bean and half the sugar. Heat gently until almost boiling, then set aside to cool.

4 Remove the vanilla bean and pour the flavored milk into a shallow dish. Beat in the eggs. Heat a sixth of the butter in the clean frying pan. Dip each slice of brioche in turn into the milk mixture, add it to the pan and cook until golden brown on both sides. Add the remaining butter as needed. As the French toast is cooked, remove the slices; keep hot.

5 Warm the apricot sauce and spoon it onto the French toast. Mix the remaining sugar with the cinnamon and sprinkle a little of the mixture over each portion.

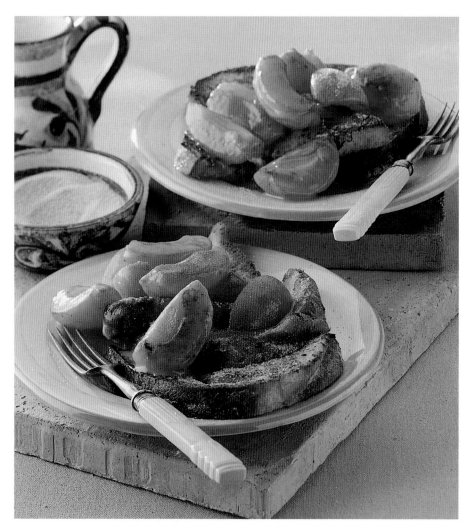

COOK'S TIP
To clarify the butter, melt it in a small saucepan, then let it stand for a few minutes. Carefully pour the clear butter on the surface (the clarified butter) into a small bowl, leaving the milky solids behind in the pan.

FRESH CHERRY <u>AND</u> HAZELNUT STRUDEL

SERVE THIS WONDERFUL OLD-WORLD TREAT AS A WARM DESSERT, OR ALLOW IT TO COOL AND OFFER IT AS AN AFTERNOON SNACK WITH TEA OR COFFEE.

SERVES SIX TO EIGHT

INGREDIENTS

- 6 tablespoons butter
- 6 tablespoons light brown sugar
- 3 egg yolks
- grated zest of 1 lemon
- ¼ teaspoon grated nutmeg
- generous 1 cup ricotta cheese
- 8 large sheets phyllo pastry, thawed if frozen
- 3 ounces ratafia biscuits or other dessert cookies, crushed
- 2½ cups cherries, pitted
- 2 tablespoons chopped hazelnuts
- confectioners' sugar, for dusting
- crème fraîche, to serve

1 Preheat the oven to 375°F. Soften 1 tablespoon of the butter. Place it in a bowl and beat in the sugar and egg yolks until light and fluffy. Beat in the lemon zest, nutmeg and ricotta, then set aside.

2 Melt the remaining butter in a small pan. Working quickly, place a sheet of phyllo on a clean dish towel and brush it generously with melted butter. Place a second sheet on top and repeat the process. Continue until all the phyllo has been layered and buttered, reserving some of the melted butter.

3 Scatter the crushed cookies over the top, leaving a 2-inch border around the outside. Spoon the ricotta mixture over the cookies, spread it lightly to cover, then scatter the cherries over the top.

4 Fold in the phyllo pastry border and use the dish towel to carefully roll up the strudel, jelly-roll style, beginning from one of the long sides of the pastry. Grease a baking sheet with the remaining melted butter.

5 Place the strudel on the baking sheet and scatter the hazelnuts over the surface. Bake for 35–40 minutes, or until the strudel is golden and crisp. Dust with confectioners' sugar and serve with a dollop of crème fraîche.

BAKED PEACHES <u>WITH A</u> LATTICE CRUST

IF YOU WOULD RATHER USE NECTARINES FOR THE RECIPE, THERE'S NO NEED TO PEEL THEM FIRST.

MAKES SIX

INGREDIENTS
  3 peaches
  juice of ½ lemon
  scant ½ cup white marzipan
  13 ounces prepared puff pastry,
    thawed if frozen
  a large pinch of ground cinnamon
  beaten egg, to glaze
  sugar, for sprinkling
For the caramel sauce
  ¼ cup sugar
  2 tablespoons cold water
  ⅔ cup heavy cream

1 Preheat the oven to 375ºF. Place the peaches in a large bowl and pour boiling water over to cover. Leave for 60 seconds, then drain the peaches and peel off the skins. Toss the skinned fruit in the lemon juice to prevent them from turning brown.

2 Divide the marzipan into six pieces and shape each to form a small round. Cut the peaches in half and remove their pits. Fill the pit cavity in each with a marzipan round.

3 Cut the puff pastry in half. Set one half aside, then cut out six rounds from the rest, making each round slightly larger than a peach half. Sprinkle a little cinnamon on each pastry round, then place a peach half, marzipan side down, on the pastry.

4 Cut the remaining pastry into lattice pastry, using a special cutter if you have one. If not, simply cut small slits in rows all over the pastry, starting each row slightly lower than the last. Cut the lattice pastry into six equal squares.

COOK'S TIP
Take care when adding the cream to the hot caramel, as the mixture is liable to spit. Pour it from a cup, protecting your hand with an oven mitt, and use a long-handled wooden spoon for stirring.

5 Dampen the edges of the pastry rounds with a little water, then drape a lattice pastry square over each peach half. Press around the edge to seal, then trim off the excess pastry and decorate with small peach leaves made from the trimmings. Transfer the peach pastries to a baking sheet. Brush with the beaten egg and sprinkle with the sugar. Bake for 20 minutes, or until the pastries are golden.

6 Meanwhile, make the caramel sauce. Heat the sugar with the water in a small pan until it dissolves. bring to a boil and continue to boil until the syrup turns a dark golden brown. Stand back and add the cream. Heat gently, stirring until smooth. Serve the peach pastries with the sauce.

PEACH <u>AND</u> RED CURRANT TARTLETS

TART RED CURRANTS AND SWEET PEACHES MAKE A WINNING COMBINATION IN THESE SIMPLE TARTLETS.

MAKES FOUR

INGREDIENTS
   2 tablespoons butter, melted
   16 × 6-inch squares of phyllo pastry,
     thawed if frozen
   confectioners' sugar, for dusting
   red currant sprigs, to decorate
For the filling
   ⅔ cup heavy cream
   4¼ ounces mixed peach and
     mango yogurt
   a few drops of pure vanilla extract
   1 tablespoon confectioners' sugar
For the topping
   2 peaches
   ½ cup red currants

COOK'S TIP
To strip red currants from their stalks, pull
the stems through the tines of a fork.

1 Preheat the oven to 375°F. Use a little of the butter to grease four cups of a standard muffin pan or four tartlet pans. Brush the pastry squares with butter, stack them in fours, then place in the pans to make four pastry shells.

2 Bake for 12–15 minutes, until golden. Cool the phyllo cases on a wire rack.

3 Make the filling. Whip the cream to soft peaks, then lightly fold in the yogurt, vanilla extract and confectioners' sugar. Divide among the pastry shells.

4 Slice the peaches and fan them out on top of the filling, with a few red currants. Decorate with red currant sprigs and dust with confectioners' sugar.

PLUM <u>AND</u> MARZIPAN PASTRIES

THESE DANISH PASTRIES CAN BE MADE WITH ANY PITTED FRUIT. TRY APRICOTS, CHERRIES OR DAMSON OR GREENGAGE PLUMS INSTEAD OF RED ONES, ADDING A GLAZE MADE FROM HONEY OR JAM.

MAKES SIX

INGREDIENTS

    13 ounces prepared puff pastry
    6 tablespoons plum jam
    ½ cup white marzipan, coarsely
      grated
    3 red plums, halved and pitted
    1 egg, beaten
    ½ cup sliced almonds
For the glaze
    2 tablespoons plum jam
    1 tablespoon water

1 Preheat the oven to 425°F. Cut the pastry into six equal squares and place on one or two dampened baking sheets

2 Spoon 1 tablespoon jam into the center of each pastry square. Divide the marzipan among them. Place half a plum, hollow side down, on top of each marzipan mound.

3 Brush the edges of the pastry with beaten egg. Bring up the corners and press them together lightly, then open out the pastry corners at the top. Glaze the pastries with a little beaten egg, then press a sixth of the flaked almonds on each.

4 Bake the pastries for 20–25 minutes, or until lightly golden.

5 Meanwhile, make the glaze by heating the jam and water in a small pan, stirring until smooth. Press the mixture through a strainer into a small bowl, then brush it over the tops of the pastries while they are still warm. Let cool on a wire rack.

YELLOW PLUM TART

IN THIS TART, GLAZED YELLOW PLUMS SIT ATOP A DELECTABLE ALMOND FILLING IN A CRISP PASTRY SHELL. WHEN THEY ARE IN SEASON, GREENGAGE PLUMS MAKE AN EXCELLENT ALTERNATIVE.

SERVES EIGHT

INGREDIENTS

1½ cups all-purpose flour
pinch of salt
6 tablespoons butter, chilled
2 tablespoons sugar
a few drops of pure vanilla extract
3 tablespoons ice water
whipped cream or custard, to serve

For the filling
⅓ cup sugar
6 tablespoons butter, softened
¾ cup ground almonds
1 egg, beaten
2 tablespoons all-purpose flour
1 pound yellow plums, halved
   and pitted

For the glaze
3 tablespoons apricot jam, strained
1 tablespoon water

1 Sift the flour and salt into a bowl, then rub in the chilled butter until the mixture resembles fine bread crumbs. Stir in the sugar, vanilla extract and enough of the ice water to make a soft dough.

COOK'S TIP
Ceramic baking beans are ideal for baking blind, but any dried beans will do. You can use them over and over again, but make sure you keep them in a special jar, separate from the rest of your dried beans, as you cannot use them for conventional cooking.

2 Knead the dough gently on a lightly floured surface until smooth, then wrap in plastic wrap and chill for 10 minutes.

3 Preheat the oven to 400ºF. Roll out the pastry and use it to line a 9-inch fluted tart pan, allowing excess pastry to overhang the top. Prick the bottom with a fork and line with baking parchment and baking beans.

4 Bake for 10 minutes, remove the paper and beans, then return the pastry shell to the oven for 10 minutes. Remove and allow to cool. Trim off any excess pastry with a sharp knife.

5 To make the filling, beat together all the ingredients except the plums. Spread on the bottom of the pastry shell. Arrange the plums on top, placing them cut side down. Make a glaze by heating the jam with the water. Stir well, then brush a little of the apricot glaze over the top of the fruit.

6 Bake the tart for 50–60 minutes, until the almond filling is cooked and the plums are tender. Warm any remaining apricot glaze and brush it over the top. Cut into slices and serve with whipped cream or custard.

APRICOT PARCELS

THESE LITTLE PHYLLO PARCELS CONTAIN A SPECIAL APRICOT AND MINCEMEAT FILLING. A GOOD WAY TO USE UP ANY MINCEMEAT AND MARZIPAN THAT HAVE BEEN IN YOUR PANTRY SINCE CHRISTMAS!

MAKES EIGHT

INGREDIENTS

    12 ounces phyllo pastry, thawed
      if frozen
    4 tablespoons butter, melted
    8 apricots, halved and pitted
    4 tablespoons mincemeat
    12 ratafia (almond paste) or other
      dessert cookies, crushed
    2 tablespoons grated marzipan
    confectioners' sugar, for dusting

COOK'S TIP
Phyllo pastry dries out quickly, so keep any squares not being used under a clean, damp dish towel. Work as quickly as possible. If the phyllo turns dry and brittle, brush it with melted butter to moisten.

1 Preheat the oven to 400°F. Cut the phyllo pastry into thirty-two 7-inch squares. Brush four of the squares with a little melted butter and stack them, giving each layer a quarter turn so that the stack acquires a star shape. Repeat to make eight stars.

2 Place an apricot half, hollow side up, in the center of each pastry star. Mix together the mincemeat, crushed cookies and marzipan and spoon a little of the mixture into the hollow in each apricot.

3 Top with another apricot half, then bring the corners of each pastry together and squeeze to make a gathered purse.

4 Place the purses on a baking sheet and brush each with a little melted butter. Bake for 15–20 minutes, or until the pastry is golden and crisp. Lightly dust with confectioners' sugar to serve. Whipped cream, flavored with a little brandy, makes an ideal accompaniment.

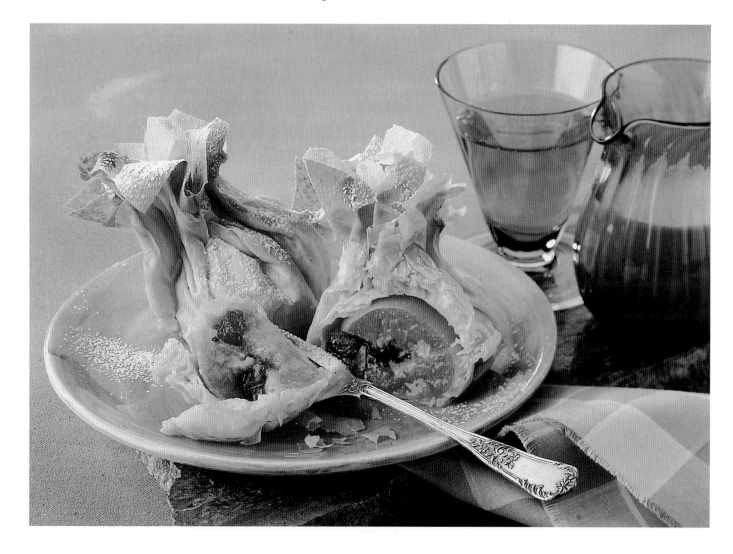

CRUNCHY-TOPPED FRESH APRICOT CAKE

ALMONDS ARE PERFECT PARTNERS FOR FRESH APRICOTS, AND THIS IS A GREAT WAY TO USE UP FIRM FRUITS. SERVE COLD AS A SNACK OR WARM WITH CUSTARD FOR A DESSERT.

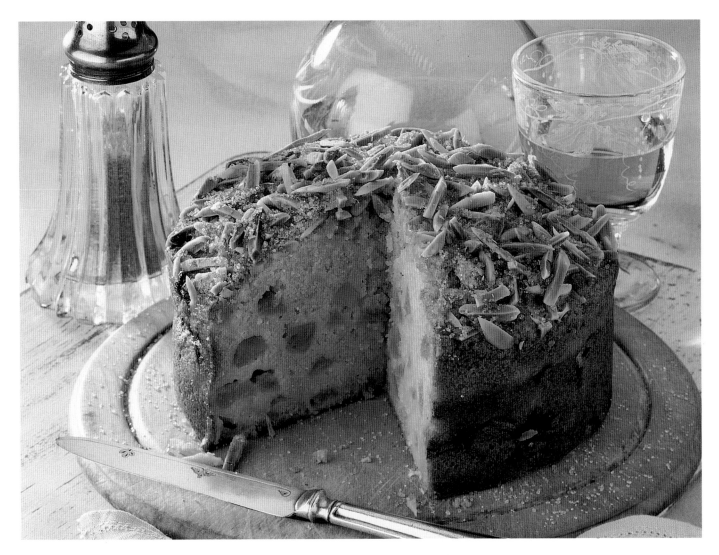

MAKES EIGHT SLICES

INGREDIENTS
  1½ cups self-rising flour
  12 tablespoons (1½ sticks) butter,
    softened
  ¾ cup granulated sugar
  1 cup ground almonds
  3 eggs
  1 teaspoon pure almond extract
  ½ teaspoon baking powder
  8 firm apricots, pitted and chopped
For the topping
  2 tablespoons demerara sugar
  ½ cup slivered almonds

1 Preheat the oven to 325°F. Grease a 7-inch round cake pan and line with baking parchment. Put all the cake ingredients, except the apricots, in a large mixing bowl and beat until creamy.

2 Fold the apricots into the cake mixture, then spoon into the prepared cake pan. Make a hollow in the center with the back of a large spoon, then scatter 1 tablespoon of the demerara sugar over for the topping, with the slivered almonds.

3 Bake for 1½ hours, or until a skewer inserted into the middle comes out clean. Sprinkle the remaining demerara sugar over the top of the cake and let cool for 10 minutes in the pan. Remove from the pan, peel off the paper and finish cooling on a wire rack.

PICKLED PEACH AND CHILE CHUTNEY

THIS IS A SPICY, RICH CHUTNEY THAT IS GREAT SERVED WITH COLD ROAST MEATS SUCH AS HAM, PORK OR TURKEY. IT IS ALSO GOOD WITH A STRONG FARMHOUSE Cheddar CHEESE.

MAKES 1 POUND

INGREDIENTS

    2 cups cider vinegar
    1⅔ cups light brown sugar
    1 cup dried dates, pitted and finely
        chopped
    1 teaspoon ground allspice
    1 teaspoon ground mace
    1 pound ripe peaches, pitted and cut
        into small chunks
    3 onions, thinly sliced
    4 fresh red chiles, seeded and finely
        chopped
    4 garlic cloves, crushed
    2-inch piece of fresh ginger root,
        finely grated
    1 teaspoon salt

1 Place the vinegar, brown sugar, dates and spices in a large saucepan and bring to a boil, stirring occasionally.

2 Add all the remaining ingredients and return to a boil. Lower the heat and simmer for 40–50 minutes, or until thick. Stir often to prevent the mixture from burning on the bottom of the pan.

3 Spoon into clean, sterilized jars and seal. When cool, store the jars in the refrigerator and use within 2 months.

COOK'S TIP
To test the consistency of the finished chutney before canning, spoon a little of the mixture onto a plate: The chutney is ready once it holds its shape.

NECTARINE RELISH

THIS SWEET AND TANGY FRUIT RELISH GOES VERY WELL WITH HOT ROAST MEATS AND GAME BIRDS, SUCH AS GUINEA FOWL, PHEASANT AND PORK. MAKE WHILE NECTARINES ARE PLENTIFUL AND KEEP TIGHTLY COVERED IN THE REFRIGERATOR TO SERVE AT CHRISTMAS FOR A SPECIAL TREAT.

MAKES 1 POUND

INGREDIENTS

    3 tablespoons olive oil
    2 Spanish onions, thinly sliced
    1 fresh green chile, seeded and finely
        chopped
    1 teaspoon finely chopped
        fresh rosemary
    2 bay leaves
    1 pound nectarines, pitted and cut
        into chunks
    1 cup raisins
    2 teaspoons crushed coriander seeds
    2 cups demerara sugar
    scant 1 cup red wine vinegar

1 Heat the oil in a large pan. Add the onions, chile, rosemary and bay leaves. Cook, stirring often, for 15–20 minutes, or until the onions are soft.

COOK'S TIP
Jars of this relish make a welcome gift. Add a colorful tag reminding the recipient to keep it in the refrigerator.

2 Add all the remaining ingredients and bring to a boil slowly, stirring often. Lower the heat and simmer, stirring occasionally, for 1 hour, or until the relish is thick and sticky.

3 Spoon into sterilized jars and seal. Cool, then chill. The relish will keep in the refrigerator for up to 5 months.

BERRY
AND
CURRANT
RECIPES

For sheer beauty, berries are hard

to beat. Make the most of their

tantalizing colors and flavors by

serving them simply, as a topping

for shortcakes or in a summer

pudding. Fresh Blueberry Muffins,

Berry Brûlée Tarts, Blackberry

Jelly—these are berries

at their best.

SUMMER PUDDING

No fruit book would be complete without this well-loved classic recipe. Don't reserve it solely for summer: it freezes well and provides a delicious dessert for Christmas Day, as a light and refreshing alternative to the traditional plum pudding.

SERVES FOUR TO SIX

INGREDIENTS

½-inch-thick slices of day-old white bread, crusts removed

6–7 cups mixed berries, such as strawberries, raspberries, black currants, red currants and blueberries

¼ cup turbinado sugar

lightly whipped heavy cream or crème fraîche, to serve

1 Trim a slice of bread to fit in the bottom of a 5-cup pudding bowl or mold, then trim another 5–6 slices to line the sides.

2 Place all the fruit in a saucepan with the sugar. Cook gently for 4–5 minutes, until the juices begin to run—it will not be necessary to add any water. Allow the mixture to cool slightly, then spoon the berries and enough of their juices to moisten into the bread-lined pudding bowl or mold. Save any leftover juice to serve with the pudding.

3 Fold over the excess bread, then cover the fruit with the remaining bread slices, trimming them to fit. Place a small plate or saucer directly on top of the pudding, fitting it inside the bowl or mold. Weight it with a 2-pound weight or a couple of full cans.

4 Leave the pudding in the refrigerator for at least 8 hours or overnight. To serve, run a knife between the pudding and the bowl or mold and turn it out onto a plate. Spoon any reserved juices over the top and serve with whipped cream or crème fraîche.

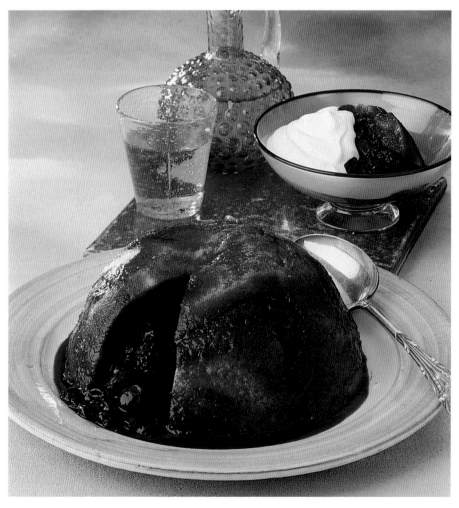

HOT BLACKBERRY AND APPLE SOUFFLES

AS THE BLACKBERRY SEASON IS SO SHORT AND THE APPLE SEASON SO LONG, IT'S ALWAYS WORTH FREEZING A BAG OF BLACKBERRIES TO HAVE ON HAND FOR TREATS LIKE THIS ONE.

2 Cook the blackberries and diced apple with the orange zest and juice in a pan for 10 minutes, or until the apple has pulped down well. Press through a strainer into a bowl. Stir in ¼ cup of the superfine sugar. Set aside to cool.

3 Put a spoonful of the fruit purée into each prepared dish and smooth the surface. Set the dishes aside.

4 Beat the egg whites in a large, greasefree bowl until they form stiff peaks. Very gradually beat in the remaining superfine sugar to make a stiff, glossy meringue mixture.

MAKES SIX

INGREDIENTS
   butter, for greasing
   ⅔ cup superfine sugar, plus extra for
      dusting
   3 cups blackberries
   1 large cooking apple, peeled, cored
      and finely diced
   grated zest and juice of 1 orange
   3 egg whites
   confectioners' sugar, for dusting

COOK'S TIP
Running a table knife around the edge of the soufflés before baking helps them to rise evenly without any part sticking to the rim of the dishes.

1 Preheat the oven to 400°F. Generously grease six ⅔-cup individual soufflé dishes with butter and dust with superfine sugar, shaking out the excess. Put a baking sheet in the oven to heat.

5 Fold in the remaining fruit purée and spoon the flavored meringue into the prepared dishes. Level the tops with a spatula, and run a table knife around the edge of each dish.

6 Place the dishes on the hot baking sheet and bake for 10–15 minutes, until the soufflés have risen well and are lightly browned. Dust the tops with confectioners' sugar and serve immediately.

SUMMER BERRY CREPES

THE DELICATE FLAVOR OF THESE FLUFFY CRÊPES CONTRASTS BEAUTIFULLY WITH TANGY BERRIES.

SERVES FOUR

INGREDIENTS
　1 cup self-rising flour
　1 large egg
　1¼ cups milk
　a few drops of pure vanilla extract
　1 tablespoon butter
　1 tablespoon sunflower oil
　confectioners' sugar, for dusting
For the fruit
　2 tablespoons butter
　¼ cup sugar
　juice of 2 oranges
　thinly pared zest of ½ orange
　3 cups mixed summer berries,
　　such as sliced strawberries,
　　yellow raspberries, blueberries
　　and red currants
　3 tablespoons Grand Marnier or other
　　orange liqueur

1 Preheat the oven to 300°F. To make the crêpes, sift the flour into a large bowl and make a well in the center. Break in the egg and gradually whisk in the milk to make a smooth batter. Stir in the vanilla extract. Set the batter aside in a cool place for up to half an hour.

2 Heat the butter and oil together in a 7-inch nonstick frying pan. Swirl to grease the pan, then pour the excess fat into a small bowl.

3 If the batter has been allowed to stand, whisk it thoroughly until smooth. Pour a little of the batter into the hot pan, swirling to cover the bottom of the pan evenly. Cook until the mixture comes away from the sides and the crêpe is golden underneath.

4 Flip over the crêpe with a large metal spatula and cook the other side briefly until golden.

5 Slide the crêpe onto a heatproof plate. Make seven more crêpes in the same way, greasing the pan with more butter and oil mixture as needed. Cover the crêpes with foil or another plate and keep them hot in the oven.

COOK'S TIP
For safety, when igniting a mixture for flambéing, use a long taper or long wooden match. Stand back as you set the mixture alight.

6 To prepare the fruit, melt the butter in a heavy frying pan, stir in the sugar and cook gently until the mixture is golden brown. Add the orange juice and zest and cook until syrupy.

7 Add the fruits and warm through, then add the liqueur and set it alight. Shake the pan to incorporate the liqueur until the flame dies down.

8 Fold the crêpes into quarters and arrange two on each plate. Spoon some of the fruit mixture over and dust with the confectioners' sugar. Serve the remaining fruit mixture separately.

FRESH BERRY PAVLOVA

PAVLOVA IS THE SIMPLEST OF DESSERTS, BUT IT CAN ALSO BE THE MOST STUNNING. FILL WITH A MIXTURE OF BERRIES IF YOU LIKE—RASPBERRIES AND BLUEBERRIES MAKE A MARVELOUS COMBINATION.

SERVES SIX TO EIGHT

INGREDIENTS

4 egg whites, at room temperature
1 cup superfine sugar
1 teaspoon cornstarch
1 teaspoon cider vinegar
½ teaspoon pure vanilla extract
1¼ cups heavy cream
⅔ cup crème fraîche
1½ cups blueberries
fresh mint sprigs,
  to decorate
confectioners' sugar, for dusting

COOK'S TIP

To begin, invert a plate on the baking parchment and draw around it with a pencil. Turn the paper over and use the circle as a guide for the meringue.

1 Preheat the oven to 275°F. Line a baking sheet with baking parchment. Beat the egg whites in a large greasefree bowl until they form stiff peaks. Gradually beat in the sugar to make a stiff, glossy meringue. Sift the cornstarch over and fold it in with the vinegar and vanilla.

2 Spoon the meringue mixture onto the paper-lined sheet, using the circle drawn on the paper as a guide (see Cook's Tip). Spread into a round, swirling the top, and bake for 1¼ hours, or until the meringue is crisp and very lightly golden. Switch off the oven, keeping the door closed, and allow the meringue to cool for 1–2 hours.

3 Carefully peel the parchment from the meringue and transfer it to a serving plate. Whip the cream in a large mixing bowl until it forms soft peaks, fold in the crème fraîche, then spoon the mixture into the center of the meringue shell. Top with the raspberries and blueberries and decorate with the mint sprigs. Sift confectioners' sugar over the top and serve at once.

GOOSEBERRY AND ELDERFLOWER FOOL

GOOSEBERRIES AND ELDERFLOWERS ARE A MATCH MADE IN HEAVEN, EACH BRINGING OUT THE FLAVOR OF THE OTHER. SERVE WITH AMARETTI OR OTHER DESSERT COOKIES FOR DIPPING.

SERVES SIX

INGREDIENTS

    4 cups gooseberries, cleaned
    2 tablespoons water
    ¼–⅓ cup sugar
    2 tablespoons elderflower cordial
    about 2 cups custard sauce (créme
      anglaise), prepared in advance
    1¼ cups heavy cream
    crushed amaretti cookies, to decorate
    amaretti cookies, to serve

1 Put the gooseberries and water in a pan. Cover and cook for 5–6 minutes, or until the berries pop open.

2 Add the sugar and elderflower cordial to the gooseberries, then stir vigorously or mash until the fruit forms a pulp. Remove the pan from the heat, spoon the gooseberry pulp into a bowl and set aside to cool.

3 Stir the custard into the fruit. Whip the cream to soft peaks, then fold it into the mixture and chill. Serve in dessert glasses, decorated with crushed amaretti and accompanied by amaretti.

FRUITS OF THE FOREST WITH WHITE CHOCOLATE CREAMS

COLORFUL FRUITS MACERATED IN A MIXTURE OF WHITE COCONUT RUM AND SUGAR MAKE A FANTASTIC ACCOMPANIMENT TO A DELIGHTFULLY CREAMY WHITE CHOCOLATE MOUSSE.

SERVES FOUR

INGREDIENTS

- 3 ounces white cooking chocolate, in squares
- ⅔ cup heavy cream
- 2 tablespoons crème fraîche
- 1 egg, separated
- 1 teaspoon powdered gelatin
- 2 tablespoons cold water
- a few drops of pure vanilla extract
- 1 cup small strawberries, sliced
- ½ cup raspberries
- ¾ cup blueberries
- 3 tablespoons superfine sugar
- 5 tablespoons white coconut rum
- strawberry leaves, to decorate (optional)

1 Melt the chocolate in a heatproof bowl set over a pan of hot water. Heat the cream in a separate pan until almost boiling, then stir into the chocolate with the crème fraîche. Cool slightly, then beat in the egg yolk.

2 Sprinkle the gelatin over the cold water in another heatproof bowl and set aside for a few minutes to soften.

COOK'S TIP
For a dramatic effect, decorate each white chocolate cream with dark chocolate leaves, made by coating the veined side of unsprayed rose leaves with melted chocolate. Let them dry before gently pulling off the leaves.

3 Set the bowl in a pan of hot water until the gelatin has dissolved completely. Stir the dissolved gelatin into the chocolate mixture and add the vanilla extract. Set aside until starting to thicken and set.

4 Brush four dariole molds or individual soufflé dishes with oil; line the bottom of each with baking parchment.

5 In a greasefree bowl, beat the egg white to soft peaks, then fold into the chocolate mixture.

6 Spoon the mixture into the prepared molds or soufflé dishes, then level the surface of each and chill for 2–3 hours, or until firm.

7 Meanwhile, place the fruits in a bowl. Add the superfine sugar and coconut rum and stir gently to mix. Cover and chill until required.

8 Ease the chocolate cream away from the rims of the molds or dishes and turn out onto dessert plates. Spoon the fruits around the outside. Decorate with the strawberry leaves, if you like, then serve at once.

FRESH STRAWBERRY ICE CREAM

YOU CAN MAKE THE ICE CREAM BY HAND IF YOU FREEZE IT OVER A PERIOD OF SEVERAL HOURS, WHISKING IT EVERY HOUR OR SO, BUT THE TEXTURE WON'T BE AS GOOD.

<u>SERVES SIX</u>

INGREDIENTS
    1¼ cups whole milk or half-and-half
    1 vanilla bean
    3 large egg yolks
    8 ounces (1½–2 cups) strawberries
    juice of ½ lemon
    ¾ cup confectioners' sugar
    1¼ cups heavy cream
    sliced strawberries, to serve

1 Put the milk into a pan, add the vanilla bean and bring to a boil over low heat. Remove from the heat. Set aside for 20 minutes, then remove the vanilla bean. Strain the warm milk into a bowl containing the egg yolks; whisk well.

2 Return the mixture to the clean pan and heat, stirring, until the custard just coats the back of the spoon. Pour the custard into a bowl, cover the surface with plastic wrap and set aside to cool.

COOK'S TIP
Use free-range eggs if possible, bought from a reputable supplier.

3 Meanwhile, purée the strawberries with the lemon juice in a food processor or blender. Press the strawberry purée through a strainer into a bowl. Stir in the confectioners' sugar and set aside.

4 Whip the cream to soft peaks, then gently but thoroughly fold it into the custard with the strawberry purée. Pour the mixture into an ice-cream maker. Churn for 20–30 minutes, or until the mixture holds its shape. Transfer the ice cream to a freezerproof container, cover and freeze until firm. Soften briefly before serving with the strawberries.

BLACK CURRANT SORBET

THIS LUSCIOUS SORBET IS EASILY MADE BY HAND, BUT IT IS IMPORTANT TO ALTERNATELY FREEZE AND BLEND OR PROCESS THE MIXTURE FIVE OR SIX TIMES TO GET THE BEST RESULT. IF YOU MAKE LOTS OF ICE CREAM AND SORBETS, IT IS WORTH INVESTING IN AN ICE-CREAM MAKER.

SERVES SIX

INGREDIENTS
1¼ cups water, plus
  2 tablespoons
½ cup sugar
2 cups black currants
2 tablespoons crème de cassis or
  other black currant liqueur
1 teaspoon lemon juice
2 egg whites

3 Pour the chilled black currant syrup into a freezerproof bowl; freeze until slushy, whisking occasionally. Beat the egg whites in a greasefree bowl until they form soft peaks, then fold into the half-frozen black currant mixture.

4 Freeze the mixture again until firm, then spoon into a food processor or blender and process. Alternately freeze and process or blend until completely smooth. Serve the sorbet straight from the freezer.

1 Pour 1¼ cups of the water into a saucepan and add the sugar. Place over low heat until the sugar has dissolved. Bring to a boil and boil rapidly for 10 minutes, then set the syrup aside to cool.

2 Meanwhile, cook the black currants with the remaining 2 tablespoons water over low heat for 5–7 minutes. Press the black currants and juice through a strainer placed over a bowl, then stir the black currant purée into the syrup with the liqueur and lemon juice. Allow to cool completely, then chill for 1 hour.

RASPBERRY AND ROSE PETAL SHORTCAKES

ROSE WATER—SCENTED CREAM AND FRESH RASPBERRIES FORM THE FILLING FOR THIS DELECTABLE DESSERT. THOUGH THEY LOOK IMPRESSIVE, THESE SHORTCAKES ARE EASY TO MAKE.

MAKES SIX

INGREDIENTS
  8 tablespoons (1 stick) unsalted
    butter, softened
  ¼ cup granulated sugar
  ½ vanilla bean, split, seeds reserved
  1 cup all-purpose flour, plus extra for
    dusting
  ⅓ cup semolina
  confectioners' sugar, for dusting
For the filling
  1¼ cups heavy cream
  1 tablespoon confectioners' sugar
  ½ teaspoon rose water
  4 cups raspberries
For the decoration
  12 miniature roses, unsprayed
  6 mint sprigs
  1 egg white, beaten
  sugar, for dusting

1 Cream the butter, sugar and vanilla seeds in a bowl until pale and fluffy. Sift the flour and semolina together, then gradually work the dry ingredients into the creamed mixture to make a cookie dough.

VARIATIONS
Other soft red summer berries, such as mulberries, loganberries and tayberries, would be equally good in this dessert.

COOK'S TIP
For best results, serve the shortcakes as soon as possible after assembling them. Otherwise, they are likely to turn soggy from the berries' liquid.

2 Gently knead the dough on a lightly floured surface until smooth. Roll out quite thinly and prick all over with a fork. Using a 3-inch fluted cutter, cut out 12 rounds. Place these on a baking sheet and chill for 30 minutes.

3 Meanwhile, make the filling. Whisk the cream with the confectioners' sugar until soft peaks form. Fold in the rose water and chill until required.

4 Preheat the oven to 350°F. To make the decoration, paint the roses and leaves with the egg white. Dust with sugar; dry on a wire rack.

5 Bake the shortcakes for 15 minutes, or until lightly golden. Lift them off the baking sheet with a metal spatula and cool on a wire rack.

6 To assemble the shortcakes, spoon the rose-water cream onto half the cookies. Add a layer of raspberries, then top with a second shortcake. Dust with confectioners' sugar. Decorate with the frosted roses and mint sprigs.

FRESH CURRANT BREAD AND BUTTER PUDDING

MIXED FRESH CURRANTS ADD A TART TOUCH TO THIS SCRUMPTIOUS HOT DESSERT.

SERVES SIX

INGREDIENTS
     8 medium-thick slices day-old bread,
       crusts removed
     4 tablespoons butter, softened
     1 cup red currants
     1 cup black currants
     4 eggs, beaten
     6 tablespoons granulated sugar
     2 cups whole milk or half-and-half
     1 teaspoon pure vanilla extract
     freshly grated nutmeg
     2 tablespoons demerara sugar
     light cream, to serve

1 Preheat the oven to 325°F.
Generously butter a 5-cup oval baking
dish.

VARIATION
A mixture of blueberries and raspberries
would work just as well as the currants.

2 Spread the slices of bread generously
with the butter, then cut them in half
diagonally. Layer the slices in the dish,
buttered side up, scattering the currants
between the layers.

3 Beat the eggs and granulated sugar
lightly together in a large mixing bowl,
then gradually beat in the milk, vanilla
extract and a large pinch of freshly
grated nutmeg.

4 Pour the milk mixture over the bread,
pushing the slices down. Scatter the
demerara sugar and a little nutmeg over
the top. Place the dish in a baking pan
and fill with hot water to come halfway
up the sides of the dish. Bake for
40 minutes, then increase the oven
temperature to 350°F and bake for
20–25 minutes more, or until the top is
golden. Cool slightly, then serve with
light cream.

CRANBERRY AND BLUEBERRY STREUSEL CAKE

CRANBERRIES ARE SELDOM USED IN SWEET DISHES, BUT ONCE THEY ARE SWEETENED, THEY HAVE A GREAT FLAVOR, AND ARE PERFECT WHEN PARTNERED WITH BLUEBERRIES.

MAKES TEN SLICES

INGREDIENTS

¾ cup butter, softened
½ cup granulated sugar
3 cups all-purpose flour
2 large eggs, beaten
1 teaspoon baking powder
1 teaspoon pure vanilla extract
1 cup cranberries
1 cup blueberries
⅓ cup light brown sugar
½ teaspoon crushed cardamom seeds
confectioners' sugar, for dusting

1 Preheat the oven to 375°F. Grease and line an 8½-inch springform pan.

2 Cream the butter and granulated sugar together until smooth, then rub in the flour with your fingers until the mixture resembles fine bread crumbs. Take out a generous 1 cup of the mixture and set aside.

3 Beat the eggs, baking powder and vanilla extract into the remaining mixture until soft and creamy. Spoon onto the bottom of the prepared pan and spread evenly. Arrange the cranberries and blueberries on top, then sprinkle the brown sugar over them.

4 Stir the cardamom seeds into the reserved flour mixture, then scatter evenly over the top of the fruit. Bake for 50–60 minutes, or until the topping is golden. Cool the cake in the pan for 10 minutes, then remove the sides. Slide the cake onto a wire rack, lifting it off the bottom of the pan. Let the cake cool, then dust with confectioners' sugar and serve with whipped cream.

FRESH BLUEBERRY MUFFINS

MAKE THESE POPULAR AMERICAN TREATS IN PAPER LINERS FOR MOISTER MUFFINS—IF YOU CAN'T FIND THEM, JUST GREASE THE PAN WELL BEFORE FILLING. THESE ARE BEST SERVED SLIGHTLY WARM.

MAKES TWELVE

INGREDIENTS
- 2½ cups all-purpose flour
- 1 tablespoon baking powder
- 6 tablespoons sugar
- 1 cup milk
- 3 eggs, beaten
- 8 tablespoons (1 stick) butter, melted
- a few drops of pure vanilla extract
- 2 cups blueberries

For the topping
- ½ cup pecans, coarsely chopped
- 2 tablespoons demerara sugar

COOK'S TIP
Don't be tempted to beat the muffin mixture; it should be fairly wet and needs to be quite lumpy. Overmixing will create tough muffins.

1 Preheat the oven to 400°F. Stand 12 paper liners in a muffin pan, or simply grease the pan well (or use lined individual pans, set on a baking sheet). Sift the flour and baking powder into a large bowl. Stir in the sugar. Mix the milk, eggs, melted butter and vanilla in a bowl and whisk lightly. Add to the flour mixture and fold together lightly.

2 Fold in the blueberries, then divide the mixture among the muffin liners. Scatter a few nuts and a little demerara sugar over the top of each. Bake for 20–25 minutes, or until the muffins are well risen and golden.

3 Remove the warm muffins from the pan; cool slightly on a wire rack.

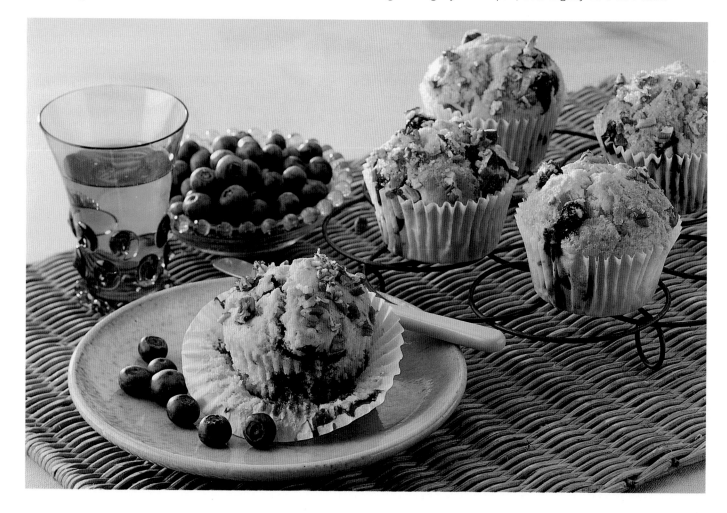

BLUEBERRY PIE

AMERICAN BLUEBERRIES OR EUROPEAN BILBERRIES CAN BE USED FOR THIS PIE. YOU MAY NEED TO ADD A LITTLE MORE SUGAR IF YOU ARE LUCKY ENOUGH TO FIND BILBERRIES.

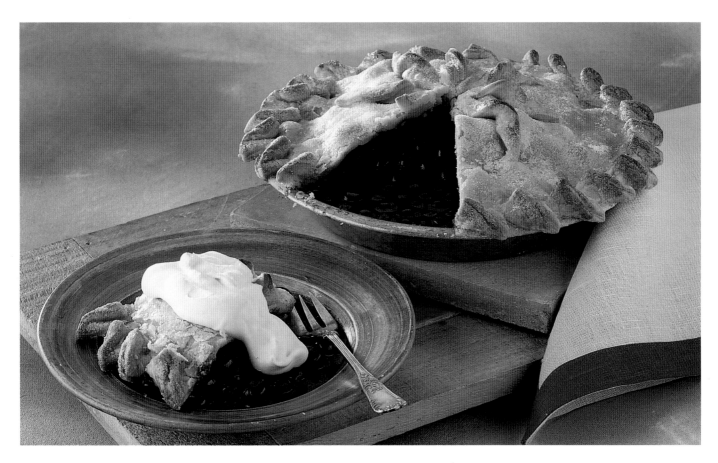

SERVES SIX

INGREDIENTS

2 × 8-ounce prepared shortcrust
  pastry sheets, thawed if frozen
7 cups blueberries
6 tablespoons sugar, plus extra for
  sprinkling
3 tablespoons cornstarch
grated zest and juice of ½ orange
grated zest of ½ lemon
½ teaspoon ground cinnamon
1 tablespoon unsalted
  butter, diced
beaten egg, to glaze
whipped cream, to serve

1 Preheat the oven to 400°F. Use one sheet of pastry to line a 9-inch pie pan, leaving the excess pastry hanging over the edges.

2 Mix the blueberries, sugar, cornstarch, orange zest and juice, lemon zest and cinnamon in a large bowl. Spoon into the pastry shell and dot with the butter. Dampen the rim of the pastry shell with a little water and top with the remaining pastry sheet.

VARIATION
Substitute a crumble topping for the top crust. The contrast with the juicy blueberry filling is sensational.

3 Cut the pastry edge at 1-inch intervals, then fold each section over on itself to form a triangle and create a sunflower edge. Trim off the excess pastry and cut out decorations from the trimmings. Attach them to the top crust with a little of the beaten egg.

4 Glaze the pastry with the egg and sprinkle with sugar. Bake for 30–35 minutes, or until golden. Serve warm or cold with whipped cream.

BERRY BRULEE TARTS

THIS QUANTITY OF PASTRY IS ENOUGH FOR EIGHT TARTLETS, SO FREEZE HALF FOR ANOTHER DAY.
THE BRÛLÉE TOPPING IS BEST ADDED NO MORE THAN TWO HOURS BEFORE SERVING THE TARTS.

MAKES FOUR

INGREDIENTS
    2¼ cups all-purpose flour
    pinch of salt
    ¼ cup ground almonds
    1 tablespoon confectioners' sugar
    10 tablespoons unsalted butter,
       chilled and diced
    1 egg yolk
    about 3 tablespoons cold water
For the filling
    4 egg yolks
    1 tablespoon cornstarch
    ¼ cup granulated sugar
    a few drops of pure vanilla extract
    1¼ cups whole milk or half-and-half
    2 cups mixed berries, such as small
       strawberries, raspberries, black
       currants and red currants
    ½ cup confectioners' sugar

1 Mix the flour, salt, ground almonds and confectioners' sugar in a bowl. Rub in the butter by hand or in a food processor until the mixture resembles fine bread crumbs. Add the egg yolk and enough cold water to form a dough. Knead the dough gently, then cut it in half and freeze half for use later.

2 Cut the remaining pastry into four equal pieces and roll out thinly.

COOK'S TIP
If you possess a culinary blowtorch—and are confident about operating it safely—use it to easily melt and caramelize the brûlée topping.

3 Use the pastry rounds to line four individual tartlet pans, letting the excess pastry hang over the edges. Chill for 30 minutes.

4 Preheat the oven to 400°F. Line the pastry with baking parchment and baking beans. Bake for 10 minutes. Remove the paper and beans and return the tartlet shells to the oven for 5 minutes, until golden. Allow the pastry to cool, then carefully trim off the excess.

5 Beat the egg yolks, cornstarch, granulated sugar and vanilla extract in a bowl.

6 Warm the milk in a heavy pan, pour it onto the egg yolks, whisking constantly, then return the mixture to the clean pan.

7 Heat, stirring, until the custard thickens, but do not let it boil. Remove from the heat, press a piece of plastic wrap directly onto the surface of the custard and allow to cool.

8 Scatter the berries in the tartlet shells and spoon the custard over them. Chill the tarts for 2 hours.

9 To serve, sift confectioners' sugar generously over the tops of the tartlets. Preheat the broiler to the highest setting. Place the tartlets under the hot broiler until the sugar melts and caramelizes. Allow the topping to cool and harden for about 10 minutes before serving the tarts.

BLACKBERRY JELLY

THIS JELLY IS ONE OF THE BEST. IT HAS TO BE MADE WITH HAND-PICKED WILD BLACKBERRIES FOR THE BEST FLAVOR. MAKE SURE YOU INCLUDE A FEW RED UNRIPE BERRIES FOR A GOOD SET.

MAKES 2 POUNDS

INGREDIENTS

    8 cups blackberries
    1¼ cups water
    juice of 1 lemon
    about 4 cups sugar
    hot buttered toast or English muffins,
        to serve

VARIATION
Red currant jelly is made in the same way, but with less sugar. Reduce the quantity to 1½ cups for every 2½ cups juice.

1 Put the fruit, water and lemon juice into a large saucepan. Cover the pan and cook for 15–30 minutes, or until the blackberries are very soft.

2 Ladle into a jelly bag or a large strainer lined with cheesecloth and set over a large bowl. Let drip overnight to obtain the maximum amount of juice.

3 Discard the fruit pulp. Measure the juice and allow 2 cups sugar to every 2½ cups juice. Place both in a large, heavy pan and bring the mixture slowly to a boil, stirring all the time until the sugar has dissolved.

4 Boil rapidly until the jelly registers 220°F on a sugar thermometer, or test for setting by spooning a small amount onto a chilled saucer. Chill for 3 minutes, then push the mixture with your finger; if wrinkles form on the surface, it is ready. Cool for 10 minutes.

5 Skim off any scum and pour the jelly into warm sterilized jars. Cover and seal while the jelly is still hot and label when the jars are cool. Serve the jelly with hot buttered toast or English muffins.

STRAWBERRY JAM

CAPTURE THE ESSENCE OF SUMMER IN A JAR OF HOMEMADE STRAWBERRY JAM.

MAKES ABOUT 3 POUNDS

INGREDIENTS
8 cups small strawberries
4 cups sugar
juice of 2 lemons
scones and créme fraîche, to serve

1 Layer the strawberries and sugar in a large bowl. Cover and leave overnight.

2 The next day, scrape the strawberries and their juice into a large, heavy pan. Add the lemon juice. Gradually bring to a boil over low heat, stirring until the sugar has dissolved.

COOK'S TIPS
For best results when making jam, don't wash the strawberries unless absolutely necessary. Instead, brush off any dirt, or wipe the strawberries with a damp cloth. If you have to wash any, pat them dry and then spread them out on a clean dish towel to dry further.

To sterilize jam jars, wash in hot soapy water, then rinse thoroughly and drain. Place the jars on a baking sheet and dry in a warm oven for 15–20 minutes.

3 Boil steadily for 10–15 minutes, or until the jam registers 220°F on a sugar thermometer. Alternatively, test for setting by spooning a small amount onto a chilled saucer. Chill for 3 minutes, then push the jam with your finger; if wrinkles form on the surface, it is ready. Cool for 10 minutes.

4 Pour the strawberry jam into warm sterilized jars, filling them right to the top. Cover and seal while the jam is still hot and label when the jars are cool. Serve with scones and créme fraîche, if you like. This jam can be stored in a cool dark place and should keep for up to 1 year.

CITRUS FRUIT RECIPES

Put the squeeze on citrus for some of the finest desserts and preserves in the good cook's repertoire. Lemon Surprise Pudding, Moist Orange and Almond Cake, Key Lime Pie and Lemon Meringue Pie are perennially popular, while new delights include Lemon Coeur à la Crème with Cointreau Oranges.

LEMON COEUR A LA CREME WITH COINTREAU ORANGES

THIS ZESTY DESSERT IS THE IDEAL CHOICE TO FOLLOW A RICH MAIN COURSE, SUCH AS ROAST PORK.

SERVES FOUR

INGREDIENTS
1 cup cottage cheese
generous 1 cup mascarpone
  cheese
¼ cup granulated sugar
grated zest and juice of 1 lemon
spirals of orange zest, to decorate
For the Cointreau oranges
4 oranges
2 teaspoons cornstarch
1 tablespoon confectioners' sugar
4 tablespoons Cointreau

1 Put the cottage cheese in a food processor or blender and process until smooth. Add the mascarpone, granulated sugar, lemon zest and juice and process briefly to mix the ingredients.

2 Line four coeur à la crème molds with cheesecloth, then divide the mixture among them. Level the surface of each, then place the molds on a plate to catch any liquid that drains from the cheese. Cover and chill overnight.

3 Make the Cointreau oranges. Squeeze the juice from two oranges and pour into a measuring cup. Add water, if necessary, to the juice to make 1 cup, then pour into a small saucepan. Blend a little of the juice mixture with the cornstarch and add to the pan with the confectioners' sugar. Heat the sauce, stirring until thickened.

4 Using a sharp knife, peel and segment the remaining oranges. Add the segments to the pan, stir to coat, then set aside. When cool, stir in the Cointreau. Cover and chill overnight.

5 Turn the molds out onto plates and surround with the oranges. Decorate with spirals of orange zest and serve at once.

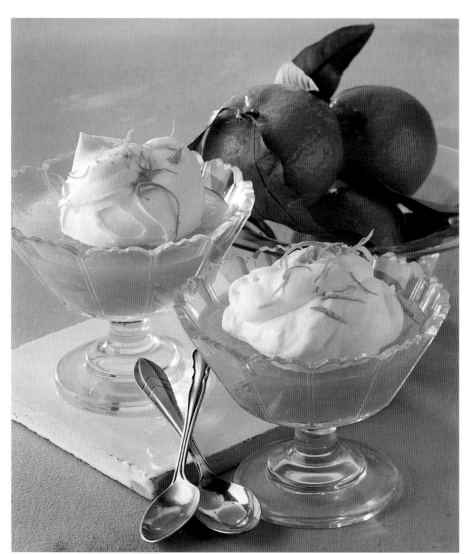

CLEMENTINE JELLY

GELATIN-BASED DESSERTS AREN'T ONLY FOR CHILDREN: THIS ADULT VERSION HAS A CLEAR FRUIT TASTE AND CAN BE MADE EXTRA SPECIAL BY ADDING A LITTLE WHITE RUM OR COINTREAU.

SERVES FOUR

INGREDIENTS
12 clementines
clear grape juice (see method
   for amount)
1 tablespoon powdered gelatin
2 tablespoons sugar
whipped cream, to decorate

VARIATION
Use four ruby grapefruit instead of clementines, if you prefer. Squeeze the juice from half of them and segment the rest, discarding any bitter white pith.

1 Squeeze the juice from eight of the clementines and pour it into a measuring cup. Add enough grape juice to make 2½ cups, then strain the juice mixture through a fine strainer.

2 Pour half the juice mixture into a pan. Sprinkle the gelatin on top, set aside for 5 minutes, then heat gently until the gelatin has dissolved. Stir in the sugar, then the remaining juice; set aside.

3 Pare the zest very thinly from the remaining fruit and set it aside. Using a small sharp knife, cut between the membrane and fruit to separate the citrus segments. Discard the membrane and white pith.

4 Place half the segments in four dessert glasses and cover with some of the liquid fruit jelly. Place in the refrigerator and allow to set.

5 When the jellies are set, arrange the remaining fruit segments on top. Carefully pour the remaining liquid jelly over and chill until set. Cut the pared clementine zest into fine shreds. Serve the jellies topped with a generous spoonful of whipped cream scattered with clementine zest shreds.

Ruby Orange Sherbet in Ginger Baskets

This superb frozen dessert is perfect for people without ice cream makers who can't be bothered with the freezing and stirring that homemade ices normally require. It is also ideal for serving at a special dinner party, as both the sherbet and ginger baskets can be made in advance and the dessert simply assembled between courses.

SERVES SIX

INGREDIENTS
  grated zest and juice of
    2 blood oranges
  1½ cups confectioners' sugar
  1¼ cups heavy cream
  scant 1 cup strained plain yogurt
  blood orange segments, to
    decorate (optional)
For the ginger baskets
  2 tablespoons unsalted butter
  1 tablespoon golden syrup or
    light corn syrup
  2 tablespoons sugar
  ¼ teaspoon ground ginger
  1 tablespoon finely chopped mixed
    citrus zest
  1 tablespoon all-purpose flour

2 Beat the heavy cream in a large bowl until the mixture forms soft peaks, then fold in the yogurt.

3 Gently stir in the orange juice mixture, then pour into a freezerproof container. Cover and freeze until firm.

6 Lightly grease two baking sheets. Using about 2 teaspoons of the mixture at a time, drop three portions of the ginger dough onto each baking sheet, spacing them well apart. Spread each one to a 2-inch circle, then bake for 12–14 minutes, or until the cookies are dark golden in color.

1 Place the orange zest and juice in a bowl. Sift the confectioners' sugar over the top and set aside for 30 minutes, then stir until smooth.

4 Make the baskets. Preheat the oven to 350°F. Place the butter, syrup and sugar in a heavy saucepan and heat gently until melted.

5 Add the ground ginger, mixed citrus zest and flour and stir until the mixture is smooth.

7 Remove the cookies from the oven and let stand on the baking sheets for 1 minute to firm slightly. Lift off with a spatula and drape over six greased individual muffin pans or upturned cups; flatten the top (which will become the bottom) and flute the edges to form a basket shape.

8 When cool, lift the baskets off the pan or cups and place on individual dessert plates. Arrange small scoops of the frozen orange sherbet in each basket. Decorate each portion with a few orange segments, if you like.

COOK'S TIP
When making the ginger baskets it is essential to work quickly. Have the greased pans or cups ready before you start. If the cookies cool and firm up before you have time to drape them all, return them to the oven for a few seconds to soften them again.

CHOCOLATE AND MANDARIN TRUFFLE LOAF

CHOCOHOLICS WILL LOVE THIS WICKEDLY RICH DESSERT. THE MANDARINS GIVE IT A DELICIOUS TANG.

SERVES EIGHT

INGREDIENTS

    14 ounces semisweet chocolate
    4 egg yolks
    3 mandarin oranges
    scant 1 cup crème
     fraîche
    2 tablespoons raisins
    chocolate curls, to decorate
For the sauce
    2 tablespoons Cointreau
    ½ cup crème fraîche

1 Grease an 8 x 4 x 2 ½-inch loaf pan and line it with plastic wrap. Break the chocolate into a large heatproof bowl. Place over a pan of hot water until melted.

2 Remove the bowl of chocolate from the heat and beat in the egg yolks.

COOK'S TIP
Chocolate-tipped mandarin slices would also make a superb decoration. Use small segments; pat dry on paper towels, then half-dip them in melted chocolate. Let sit on baking parchment until the chocolate has set.

3 Pare the zest from the mandarins, taking care to leave the pith behind. Cut the zest into slivers.

4 Stir the slivers of mandarin zest into the chocolate with the crème fraîche and raisins. Beat until smooth, then spoon the mixture into the prepared loaf pan and chill for 4 hours.

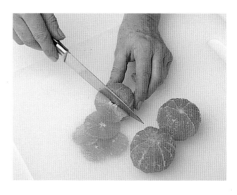

5 Cut the pith and any remaining zest from the mandarins, then slice thinly.

6 For the sauce, stir the Cointreau into the crème fraîche. Remove the truffle loaf from the pan, peel off the plastic wrap and slice. Serve each slice on a dessert plate with some sauce and mandarin slices, and decorate.

LEMON AND LIME CHEESECAKE

TANGY LEMON CHEESECAKE IS ALWAYS A HIT. THE LIME SYRUP MAKES THIS A CITRUS SENSATION.

2 Make the topping. Place the lemon zest and juice in a small saucepan and sprinkle the gelatin over. Let soften for 5 minutes. Heat gently until the gelatin has melted, then set the mixture aside to cool slightly. Beat the ricotta cheese and sugar in a bowl. Stir in the cream and egg yolks, then beat in the cooled gelatin mixture.

3 Beat the egg whites in a greasefree bowl until they form soft peaks. Fold them into the cheese mixture. Spoon onto the crust, level the surface and chill for 2–3 hours.

4 Meanwhile, make the lime syrup. Place the lime zest, juice and sugar in a small saucepan. Bring to a boil, stirring, then boil the syrup for 5 minutes. Stir in the arrowroot mixture and continue to stir until the syrup boils again and thickens slightly. Cool, then chill until required.

5 Spoon the lime syrup over the set cheesecake. Remove from the pan and cut into slices to serve.

MAKES EIGHT SLICES

INGREDIENTS
    5 ounces digestive biscuits or graham
      crackers (1½ cups ground)
    3 tablespoons butter
For the topping
    grated zest and juice of 2 lemons
    2 teaspoons powdered gelatin
    generous 1 cup ricotta
      cheese
    ⅓ cup sugar
    ⅔ cup heavy cream
    2 eggs, separated
For the lime syrup
    finely pared zest and juice of 3 limes
    ⅓ cup sugar
    1 teaspoon arrowroot mixed with
      2 tablespoons water

1 Lightly grease an 8-inch round springform pan. Place the biscuits or graham crackers in a food processor or blender and process until they form fine crumbs. Melt the butter in a large saucepan, then stir in the crumbs until well coated. Spoon into the prepared pan, press the crumbs down well in an even layer, then chill.

LEMON SURPRISE PUDDING

THE SURPRISE IN THIS MUCH-LOVED DESSERT IS THE UNEXPECTED SAUCE CONCEALED BENEATH THE DELECTABLE SPONGE.

SERVES FOUR

INGREDIENTS
  4 tablespoons butter, plus extra
    for greasing
  grated zest and juice of 2 lemons
  ½ cup superfine sugar
  2 eggs, separated
  ½ cup self-rising flour
  1¼ cups milk

1 Preheat the oven to 375ºF. Use a little butter to grease a 5-cup baking dish.

2 Beat the lemon zest, 4 tablespoons butter and sugar in a bowl until pale and fluffy. Add the egg yolks and flour and beat together well. Gradually beat in the lemon juice and milk (don't be alarmed if the mixture curdles horribly!). In a greasefree bowl, beat the egg whites until they form stiff peaks.

3 Fold the egg whites lightly into the lemon mixture, then pour into the prepared baking dish.

4 Place the dish in a roasting pan and pour in hot water to come halfway up the side of the dish. Bake for about 45 minutes, until golden. Serve at once.

CREPES SUZETTE

SIMPLY SUPERB—THAT'S THE VERDICT ON THIS PERENNIALLY POPULAR DESSERT. THESE CRÊPES DESERVE NOTHING LESS THAN THE BEST-QUALITY VANILLA ICE CREAM YOU CAN FIND.

SERVES FOUR

INGREDIENTS
  8 crêpes (see Summer Berry Crêpes
    for method)
  2 tablespoons unsalted butter
  ¼ cup sugar
  juice of 2 oranges
  juice of ½ lemon
  ¼ cup Cointreau or other orange
    liqueur
  best-quality vanilla ice cream,
    to serve

COOK'S TIP
Crêpes freeze well and can be reheated by the method described in step 1, or simultaneously thawed and reheated in the microwave. A stack of eight crêpes, interleaved with waxed paper, will take 2–3 minutes on High (100 percent power). Be sure to cover the top crêpe with paper as well.

1 Warm the cooked crêpes between two plates placed over a saucepan of simmering water.

2 Melt the butter in a heavy frying pan. Stir in the sugar and cook over medium heat, tilting the pan occasionally, until the mixture is golden brown. Add the orange and lemon juices and stir until the caramel has completely dissolved.

3 Add a crêpe to the pan. Using kitchen tongs, fold it in half, then in half again. Slide to the side of the pan. Repeat with the remaining crêpes

4 When all the crêpes have been folded in the sauce, pour the Cointreau over and carefully set it alight. Shake the pan until the flames die down. Divide the crêpes and sauce among dessert plates and serve at once with vanilla ice cream.

CITRUS FRUIT FLAMBE
WITH PISTACHIO PRALINE

A FRUIT FLAMBE MAKES A DRAMATIC FINALE FOR A DINNER PARTY. TOPPING THIS REFRESHING CITRUS FRUIT DESSERT WITH CRUNCHY PISTACHIO PRALINE MAKES IT EXTRA SPECIAL.

SERVES FOUR

INGREDIENTS
    4 oranges
    2 ruby grapefruit
    2 limes
    4 tablespoons butter
    ⅓ cup light brown sugar
    3 tablespoons Cointreau
    fresh mint sprigs, to decorate
For the praline
    oil, for greasing
    ½ cup granulated sugar
    ½ cup pistachio nuts

4 Heat the butter and brown sugar together in a heavy frying pan until the sugar has melted and the mixture is golden. Strain the citrus juices into the pan and continue to cook, stirring occasionally, until the juice has reduced and is syrupy.

5 Add the fruit segments and warm through without stirring. Pour the Cointreau over and set it alight. As soon as the flames die down, spoon the fruit flambé into serving dishes. Scatter some praline over each portion and decorate with mint. Serve at once.

1 First, make the pistachio praline. Brush a baking sheet lightly with oil. Place the granulated sugar and nuts in a small, heavy saucepan and cook gently, swirling the pan occasionally, until the sugar has melted.

2 Continue to cook over fairly low heat until the nuts start to pop and the sugar has turned a dark golden color. Pour onto the oiled baking sheet and set aside to cool. Using a sharp knife, chop the praline into rough chunks.

3 Cut off all the zest and pith from the citrus fruit. Holding each fruit in turn over a large bowl, cut between the membranes so that the segments fall into the bowl, with any juice.

COOK'S TIP
If desired, use a rolling pin or toffee hammer to break up the praline.

COLD LEMON SOUFFLE <u>WITH</u> CARAMELIZED ALMOND TOPPING

THIS TERRIFIC-TO-LOOK-AT, REFRESHING DESSERT SOUFFLE IS LIGHT AND LUSCIOUS.

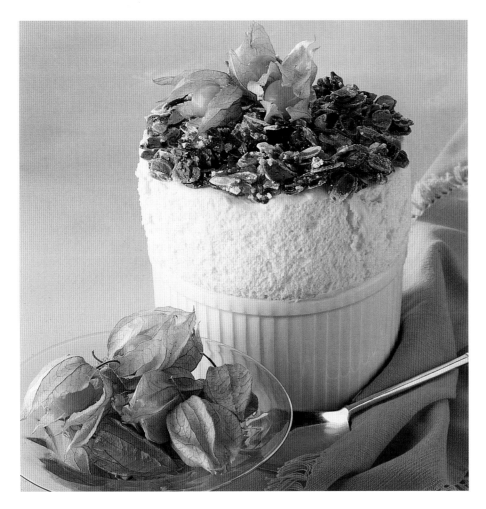

2 Put the lemon zest and egg yolks in a bowl. Add 6 tablespoons of the granulated sugar and whisk until creamy.

3 Place the lemon juice in a small heatproof bowl and sprinkle the gelatin over. Set aside for 5 minutes, then place the bowl in a pan of simmering water. Heat, stirring occasionally, until the gelatin has dissolved. Cool slightly, then stir the gelatin mixture into the egg yolk mixture.

4 In a separate bowl, lightly whip the cream to soft peaks. Fold into the egg yolk mixture and set aside.

5 Beat the egg whites in a greasefree bowl until stiff peaks form. Gradually beat in the remaining sugar until the mixture is stiff and glossy. Quickly and lightly fold the whites into the yolk mixture. Pour into the prepared dish, smooth the surface and chill for 4–5 hours, or until set.

6 Make the decoration. Brush a baking sheet lightly with oil. Preheat the broiler. Scatter the almonds over the sheet and sift the confectioners' sugar over. Broil until the nuts are golden and the sugar has caramelized. Allow to cool, then remove the mixture from the sheet with a spatula and break it into pieces.

SERVES SIX

INGREDIENTS
  oil, for greasing
  grated zest and juice of
   3 large lemons
  5 large eggs, separated
  ½ cup granulated sugar
  1½ tablespoons powdered gelatin
  scant 2 cups heavy cream
For the decoration
  ¾ cup sliced almonds
  ¾ cup confectioners' sugar
  3 physalis (cape gooseberries)

COOK'S TIP
When peeling off the soufflé collar, hold the blade of a knife against the set soufflé so that it keeps its shape.

1 Make a soufflé collar. Cut a strip of baking parchment long enough to fit around a 3¾-cup soufflé dish and wide enough to extend 3 inches above the rim. Fit the strip around the dish, tape, then tie it around the top of the dish with string. Brush the inside of the paper lightly with oil.

7 When the soufflé has set, carefully peel off the paper. Pile the caramelized almonds on top of the soufflé and decorate with the physalis.

LEMON ROULADE <u>WITH</u> LEMON CURD CREAM

THIS FEATHERLIGHT ROULADE FILLED WITH A RICH LEMON CURD CREAM MAKES A MARVELOUS DESSERT OR SNACK~TIME TREAT. THE LEMON CURD CAN BE MADE AHEAD AND KEPT IN THE REFRIGERATOR.

<u>MAKES EIGHT SLICES</u>

INGREDIENTS
    4 eggs, separated
    ½ cup granulated sugar
    finely grated zest of 2 lemons
    1 teaspoon pure vanilla extract
    ¼ cup ground almonds
    ⅓ cup all-purpose flour, sifted
    3 tablespoons confectioners' sugar
For the lemon curd cream
    1¼ cups heavy cream
    4 tablespoons fresh lemon curd
        (recipe below right)

1 Preheat the oven to 375°F. Grease a 13 x 9-inch jelly roll pan and line with baking parchment.

2 In a large bowl, beat the egg yolks with half the granulated sugar until light and foamy. Beat in the lemon zest and vanilla extract, then lightly fold in the ground almonds and flour using a large metal spoon or spatula.

COOK'S TIP
Having filled and rolled the roulade, keep it wrapped in the baking parchment and hold it together for about a minute to allow the shape to set before removing the paper and transferring the roulade to a plate.

3 Beat the egg whites in a greasefree bowl until they form stiff, glossy peaks. Gradually beat in the remaining granulated sugar to form a stiff meringue. Stir half the meringue mixture into the egg yolk mixture and fold in the rest.

4 Pour into the prepared pan, level the surface with a spatula and bake for 10 minutes, or until risen and spongy to the touch. Cover loosely with a sheet of baking parchment and a damp dish towel. Let cool in the pan.

5 Make the lemon cream. Whip the cream, then lightly fold in the lemon curd.

6 Sift the confectioners' sugar liberally over a piece of baking parchment. Turn the sponge out onto it. Peel off the lining paper and spread the lemon curd cream over the surface of the sponge, leaving a border around the edge.

7 Using the paper underneath as a guide, roll up the sponge from one of the long sides. Place on a serving platter with the seam underneath. Cut the roulade into slices to serve.

FRESH LEMON CURD
Put the grated zest and juice of 3 lemons into a pan with ½ cup sugar. Bring to a boil, stirring until the sugar has dissolved. Stir in 1 tablespoon cornstarch mixed to a paste with 1 tablespoon cold water. Off the heat, beat in 2 egg yolks. Return to low heat and beat for about 2 minutes; remove from the heat. Gradually beat in 4 tablespoons butter, at room temperature. Pour into a sterilized jar, cover and seal at once. Let cool, then chill. Use within 2–3 weeks. Makes 1 pound.

LEMON MERINGUE PIE

CRISP SHORTCRUST IS FILLED WITH A MOUTHWATERING LEMON CREAM FILLING AND TOPPED WITH SOFT GOLDEN MERINGUE. THIS CLASSIC OPEN TART NEVER FAILS TO PLEASE. POPULAR WITH ADULTS AND CHILDREN, IT IS THE ESSENTIAL SUNDAY LUNCH DESSERT.

2 Meanwhile, make the filling. Place all the ingredients in a bowl, mix lightly and let soak for 1 hour.

3 Preheat the oven to 400°F. Beat the filling until smooth and pour into the chilled pastry shell. Bake for 20 minutes, or until the filling has just set and the pastry is golden. Remove from the oven and cool on a wire rack for 30 minutes, or until a skin has formed on the surface. Lower the oven temperature to 350°F.

4 Make the topping. Beat the egg whites in a greasefree bowl until they form stiff peaks. Beat in the superfine sugar to form a glossy meringue. Spoon on top of the set lemon filling and spread over, making sure you spread the meringue right to the rim of the pie shell. Swirl the meringue slightly.

5 Bake the pie for 20–25 minutes, or until the meringue is crisp and golden brown. Allow to cool on a wire rack for 10 minutes before serving.

SERVES SIX

INGREDIENTS
   1 cup all-purpose flour
   pinch of salt
   4 tablespoons butter
   ¼ cup solid vegetable shortening or lard
   1 tablespoon granulated sugar
   about 1 tablespoon ice water
For the filling
   3 large egg yolks
   2 tablespoons granulated sugar
   grated zest and juice of 1 lemon
   ½ cup fresh white bread crumbs
   1 cup milk
For the topping
   3 large egg whites
   ½ cup superfine sugar

1 Sift the flour and salt into a bowl. Rub in the butter and shortening or lard until the mixture resembles fine bread crumbs. Stir in the sugar and add enough ice water to make a soft dough. Roll out the pastry on a lightly floured surface and use it to line an 8½-inch pie plate or pan. Chill until required.

FRESH LEMON TART

THIS TART SHOULD BE SERVED AT ROOM TEMPERATURE IF THE ZESTY LEMON FLAVOR IS TO BE ENJOYED TO THE UTMOST.

SERVES SIX TO EIGHT

INGREDIENTS
   12-ounce package prepared rich
      sweet shortcrust pastry, thawed
      if frozen
For the filling
   3 eggs
   ½ cup sugar
   1 cup ground almonds
   7 tablespoons heavy cream
   grated zest and juice of 2 lemons
For the topping
   2 thin-skinned unwaxed lemons,
      thinly sliced
   scant 1 cup sugar
   7 tablespoons water

COOK'S TIP
If you prefer not to candy the lemons, dust the tart with confectioners' sugar.

1 Roll out the pastry and use it to line a deep 9-inch fluted tart pan. Prick the bottom and chill for 30 minutes.

2 Preheat the oven to 400°F. Line the pastry with baking parchment and baking beans and bake for 10 minutes. Remove the paper and beans and return the pastry shell to the oven for 5 minutes more.

3 Meanwhile, make the filling. Beat the eggs, sugar, almonds and cream in a bowl until smooth. Beat in the lemon zest and juice. Pour the filling into the pastry shell. Lower the oven temperature to 375°F and bake for 20 minutes, or until the filling has set and the pastry is golden.

4 Make the topping. Place the lemon slices in a pan and pour in water to cover. Simmer for 15–20 minutes, or until the skins are tender, then drain.

5 Place the sugar in a saucepan and stir in the measured water. Heat gently until the sugar has dissolved, stirring constantly, then boil for 2 minutes. Add the lemon slices and cook for 10–15 minutes, until the skins become shiny and candied.

6 Lift out the candied lemon slices and arrange them over the top of the tart. Return the syrup to the heat and boil until reduced to a thick glaze. Brush this over the tart and allow to cool completely before serving.

KEY LIME PIE

THIS IS ONE OF AMERICA'S FAVORITES. AS THE NAME SUGGESTS, IT ORIGINATED IN THE FLORIDA KEYS.

MAKES TEN SLICES

INGREDIENTS
    2 cups all-purpose flour
    8 tablespoons (1 stick) chilled
      butter, diced
    2 tablespoons granulated sugar
    2 egg yolks
    pinch of salt
    2 tablespoons cold water
    thinly pared lime zest and mint
      leaves, to decorate
For the filling
    4 eggs, separated
    14-ounce can condensed milk
    grated zest and juice of 3 limes,
      preferrably Key limes
    2 tablespoons superfine sugar
For the topping
    1¼ cups heavy cream
    2–3 Key limes, thinly sliced

3 Preheat the oven to 400°F. Trim off the excess pastry from around the edge of the pastry shell using a large, sharp knife and line the pastry shell with baking parchment and baking beans.

4 Bake the pastry shell for 10 minutes. Remove the paper and beans and return the pastry shell to the oven for 10 minutes.

6 In a greasefree bowl, beat the egg whites to stiff peaks. Beat in the superfine sugar, then fold into the lime mixture.

7 Lower the oven temperature to 325°F. Pour the lime filling into the pastry shell. Bake for 20–25 minutes, or until it has set and is starting to brown. Cool, then chill.

1 Sift the flour into a mixing bowl and, using your fingertips, rub in the butter until the mixture resembles fresh bread crumbs. Add the granulated sugar, egg yolks, salt and water. Mix to a soft dough.

2 Roll out the pastry on a lightly floured surface and use to line a deep 8½-inch fluted flan pan, allowing the excess pastry to hang over the edge. Prick the pastry bottom and chill for at least 30 minutes.

5 Meanwhile, make the filling. Beat the egg yolks in a large bowl until light and creamy, then beat in the condensed milk, with the lime zest and juice, until well combined. Continue to beat until the mixture is thick.

COOK'S TIP
You can make the pastry in a food processor, but take care not to overprocess the dough. Use the pulse button and process for a few seconds at a time; switch off the motor the moment the dough clumps together.

8 Just before serving, whip the heavy cream for the topping and spoon it around the edge of the pie. Cut the lime slices once from the center to the edge, then twist each slice and arrange between the spoonfuls of cream. Decorate with lime zest and mint leaves.

MOIST ORANGE AND ALMOND CAKE

THE KEY TO THIS RECIPE IS TO COOK THE ORANGE SLOWLY FIRST, SO IT IS FULLY TENDER BEFORE BEING BLENDED. DON'T USE A MICROWAVE TO SPEED THINGS UP—THIS MAKES ORANGE SKIN TOUGH.

SERVES EIGHT

INGREDIENTS

1 large orange
3 eggs
1 cup granulated sugar
1 teaspoon baking powder
2 cups ground almonds
¼ cup all-purpose flour
confectioners' sugar, for dusting
whipped cream and orange slices
  (optional), to serve

1 Wash the orange and pierce it with a skewer. Put it in a deep saucepan and pour in water to cover completely. Bring to a boil, then lower the heat, cover and simmer for 1 hour, or until the skin is very soft. Drain, then cool.

COOK'S TIP
For a treat, serve this with spiced poached kumquats.

2 Preheat the oven to 350°F. Grease an 8-inch round cake pan and line it with baking parchment. Cut the cooled orange in half and discard the seeds. Place the orange, skin and all, in a blender or food processor and purée until smooth and pulpy.

3 In a bowl, beat the eggs and sugar until thick. Fold in the baking powder, almonds and flour, then fold in the purée.

4 Pour into the prepared pan, level the surface and bake for 1 hour, or until a skewer inserted into the middle comes out clean. Cool the cake in the pan for 10 minutes, then turn out onto a wire rack, peel off the lining paper and cool completely. Dust the top liberally with confectioners' sugar and serve with whipped cream. For added color, tuck thick orange slices under the cake just before serving.

LEMON <u>AND</u> LIME SYRUP CAKE

*THIS CAKE IS PERFECT FOR BUSY COOKS, AS IT CAN BE MIXED IN MOMENTS AND NEEDS NO ICING.
THE SIMPLE TANGY LIME TOPPING TRANSFORMS IT INTO A FABULOUSLY MOIST CAKE.*

SERVES EIGHT

INGREDIENTS

    2 cups self-rising flour
    1 teaspoon baking powder
    1 cup sugar
    ½ pound (2 sticks) butter, softened
    4 eggs, beaten
    grated zest of 2 lemons
    2 tablespoons lemon juice
For the topping
    finely pared zest of 1 lime
    juice of 2 limes
    ⅔ cup sugar

1 Make the cake. Preheat the oven to 325°F. Grease and line an 8-inch round cake pan. Sift the flour and baking powder into a large bowl. Add the sugar, butter and eggs and beat together well until the mixture is smooth, creamy and fluffy.

2 Beat in the lemon zest and juice. Spoon the mixture into the prepared pan, then smooth the surface and make a shallow indentation in the top with the back of a spoon.

3 Bake for 1¼–1½ hours, or until the cake is golden on top and spongy when lightly pressed and a skewer inserted in the center comes out clean.

4 Meanwhile, mix the topping ingredients together. As soon as the cake is done, remove it from the oven and pour the topping over the surface. Allow the cake to cool in the pan.

VARIATION
Use lemon zest and juice instead of lime for the topping if you prefer. You will need only one large lemon.

SPICED POACHED KUMQUATS

KUMQUATS ARE NOT AVAILABLE THROUGHOUT THE YEAR, BUT THEY ARE UNDOUBTEDLY AT THEIR BEST JUST BEFORE THE CHRISTMAS SEASON. THESE FRUITS CAN BE CANNED AND GIVEN AS PRESENTS. THEIR MARVELOUS SPICY-SWEET CITRUS FLAVOR COMPLEMENTS BOTH SWEET AND SAVORY DISHES.

SERVES SIX

INGREDIENTS
4 cups kumquats
½ cup sugar
⅔ cup water
1 small cinnamon stick
1 star anise
a citrus leaf, to decorate

1 Cut the kumquats in half and discard the seeds. Place the kumquats in a saucepan with the sugar, water and spices. Cook over gentle heat, stirring until the sugar has dissolved.

2 Increase the heat, cover the pan and boil the mixture for 8–10 minutes, until the kumquats are tender. To can the kumquats, spoon them into warm, sterilized jars, seal and label.

3 If you want to serve the spiced kumquats soon after making them, let the mixture cool, then chill it. Decorate with a citrus leaf, if you like.

COOK'S TIP
Try these delectable treats with baked ham or roast pork. They would also make a perfect accompaniment for moist almond or chocolate cake.

THREE-FRUIT MARMALADE

SEVILLE ORANGES HAVE A FINE FLAVOR AND ARE THE BEST VARIETY FOR MARMALADE. SWEET ORANGES CAN BE USED IN A PINCH, BUT THEY TEND TO MAKE THE MARMALADE CLOUDY.

MAKES 5–5¼ POUNDS

INGREDIENTS
2 Seville oranges
2 lemons
1 grapefruit
7½ cups water
6¾ cups sugar
croissants, to serve (optional)

1 Wash the fruit, halve and squeeze their juice. Pour into a large, heavy saucepan or preserving pan. Place the seeds and pulp in a square of cheesecloth, gather the sides into a bag and tie the neck tightly with string. Tie the bag to the handle of the pan so that it dangles in the citrus juice.

2 Cut the citrus skins into thin wedges; scrape off and discard the membranes and pith. Cut the rinds into slivers and add to the pan with the measured water. Bring to a simmer and cook gently for 2 hours, until the rinds are very tender and the water has reduced by half. Test the rinds for softness by pressing a cooled piece with a finger.

3 Lift out the cheesecloth bag, squeezing out the juice into the pan. Discard the bag. Stir the sugar into the pan and heat very gently, stirring occasionally, until all the sugar has dissolved.

4 Bring the mixture to a boil and boil for 10–15 minutes, or until the marmalade registers 220°F.

5 Alternatively, test the marmalade for setting by pouring a small amount onto a chilled saucer. Chill for 2 minutes, then push the marmalade with your finger; if wrinkles form on the surface, it is ready. Cool for 15 minutes.

6 Stir the marmalade and pour it into warm, sterilized jars. Cover with waxed paper disks. Seal and label when cool. Store in a cool, dark cupboard. Serve with warm croissants, if you like.

COOK'S TIP
Allowing the marmalade to cool slightly before canning lets it set enough to prevent the fruit from sinking. Stir before pouring it into the jars.

EXOTIC FRUIT RECIPES

Who can resist the colors, textures and flavors of exotic fruits? Now that many varieties are widely available all year, there's every excuse for taking the taste trip and trying such delights as Lychee and Elderflower Sorbet, Passion Fruit Crème Caramels with Dipped Physalis or Exotic Fruit Sushi.

COLD MANGO SOUFFLES TOPPED WITH TOASTED COCONUT

FRAGRANT, FRESH MANGO IS ONE OF THE MOST DELICIOUS EXOTIC FRUITS AROUND, WHETHER IT IS SIMPLY SERVED IN SLICES OR USED AS THE BASIS FOR AN ICE CREAM OR SOUFFLÉ.

MAKES FOUR

INGREDIENTS
4 small mangoes, peeled, pitted
 and chopped
2 tablespoons water
1 tablespoon powdered gelatin
2 egg yolks
½ cup sugar
½ cup milk
grated zest of 1 orange
1¼ cups heavy cream
toasted flaked or coarsely shredded
 coconut, to decorate

COOK'S TIP
Cool and creamy, these are great after a curry. Add some juicy pieces of fresh mango on the side, if you like.

1 Place a few pieces of mango in the bottom of each of four ⅔-cup ramekins. Wrap a greased collar of baking parchment around the outside of each dish, extending well above the rim. Secure with tape, then tie tightly with string.

2 Pour the water into a small heatproof bowl and sprinkle the gelatin over the surface. Leave for 5 minutes, or until soft. Place the bowl in a pan of hot water, stirring occasionally, until the gelatin has dissolved.

3 Meanwhile, beat the egg yolks with the sugar and milk in another heatproof bowl. Place the bowl over a saucepan of simmering water and continue to beat until the mixture is thick and frothy. Remove from the heat and continue beating until the mixture cools. Beat in the liquid gelatin.

4 Purée the remaining mango pieces in a food processor or blender, then fold the purée into the egg yolk mixture with the orange zest. Set the mixture aside until it starts to thicken.

5 Whip the heavy cream to soft peaks. Reserve 4 tablespoons and fold the rest into the mango mixture. Spoon into the ramekins until the mixture is 1 inch above the rim of each dish. Chill for 3–4 hours, or until set.

6 Carefully remove the paper collars from the soufflés. Spoon a little of the reserved cream on top of each soufflé and decorate with some toasted flaked or coarsely shredded coconut.

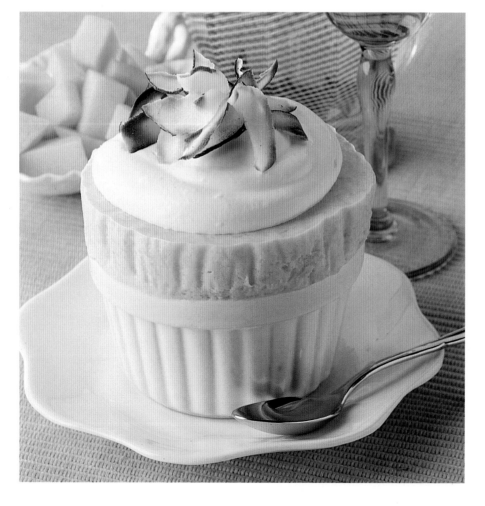

PASSION FRUIT CREME CARAMELS WITH DIPPED PHYSALIS

PASSION FRUIT HAS AN AROMATIC FLAVOR THAT REALLY PERMEATES THESE CRÈME CARAMELS.
USE SOME OF THE CARAMEL TO DIP PHYSALIS TO CREATE A UNIQUE DECORATION.

MAKES FOUR

INGREDIENTS
 generous ¾ cup sugar
 5 tablespoons water
 4 passion fruit
 4 physalis (cape gooseberries)
 3 eggs plus 1 egg yolk
 ⅔ cup heavy cream
 ⅔ cup whole milk or half-and-half

1 Place ⅔ cup of the sugar in a heavy saucepan. Add the water and heat the mixture gently until the sugar has dissolved. Increase the heat and boil until the syrup turns a dark golden color.

2 Meanwhile, cut each passion fruit in half. Scoop out the seeds from the passion fruit into a strainer set over a bowl. Press the seeds against the strainer to extract all their juice. Spoon a few of the seeds into each of four ⅔-cup ramekins. Set the juice aside.

3 Peel back the papery casing from each physalis and dip the orange berries into the caramel. Place on a sheet of baking parchment and set aside. Pour the remaining caramel carefully into the ramekins.

4 Preheat the oven to 300°F. Beat the eggs, egg yolk and remaining sugar in a bowl. Beat in the cream and milk, then the passion fruit juice. Strain through a strainer into each ramekin, then place the ramekins in a baking pan. Pour in hot water to come halfway up the sides of the dishes; bake for 40–45 minutes, or until just set.

5 Remove the custards from the pan and let cool, then cover and chill them for 4 hours before serving. Run a knife between the edge of each ramekin and the custard and invert each in turn onto a dessert plate. Shake the ramekins firmly to release the custards. Decorate each with a dipped physalis.

LYCHEE <u>AND</u> ELDERFLOWER SORBET

THE FLAVOR OF ELDERFLOWERS IS FAMOUS FOR BRINGING OUT THE ESSENCE OF GOOSEBERRIES,
BUT WHAT IS LESS WELL KNOWN IS HOW WONDERFULLY IT COMPLEMENTS LYCHEES.

SERVES FOUR

INGREDIENTS
   ¾ cup sugar
   1⅔ cups water
   1¼ pounds fresh lychees, peeled
   and pitted
   1 tablespoon elderflower cordial
   dessert cookies, to serve

COOK'S TIP
Switch the freezer to the coldest setting
before making the sorbet—the faster the
mixture freezes, the smaller the ice
crystals that form and the better the final
texture will be. To ensure rapid freezing,
use a metal freezerproof container and
place it directly on the freezer shelf.

1 Place the sugar and water in a
saucepan and heat gently until the
sugar has dissolved. Increase the heat
and boil for 5 minutes, then add the
lychees. Lower the heat and simmer for
7 minutes. Remove from the heat and
set aside to cool.

2 Purée the fruit and syrup in a
blender or food processor. Place a
strainer over a bowl and pour the purée
into it. Press through as much of the
purée as possible with a spoon.

3 Stir the elderflower cordial into the
strained purée, then pour the mixture
into a freezerproof container. Freeze
for 2 hours, until ice crystals start to
form around the edges.

4 Remove the sorbet from the freezer
and process briefly in a food processor
or blender to break up the crystals.
Repeat this process twice more, then
freeze until firm. Transfer to the
refrigerator for 10 minutes to soften
before serving in scoops, with cookies.

EXOTIC FRUIT SUSHI

THIS IDEA CAN BE ADAPTED TO INCORPORATE A WIDE VARIETY OF FRUITS, BUT TO KEEP TO THE EXOTIC THEME TAKE YOUR INSPIRATION FROM THE TROPICS. THE SUSHI NEEDS TO CHILL OVERNIGHT TO ENSURE THAT THE RICE MIXTURE FIRMS PROPERLY, SO BE SURE YOU START THIS IN GOOD TIME.

SERVES FOUR

INGREDIENTS
⅔ cup short-grain rice
1½ cups water
1⅔ cups coconut milk
⅓ cup sugar
a selection of exotic fruit, such as
1 mango, 1 kiwi fruit, 2 figs and
1 star fruit, thinly sliced
2 tablespoons apricot jam, strained
For the raspberry sauce
2 cups raspberries
¼ cup confectioners' sugar

COOK'S TIP
To cut the rice mixture into bars, turn
out of the pan, cut in half lengthwise,
then make 7 crosswise cuts for 16 bars.
Shape into ovals with damp hands.

1 Rinse the rice well under cold running
water, drain and place in a saucepan
with 1¼ cups of the water. Pour in ¾ cup
of the coconut milk. Cook over very low
heat for 25 minutes, stirring often and
gradually adding the remaining coconut
milk, until the rice has absorbed all the
liquid and is tender.

2 Grease a shallow 7-inch square
pan and line it with plastic wrap. Stir
2 tablespoons of the sugar into the rice
mixture and pour it into the prepared
pan. Cool, then chill overnight.

3 Cut the rice mixture into 16 small
bars, shape into ovals and flatten the
tops. Place on a baking sheet lined with
baking parchment. Arrange the sliced
fruit on top, using one type of fruit only
for each piece of sushi.

4 Place the remaining sugar in a small
pan with the remaining ¼ cup water.
Bring to a boil, then lower the heat and
simmer until thick and syrupy. Stir in
the jam and cool slightly.

5 To make the sauce, purée the
raspberries with the confectioners'
sugar in a food processor or blender.
Press through a strainer, then divide
among four small bowls. Arrange a few
different fruit sushi on each plate and
spoon a little of the cool apricot syrup
over. Serve with the sauce.

LemonGrass Skewers <u>with</u> Lime Cheese

Grilled fruits make a fine finale to a barbecue, whether they are cooked over the coals or under a hot broiler. The lemongrass skewers give the fruit a subtle citrus tang. The fruits used here make an ideal exotic mix, but almost any soft fruit can be substituted.

SERVES FOUR

INGREDIENTS

    4 long fresh lemongrass stalks
    1 mango, peeled, pitted and cut
        into chunks
    1 papaya, peeled, seeded and cut
        into chunks
    1 star fruit, cut into thick slices
        and halved
    8 fresh bay leaves
    a nutmeg
    ¼ cup maple syrup
    ⅓ cup demerara sugar
For the lime cheese
    ⅔ cup cottage cheese or low-fat
        cream cheese
    ½ cup heavy cream
    grated zest and juice of ½ lime
    2 tablespoons confectioners' sugar

1 Prepare the grill or preheat the broiler. Cut the top of each lemongrass stalk into a point with a sharp knife. Discard the outer leaves, then use the back of the knife to bruise the length of each stalk to release the aromatic oils. Thread each stalk, skewer-style, with the fruit pieces and bay leaves.

2 Support a piece of foil on a baking sheet and roll up the edges to make a rim. Grease the foil, lay the kebabs on top and grate a little nutmeg over each. Drizzle the maple syrup over and dust liberally with the demerara sugar. Grill for 5 minutes, until lightly charred.

3 Meanwhile, make the lime cheese. Mix together the cheese, cream, grated lime zest and juice and confectioners' sugar in a bowl. Serve at once with the lightly charred fruit kebabs.

COOK'S TIP
Only fresh lemongrass will work as skewers for this recipe.

Coconut Jelly <u>with</u> Star Anise Fruits

Serve this dessert after any Asian-style meal with plenty of refreshing exotic fruit.

SERVES FOUR

INGREDIENTS

    1 cup cold water
    ⅓ cup sugar
    1 tablespoon powdered gelatin
    1⅔ cups canned coconut milk
For the syrup and fruit
    1 cup water
    3 star anise
    ¼ cup sugar
    1 star fruit, sliced
    12 lychees, peeled and pitted
    1 cup blackberries

1 Pour the water into a saucepan and add the sugar. Heat gently until the sugar has dissolved. Sprinkle the gelatin over and continue to heat the mixture gently, stirring occasionally, until the gelatin has dissolved. Stir in the coconut milk, remove from the heat and set aside to cool.

2 Grease a 7-inch square cake pan. Line with plastic wrap. Pour in the coconut milk mixture and chill until set.

3 To make the syrup, combine the water, star anise and sugar in a pan. bring to a boil, stirring, then lower the heat and simmer for 10–12 minutes, until syrupy. Place the fruit in a heatproof bowl and pour the hot syrup over it. Cool, then chill.

4 To serve, cut the coconut jelly into diamonds and remove from the pan. Arrange the coconut jelly on individual plates, adding a few of the fruits and their syrup to each portion.

PAPAYA BAKED <u>WITH</u> GINGER

GINGER ENHANCES THE FLAVOR OF PAPAYA IN THIS RECIPE, WHICH TAKES NO MORE THAN TEN MINUTES TO PREPARE! DON'T OVERCOOK PAPAYA, OR THE FLESH WILL BECOME VERY WATERY.

SERVES FOUR

INGREDIENTS

2 ripe papayas

2 pieces preserved ginger in syrup, drained, plus 1 tablespoon syrup from the jar

8 amaretti or other dessert cookies, coarsely crushed

3 tablespoons raisins

shredded, finely pared zest and juice of 1 lime

¼ cup pistachio nuts, chopped

1 tablespoon light brown sugar

¼ cup crème fraîche, plus extra to serve

VARIATION

Use strained plain yogurt and almonds instead of crème fraîche and pistachios.

1 Preheat the oven to 400°F. Cut the papayas in half and scoop out their seeds. Place the halves in a baking dish and set aside. Cut the preserved ginger into fine matchsticks.

2 Make the filling. Place the crushed amaretti cookies, ginger matchsticks and raisins in a bowl.

3 Stir in the lime zest and juice and two-thirds of the nuts, then add the sugar and the crème fraîche. Mix well.

4 Fill the papaya halves and drizzle with the ginger syrup. Sprinkle with the remaining nuts. Bake for about 25 minutes, or until tender. Serve with extra crème fraîche.

EXOTIC FRUIT SALAD WITH PASSION FRUIT DRESSING

PASSION FRUIT MAKES A SUPERB DRESSING FOR ANY FRUIT, BUT REALLY BRINGS OUT THE FLAVOR OF EXOTIC VARIETIES. YOU CAN EASILY DOUBLE THE RECIPE, THEN SERVE THE REST FOR BREAKFAST.

SERVES SIX

INGREDIENTS
   1 mango
   1 papaya
   2 kiwi fruit
   coconut or vanilla ice cream, to serve
For the dressing
   3 passion fruit
   thinly pared zest and juice of 1 lime
   1 teaspoon hazelnut or walnut oil
   1 tablespoon honey

COOK'S TIP
A clear golden honey scented with orange blossom or acacia blossom would be perfect for the dressing.

1 Peel the mango, cut it into three slices, then cut the flesh into chunks and place it in a large bowl. Peel the papaya and cut it in half. Scoop out the seeds, then chop the flesh.

2 Cut both ends off each kiwi fruit, then stand them on a board. Using a small, sharp knife, cut off the skin from top to bottom. Cut each kiwi fruit in half lengthwise, then cut into thick slices. Combine all the fruit in a large bowl.

3 Make the dressing. Cut each passion fruit in half and scoop the seeds out into a strainer set over a small bowl. Press the seeds well to extract all their juices. Lightly beat the remaining dressing ingredients into the passion fruit juice, then pour the dressing over the fruit. Mix gently to combine. Let chill for 1 hour before serving with scoops of coconut or vanilla ice cream.

TROPICAL FRUIT GRATIN

THIS OUT-OF-THE-ORDINARY GRATIN IS STRICTLY FOR GROWN-UPS. A COLORFUL COMBINATION OF FRUIT IS TOPPED WITH A SIMPLE SABAYON BEFORE BEING FLASHED UNDER THE BROILER.

SERVES FOUR

INGREDIENTS
2 tamarillos
½ sweet pineapple
1 ripe mango
1½ cups blackberries
½ cup sparkling white wine
½ cup sugar
6 egg yolks

VARIATION
Although boiling drives off the alcohol in the wine, children do not always appreciate the flavor, so substitute orange juice if making the gratin for them. White grape juice or pineapple juice would also work well.

1 Cut each tamarillo in half lengthwise and then into thick slices. Cut the zest and core from the pineapple and take spiral slices off the outside to remove the eyes. Cut the flesh into chunks. Peel the mango, cut it in half and cut the flesh from the pit in slices.

2 Divide all the fruit, including the blackberries, among four 5½-inch gratin dishes set on a baking sheet and set aside. Heat the wine and sugar in a saucepan until the sugar has dissolved. Bring to a boil and cook for 5 minutes.

3 Put the egg yolks in a large heatproof bowl. Place the bowl over a pan of simmering water and beat until pale. Slowly pour in the hot sugar syrup, beating all the time, until the mixture thickens. Preheat the broiler.

4 Spoon the mixture over the fruit. Place the baking sheet holding the dishes on a low shelf under the hot broiler until the topping is golden. Serve hot.

GRILLED PINEAPPLE WITH PAPAYA SAUCE

PINEAPPLE COOKED THIS WAY TAKES ON A SUPERB FLAVOR AND IS SENSATIONAL WHEN SERVED WITH THE PAPAYA SAUCE.

SERVES SIX

INGREDIENTS
1 sweet pineapple
melted butter, for greasing
   and brushing
2 pieces drained preserved ginger in
   syrup, cut into fine matchsticks,
   plus 2 tablespoons of the syrup
   from the jar
2 tablespoons demerara sugar
pinch of ground cinnamon
fresh mint sprigs, to decorate
For the sauce
1 ripe papaya, peeled and seeded
¾ cup apple juice

1 Peel the pineapple and take spiral slices off the outside to remove the eyes. Cut it crosswise into six slices, each 1 inch thick. Line a baking sheet with a sheet of foil, rolling up the sides to make a rim. Grease the foil with melted butter. Preheat the broiler.

2 Arrange the pineapple slices on the lined baking sheet. Brush with butter, then top with the ginger matchsticks, sugar and cinnamon. Drizzle the ginger syrup over. Broil for 5–7 minutes, or until the slices are golden and lightly charred on top.

3 Meanwhile, make the sauce. Cut a few slices from the papaya and set aside, then purée the rest with the apple juice in a blender or food processor.

4 Press the purée through a strainer placed over a bowl, then stir in any juices from cooking the pineapple. Serve the pineapple slices with a little sauce drizzled around each plate. Decorate with the reserved papaya slices and the mint sprigs.

COOK'S TIP
Try the papaya sauce with savory dishes too. It tastes great with grilled chicken and game birds as well as pork and lamb.

JAMAICAN FRUIT TRIFLE

THIS TRIFLE IS ACTUALLY BASED ON A CARIBBEAN FOOL THAT CONSISTS OF FRUIT STIRRED INTO THICK VANILLA-FLAVORED CREAM. THIS VERSION IS MUCH LESS RICH, REDRESSING THE BALANCE WITH PLENTY OF FRUIT, AND WITH CREME FRAICHE REPLACING SOME OF THE CREAM.

2 Whip the heavy cream to very soft peaks, then lightly but thoroughly fold in the crème fraîche, sifted confectioners' sugar, vanilla extract and rum.

3 Fold the drained chopped pineapple into the cream mixture. Place the chopped papayas and mangoes in a large bowl and pour the lime juice over. Gently stir the fruit mixture to combine. Shred the pared lime zest.

4 Divide the fruit mixture and the pineapple cream among eight dessert plates. Decorate with the lime shreds, toasted coconut and a few small pineapple leaves, if you like, and serve at once.

SERVES EIGHT

INGREDIENTS
1 large sweet pineapple, peeled and cored, about 12 ounces
1¼ cups heavy cream
scant 1 cup crème fraîche
¼ cup confectioners' sugar, sifted
2 teaspoons pure vanilla extract
2 tablespoons white or coconut rum
3 papayas, peeled, seeded and chopped
3 mangoes, peeled, pitted and chopped
thinly pared zest and juice of 1 lime
⅓ cup coarsely shredded or flaked coconut, toasted

1 Cut the pineapple into large chunks, place in a food processor or blender and process briefly until chopped. Pour into a strainer placed over a bowl and leave for 5 minutes, so that most of the juice drains from the fruit.

COOK'S TIP
It is important to let the pineapple purée drain thoroughly, otherwise the pineapple cream will be watery. Don't throw away the drained pineapple juice—mix it with sparkling mineral water for a refreshing drink.

POMEGRANATE JEWELED CHEESECAKE

THIS LIGHT CHEESECAKE IS FLAVORED WITH COCONUT AND HAS A STUNNING POMEGRANATE GLAZE.

SERVES EIGHT

INGREDIENTS

8 ounces oat biscuits or graham
   crackers (1½ cups crumbed)
6 tablespoons unsalted butter, melted
For the filling
3 tablespoons orange juice
1 tablespoon powdered gelatin
generous 1 cup mascarpone
   cheese
scant 1 cup full-fat cream cheese
¾ cup confectioners' sugar, sifted
scant 1 cup coconut cream
2 egg whites
For the topping
2 pomegranates, peeled and
   seeds separated
grated zest and juice of 1 orange
2 tablespoons granulated sugar
1 tablespoon arrowroot, mixed to a
   paste with 2 tablespoons kirsch

2 For the filling, pour the orange juice into a heatproof bowl, sprinkle the gelatin on top and set aside for 5 minutes, until softened. Place the bowl in a pan of hot water and stir until the gelatin has dissolved.

3 In a bowl, beat together both cheeses and the confectioners' sugar, then beat in the coconut cream. Beat the egg whites in a greasefree bowl to soft peaks. Quickly stir the melted gelatin into the coconut mixture and fold into the egg whites. Pour over the crust in the pan, level and chill until set.

4 Make the cheesecake topping. Place the pomegranate seeds in a saucepan and add the orange zest and juice and granulated sugar. Bring to a boil, then lower the heat, cover and simmer for 5 minutes. Add the arrowroot paste and heat, stirring constantly, until thickened. Allow to cool, stirring occasionally.

5 Pour the glaze over the top of the set cheesecake, then chill. To serve, run a knife between the edge of the pan and the cheesecake, then remove the side of the pan.

1 Grease a 9-inch springform pan. Crumb the biscuits or graham crackers in a food processor or blender. Add the melted butter and process briefly to combine. Spoon into the prepared pan, press the mixture in well, then chill.

COOK'S TIP
If you do not have a blender or food processor, crumb the biscuits or graham crackers by placing them in a large, strong plastic bag and crushing them with a rolling pin. For the best results, crush the crumbs as finely as possible.

BANANA AND MASCARPONE CREAMS

IF YOU ARE A FAN OF BANANA PUDDING, YOU'LL LOVE THIS RECIPE. IT IS A GROWN-UP VERSION OF AN OLD FAVORITE. NO ONE WILL GUESS THAT THE SECRET IS PREPARED CUSTARD SAUCE.

SERVES FOUR TO SIX

INGREDIENTS
  generous 1 cup mascarpone
    cheese
1¼ cups custard sauce (créme
  anglaise), prepared in advance
  ⅔ cup plain strained yogurt
  4 bananas
  juice of 1 lime
  ½ cup pecans,
    coarsely chopped
  ½ cup maple syrup

VARIATION
Use honey instead of maple syrup and walnuts instead of pecans, if you like. Also, try layering in some crumbled cookies, such as amaretti or ratafia (almond paste), shortbread crumbs or crushed meringues. Or add a handful of finely grated dark or white chocolate.

1 Combine the mascarpone, custard sauce and yogurt in a large bowl and beat together until smooth. Make this mixture up to several hours ahead, if you like. Cover and chill, then stir before using.

2 Slice the bananas diagonally and place in a separate bowl. Pour the lime juice over and toss together until the bananas are coated in the juice.

3 Divide half the custard mixture among four or six dessert glasses and top each portion with a generous spoonful of the banana mixture.

4 Spoon the remaining custard mixture into the glasses and top with the rest of the bananas. Scatter the nuts over the top. Drizzle maple syrup over each dessert and chill for 30 minutes before serving.

BANANAS WITH LIME AND CARDAMOM SAUCE

SERVE THESE BANANAS WITH VANILLA ICE CREAM, OR SPOON THEM OVER FOLDED CRÊPES.

SERVES FOUR

INGREDIENTS
  6 small bananas
  4 tablespoons butter
  seeds from 4 cardamom
    pods, crushed
  ½ cup sliced almonds
  thinly pared zest and juice
    of 2 limes
  ⅓ cup light brown sugar
  2 tablespoons dark rum
  vanilla ice cream, to serve

VARIATION
If you prefer not to use alcohol in your cooking, replace the rum with orange juice or even pineapple juice.

1 Peel the bananas and cut them in half lengthwise. Heat half the butter in a large frying pan. Add half the bananas and cook until the undersides are golden. Turn carefully, using a spatula. Cook until golden.

2 As they cook, transfer the bananas to a heatproof serving dish. Cook the remaining bananas in the same way.

3 Melt the remaining butter, then add the cardamom seeds and almonds. Cook, stirring, until golden.

4 Stir in the lime zest and juice, then the sugar. Cook, stirring, until the mixture is smooth, bubbling and slightly reduced. Stir in the rum. Pour the sauce over the bananas and serve immediately, with vanilla ice cream.

TOFFEE BANANAS

Although the method for this recipe sounds simple, it can be a bit tricky to master. You need to work fast, especially when dipping the fruit in the caramel, as it will cool and set quite quickly. The luscious results, however, are worth the effort.

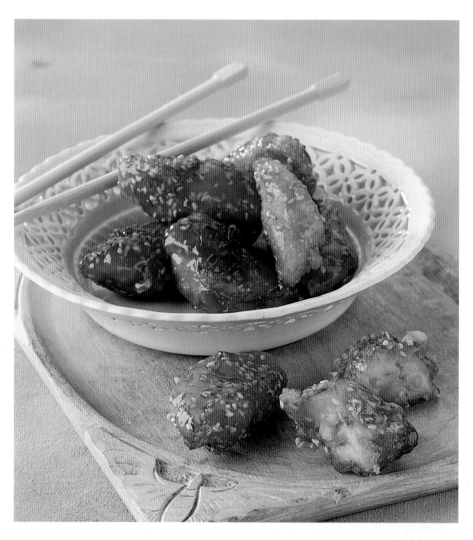

2 Heat the peanut, sunflower or corn oil in a deep pan until it registers 350°F, or until a cube of bread added to the oil turns pale brown in 45 seconds.

3 Using a fork, remove a piece of banana from the batter, allowing the excess batter to drain back into the bowl. Gently lower the piece of banana into the hot oil. Add more pieces in the same way; do not overcrowd the pan. Fry for about 2 minutes, or until the coating is golden.

4 As they are cooked, remove the banana fritters from the oil with a slotted spoon and place on paper towels to drain. Cook the rest of the battered bananas in the same way.

SERVES FOUR

INGREDIENTS
4 firm bananas
¾ cup all-purpose flour
½ cup cornstarch
2 teaspoons baking powder
¾ cup water
1 teaspoon sesame oil
peanut, sunflower or corn oil, for
   deep-frying
For the caramel
1 cup sugar
2 tablespoons sesame seeds
¼ cup water

1 Peel the bananas, then cut them diagonally into thick slices. Sift the flour, cornstarch and baking powder into a large bowl. Quickly beat in the water and sesame oil, taking care not to overmix. Stir in the bananas until coated.

5 When all the banana pieces have been fried, make the caramel. Mix the sugar, sesame seeds and water in a pan. Heat gently, stirring occasionally, until the sugar has dissolved. Raise the heat slightly and continue cooking, without stirring, until the syrup becomes a light caramel. Remove from the heat.

6 Have ready a bowl of ice water. Working quickly, drop one fritter at a time into the hot caramel. Flip over with a fork, remove immediately and plunge the piece into the ice water. Remove from the water quickly (using your fingers for speed, but taking care) and drain on a wire rack while coating the rest. Serve immediately.

HOT DATE PUDDINGS WITH TOFFEE SAUCE

FRESH DATES MAKE THIS PUDDING LESS RICH THAN THE CONVENTIONAL DRIED DATE VERSION, BUT IT IS STILL A BIT OF AN INDULGENCE! IT IS PREFERABLE TO PEEL THE DATES, AS THEY CAN BE RATHER TOUGH: SIMPLY SQUEEZE THEM BETWEEN YOUR THUMB AND FOREFINGER AND THE SKINS WILL POP OFF.

SERVES SIX

INGREDIENTS
- 4 tablespoons butter, softened
- ½ cup light brown sugar
- 2 eggs, beaten
- 1 cup self-rising flour
- ½ teaspoon baking soda
- 1 cup fresh dates, peeled, pitted and chopped
- 5 tablespoons boiling water
- 2 teaspoons very strong black coffee

For the toffee sauce
- ½ cup light brown sugar
- ¼ cup butter
- ¼ cup heavy cream
- 2 tablespoons brandy

1 Preheat the oven to 350°F. Place a baking sheet in the oven to heat up. Grease six individual pudding molds or pans. Cream the butter and sugar in a mixing bowl until pale and fluffy. Gradually add the eggs, beating well after each addition.

2 Sift the flour and baking soda together and fold into the creamed mixture. Put the dates in a heatproof bowl, pour the boiling water over and mash with a potato masher. Add the coffee, then stir the paste into the creamed mixture.

3 Spoon the mixture into the prepared molds or pans. Place on the hot baking sheet and bake for 20 minutes.

4 Meanwhile, make the toffee sauce. Put all the ingredients in a pan and heat very gently, stirring occasionally, until the mixture is smooth. Increase the heat and boil for 1 minute.

5 Turn the warm puddings out onto individual dessert plates. Spoon a generous amount of sauce over each portion and serve at once.

COOK'S TIP
The sauce is a great standby. Try it on poached apple or pear slices, over ice cream or with a steamed pudding.

RUM AND BANANA WAFFLES

TO SAVE TIME, THESE SCRUMPTIOUS DESSERT WAFFLES CAN BE MADE IN ADVANCE, WRAPPED TIGHTLY, FROZEN, AND THEN WARMED THROUGH IN THE OVEN JUST BEFORE SERVING.

SERVES FOUR

INGREDIENTS
   2 cups all-purpose flour
   2 teaspoons baking powder
   1 teaspoon baking soda
   1 tablespoon granulated sugar
   2 eggs
   4 tablespoons butter, melted
   ¾ cup milk, plus additional
      if needed
   1¼ cups buttermilk
   1 teaspoon pure vanilla extract
   light cream, to serve
For the bananas
   6 bananas, thickly sliced
   1 cup pecans, broken
      into pieces
   ⅓ cup demerara sugar
   5 tablespoons maple syrup
   3 tablespoons dark rum

2 Add the buttermilk and vanilla to the batter and mix well. Cover and let stand for 30 minutes. Preheat the oven to 300°F.

3 Heat a handheld waffle iron over the heat. Stir the batter and add more milk if required (the consistency should be quite thick). Open the waffle iron and pour some batter over two-thirds of the surface. Close it and wipe off any excess batter.

4 Cook for 3–4 minutes, carefully turning the waffle iron over once during cooking. If using an electric waffle maker, follow the manufacturer's instructions for cooking.

5 When the batter stops steaming, open the iron and lift out the waffle with a fork. Put it on a heatproof plate and keep it hot in the oven. Repeat with the remaining batter to make eight waffles in all. Preheat the broiler.

6 Cook the bananas. Spread them out on a large shallow baking tin and top with the pecans. Scatter the demerara sugar over. Mix the maple syrup and rum together and spoon over.

7 Broil for 3–4 minutes, or until the sugar begins to bubble. Serve on top of the waffles with light cream.

1 Sift the dry ingredients into a large mixing bowl. Make a well in the center. Add the eggs, melted butter and milk. Beat together, gradually incorporating the flour mixture, until smooth.

COOK'S TIP
If you don't own a waffle iron, prepare the batter as directed, but make small pancakes in a heavy frying pan. Alternatively, use frozen waffles, and reheat as directed on the package before serving with the hot banana topping.

VARIATIONS
Use other fruits for the waffle topping, if you like. Small chunks of fresh or drained canned pineapple, thin wedges of peaches or nectarines, or even orange slices would be delicious alternatives to the banana.

MANGO AND TAMARILLO PASTRIES

THESE LITTLE FRUIT-TOPPED PASTRIES GO VERY WELL WITH A CUP OF AFTERNOON TEA.

MAKES EIGHT

INGREDIENTS
    8 ounces prepared puff pastry
      (12 × 10-inch rectangle)
    1 egg yolk, lightly beaten
    ½ cup white marzipan
    8 teaspoons ginger or apricot conserve
    1 mango, peeled and thinly sliced off
      the pit
    2 tamarillos, halved and sliced
    sugar, for sprinkling

1 Preheat the oven to 400°F. Cut the pastry into 8 rectangles. Place on baking sheets.

VARIATION
Use apricot slices instead of tamarillos, or a mixture of plums and peaches.

2 Using a sharp knife, score the surface of each piece of pastry into a diamond pattern, then brush with the egg yolk to glaze. Cut eight thin slices of marzipan and lay one slice on each pastry rectangle. Top each with a teaspoon of the ginger or apricot conserve and spread over evenly.

3 Top the pastry rectangles with alternate slices of mango and tamarillo. Sprinkle with some of the sugar, then bake for 15–20 minutes, until the pastry is well puffed up and golden. Remove the pastries to a wire rack to cool. Sprinkle with more sugar before serving.

EXOTIC FRUIT TART

THIS IS A GOOD WAY TO MAKE THE MOST OF A SMALL SELECTION OF EXOTIC FRUIT.

SERVES EIGHT

INGREDIENTS
  1½ cups all-purpose flour
  4 tablespoons unsalted butter
  2 tablespoons solid vegetable
    shortening
  ¼ cup granulated sugar
  2 egg yolks
  about 1 tablespoon cold water
  scant ½ cup apricot conserve,
    strained and warmed
For the filling
  ⅔ cup heavy cream, plus extra to serve
  generous 1 cup mascarpone cheese
  ¼ cup confectioners' sugar, sifted
  grated zest of 1 orange
  3 cups mixed prepared fruits, such
    as mango, papaya, star fruit, kiwi
    fruit and blackberries
  6 tablespoons apricot conserve,
    strained
  1 tablespoon white or coconut rum

1 Sift the flour into a bowl and rub in the butter and solid vegetable shortening until the mixture resembles fine bread crumbs. Stir in the granulated sugar. Add the egg yolks and enough cold water to make a soft dough. Thinly roll out the pastry between two sheets of plastic wrap and use the pastry to line a 14 × 4½-inch fluted tart pan. Allow the excess pastry to hang over the edge of the pan and chill for 30 minutes.

2 Preheat the oven to 400°F. Prick the base of the pastry shell and line with baking parchment and baking beans. Bake for 10–12 minutes. Lift out the paper and beans and return the pastry shell to the oven for 5 minutes. Trim off the excess pastry and brush the inside of the shell with the warmed apricot conserve to form a seal. Let cool on a wire rack.

3 Make the filling. Whip the cream to soft peaks, then stir it into the mascarpone with the confectioners' sugar and orange zest. Spread in the cooled pastry shell and top with the prepared fruits. Warm the apricot conserve with the rum and drizzle or brush over the fruits to make a glaze. Serve with extra cream.

COOK'S TIP
You can also use a 9-inch round tart pan for this recipe.

MANGO PIE

THIS RECIPE COMES STRAIGHT FROM THE CARIBBEAN AND CAPTURES ALL THE SUNSHINE FLAVORS OF THAT EXOTIC SETTING. FOR THE TASTIEST PIE, BE SURE THE MANGOES ARE RIPE.

SERVES SIX

INGREDIENTS
  1½ cups all-purpose flour
  pinch of salt
  6 tablespoons unsalted butter,
    chilled and diced
  2 tablespoons solid vegetable
    shortening, chilled and diced
  1 tablespoon sugar, plus extra
    for sprinkling
  about 3 tablespoons cold water
  beaten egg, to glaze
  vanilla ice cream, to serve
For the filling
  2 ripe mangoes
  3 tablespoons fresh lime juice
  ½ cup sugar
  1 tablespoon arrowroot mixed to a
    paste with 1 tablespoon water

1 Sift the flour and salt into a large mixing bowl. Rub in the butter and solid vegetable shortening with your fingertips until the mixture resembles fine bread crumbs, then stir in the sugar. Add just enough of the cold water to make a dough.

VARIATIONS
Make the pie using one mango and one papaya, peeled, seeded and sliced. Add a little ground cinnamon and some freshly grated nutmeg to the filling for a sweet spice flavor.

COOK'S TIP
If the top of the pie begins to brown too much during baking, simply cover it loosely with a piece of foil.

2 Knead lightly, then roll out two-thirds of the pastry and use it to line a 7-inch pie dish. Wrap the remaining pastry in plastic wrap and chill both the pastry and the pastry shell for 30 minutes.

3 Meanwhile, make the filling. Peel the mangoes and slice the flesh off the pit. Reserve half the sliced mango and coarsely chop the rest.

4 Place the chopped mango in a saucepan with the lime juice and sugar. Cover and cook for 10 minutes, or until soft. Pour in the arrowroot paste and cook, stirring all the time, until thickened. Set the filling aside to cool.

5 Preheat the oven to 375°F. Pour the cooled mango filling into the chilled pastry shell and top with the reserved mango slices. Roll out the remaining pastry to make a top crust.

6 Dampen the rim of the pastry shell and add the top crust. Crimp the edges to seal, then cut a cross in the center to allow the steam to escape.

7 Glaze the pastry with the beaten egg and sprinkle lightly with sugar. Bake for 35–40 minutes, until the pastry is golden brown. Cool slightly on a wire rack. Serve warm with vanilla ice cream.

BANANA AND PECAN BREAD

BANANAS AND PECANS JUST SEEM TO BELONG TOGETHER. THIS IS A MOIST AND DELICIOUS TEA BREAD.
SPREAD IT WITH CREAM CHEESE OR JAM, OR SERVE AS A DESSERT WITH WHIPPED CREAM.

MAKES A 2-POUND LOAF

INGREDIENTS
    8 tablespoons (1 stick) butter,
        softened
    1 cup light brown sugar
    2 large eggs, beaten
    3 ripe bananas
    ¾ cup pecans, coarsely chopped
    2 cups self-rising flour
    ½ teaspoon ground apple pie spice

1 Preheat the oven to 350°F.
Generously grease a 9 x 5 x 3-inch loaf
pan and line it with baking parchment.
Cream the butter and brown sugar in a
large mixing bowl until the mixture is
light and fluffy. Gradually add the
eggs, beating after each addition, until
well combined.

2 Peel and then mash the bananas
with a fork. Add them to the creamed
mixture with the chopped pecans. Beat
until well combined.

COOK'S TIP
If the mixture shows signs of curdling
when you add the eggs, stir in a little
of the flour to stabilize it.

3 Sift the flour and apple pie spice
together and fold into the banana
mixture. Spoon into the pan, level the
surface and bake for 1–1¼ hours, or
until a skewer inserted into the middle
of the loaf comes out clean. Cool for
10 minutes in the pan, then invert the
pan on a wire rack. Lift off the pan, peel
off the lining paper and cool completely.

DATE AND WALNUT BROWNIES

THESE RICH BROWNIES ARE GREAT FOR AN AFTERNOON SNACK, BUT THEY ALSO MAKE A FANTASTIC
DESSERT. REHEAT SLICES BRIEFLY IN THE MICROWAVE OVEN AND SERVE WITH CREME FRAICHE.

MAKES TWELVE

INGREDIENTS
    12 ounces semisweet chocolate,
        broken into squares
    ½ pound (2 sticks) butter, diced
    3 large eggs
    ½ cup granulated sugar
    1 teaspoon pure vanilla extract
    ¾ cup all-purpose flour, sifted
    1½ cups fresh dates, peeled, pitted
        and chopped
    1¾ cups walnut pieces
    confectioners' sugar, for dusting

COOK'S TIP
When melting the chocolate and butter,
keep the water in the pan beneath hot,
but do not let it approach boiling point.
Chocolate is notoriously sensitive to heat;
it is vital not to let it get too hot or it
may stiffen into an unmanageable mass.

1 Preheat the oven to 375°F.
Generously grease a 12 x 8-inch
baking pan and line with baking
parchment.

2 Put the chocolate and butter in a
large heatproof bowl. Place the bowl
over a pan of hot water and leave until
both have melted. Stir until smooth,
then lift the bowl out and cool slightly.

3 In a separate bowl, beat the eggs,
granulated sugar and vanilla. Beat into
the chocolate mixture, then fold in the
flour, dates and nuts. Pour into the pan.

4 Bake for 30–40 minutes, until firm
and the mixture comes away from the
sides of the pan. Cool in the pan, then
turn out, remove the paper and dust
with confectioners' sugar.

MANGO CHUTNEY

THIS CLASSIC CHUTNEY IS CONVENTIONALLY SERVED WITH CURRIES AND INDIAN PAPPADAMS, BUT IT IS ALSO DELICIOUS WITH BAKED HAM OR A TRADITIONAL ENGLISH CHEESE PLOUGHMAN'S LUNCH.

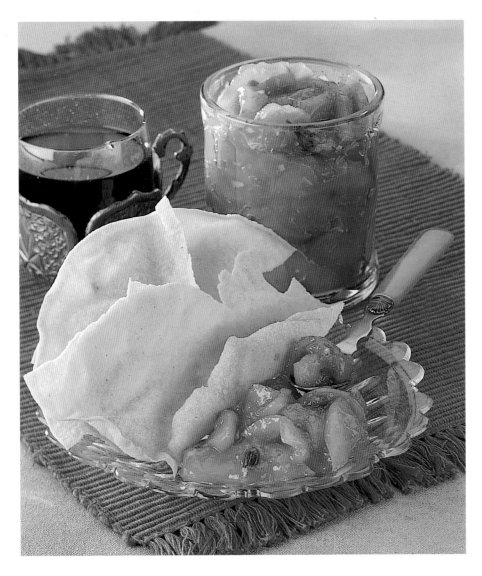

MAKES 1 POUND

INGREDIENTS
    3 firm green mangoes
    ⅔ cup cider vinegar
    ⅔ cup light brown sugar
    1 small red finger chile or jalapeño,
        split
    1-inch piece of fresh ginger root,
        peeled and finely chopped
    1 garlic clove, finely chopped
    5 cardamom pods, bruised
    ½ teaspoon coriander seeds, crushed
    1 bay leaf
    ½ teaspoon salt

2 Place the mango pieces in a large saucepan, add the vinegar and cover. Cook over low heat for 10 minutes.

3 Stir in the brown sugar, chile, ginger, garlic, bruised cardamoms and coriander. Add the bay leaf and salt. Bring to a boil slowly, stirring often.

4 Lower the heat and simmer, uncovered, for 30 minutes, or until the mixture is thick and syrupy.

1 Peel the mangoes and cut the flesh off the pit. Slice the mangoes lengthwise, then cut across into small chunks or thin wedges.

5 Ladle into hot sterilized jars, seal and label. Store for 1 week before eating. Keep chilled after opening.

PAPAYA AND LEMON RELISH

THIS CHUNKY RELISH IS BEST MADE WITH A FIRM, UNRIPE PAPAYA. IT SHOULD BE LEFT FOR A WEEK BEFORE EATING TO ALLOW ALL THE FLAVORS TO MELLOW. STORE THE UNOPENED JARS IN A COOL PLACE, AWAY FROM SUNLIGHT. SERVE WITH ROAST MEATS OR WITH A ROBUST CHEESE AND CRACKERS.

MAKES 1 POUND

INGREDIENTS

1 large unripe papaya
1 onion, thinly sliced
⅓ cup raisins
1 cup red wine vinegar
juice of 2 lemons
⅔ cup elderflower
  cordial
¾ cup turbinado sugar
1 cinnamon stick
1 fresh bay leaf
½ teaspoon hot paprika
½ teaspoon salt

1 Peel the papaya and cut it in half lengthwise. Remove the seeds with a small teaspoon. Cut the flesh into small chunks and place them in a large saucepan.

2 Add the onion slices and raisins to the papaya chunks, then stir in the vinegar. Bring to a boil, lower the heat and simmer for 10 minutes.

3 Add all the remaining ingredients and bring to a boil, stirring all the time. Check that all the sugar has dissolved, then lower the heat and simmer for 50–60 minutes, or until the relish is thick and syrupy.

4 Ladle into hot sterilized jars. Seal, label and store for 1 week before using. Keep chilled after opening.

MELON, GRAPE, FIG AND RHUBARB RECIPES

Whether alone or with other fruits, melons, rhubarb, figs and grapes make wonderful desserts, pies, cakes and preserves. Don't miss Red Grape and Cheese Tartlets, One-Crust Rhubarb Pie or Yogurt and Fig Cake.

MELON TRIO WITH GINGER COOKIES

THE EYE-CATCHING COLORS OF THESE THREE DIFFERENT MELONS REALLY MAKE THIS DESSERT, WHILE THE CRISP COOKIES PROVIDE A PERFECT CONTRAST IN TEXTURE.

SERVES FOUR

INGREDIENTS

¼ watermelon
½ honeydew melon
½ charentais melon
¼ cup preserved ginger syrup
For the cookies
2 tablespoons unsalted butter
2 tablespoons sugar
1 teaspoon honey
¼ cup all-purpose flour
¼ cup deluxe glacé
  mixed fruit, finely chopped
1 piece of preserved ginger in syrup,
  drained and finely chopped
2 tablespoons sliced almonds

1 Remove the seeds from the melons, cut them into wedges, then slice off the zest. Cut all the flesh into chunks and mix in a bowl. Stir in the ginger syrup, cover and chill until ready to serve.

2 Meanwhile, make the cookies. Preheat the oven to 350°F. Melt the butter, sugar and honey in a saucepan. Remove from the heat and stir in the remaining ingredients.

3 Line a baking sheet with baking parchment. Space four spoonfuls of the mixture on the paper at regular intervals, leaving plenty of room for spreading. Flatten the mixture slightly into rounds and bake for 15 minutes, or until the tops are golden.

4 Let the cookies cool on the baking sheet for 1 minute, then lift each one in turn, using a metal spatula, and drape over a rolling pin to cool and harden. Repeat with the remaining mixture to make eight cookies in all.

5 Serve the melon chunks with some of the syrup and the ginger cookies.

COOK'S TIP
For an even prettier effect, scoop the melon flesh into balls with the large end of a melon baller.

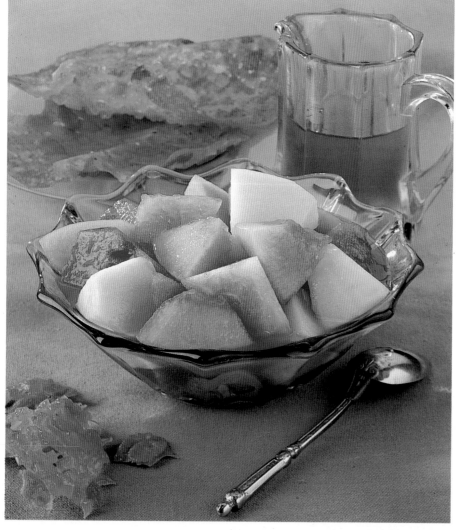

PORT-STEWED RHUBARB
WITH VANILLA DESSERTS

RHUBARB IS ONE OF THOSE FRUITS THAT SELDOM REALIZES ITS FULL POTENTIAL. IT HAS QUITE A SHORT SEASON, SO IF YOU CAN REMEMBER, IT IS WORTH FREEZING SOME FOR USE LATER IN THE YEAR.

2 Meanwhile, pour the water into a ramekin and sprinkle the gelatin over the surface. Set aside to soften for 5 minutes. Place the ramekin in a pan of hot water and set aside until the gelatin is dissolved, stirring occasionally.

3 Add the gelatin mixture to the hot milk mixture and stir until dissolved. Remove the vanilla bean and pour the mixture into the molds or pans. Cool, then chill overnight, or until set.

4 Put the sugar in a pan and add the water, orange zest and juice and cinnamon stick. Bring to a boil over low heat, stirring occasionally until the sugar has dissolved. Increase the heat and boil for 1 minute.

5 Add the port, let the syrup return to a boil, then lower the heat and simmer for 15 minutes, or until it has reduced and thickened. Remove the orange zest and cinnamon stick, add the rhubarb, cover and simmer gently for 2–3 minutes without stirring. Cool.

6 To serve, run a knife around the edge of each vanilla dessert to loosen it, then unmold on to a dessert plate. Serve each dessert with a spoonful or two of the rhubarb with its syrup.

COOK'S TIP
Rhubarb yields a lot of juice when cooked, so make sure the syrup has reduced well before adding the fruit.

SERVES FOUR

INGREDIENTS
½ cup sugar
⅔ cup water
pared zest and juice of 1 orange
1 cinnamon stick
1¼ cups ruby port
10 ounces rhubarb, cut into 1-inch
   pieces (2 cups)
For the vanilla desserts
   ¾ vanilla pod
   ¾ cup heavy cream
   ¾ cup whole milk or half-and-half
   3 tablespoons sugar
   2 tablespoons water
   1½ teaspoons powdered gelatin

1 Start by making the vanilla desserts. Grease four individual pudding molds or pans. Split the vanilla pod and scrape the seeds into a saucepan. Add the bean, cream, milk and sugar. Simmer gently, stirring, for 5 minutes.

FIG <u>AND</u> WALNUT TORTE

THIS RECIPE IS BASED ON THE TRADITIONAL MIDDLE EASTERN SPECIALITY BAKLAVA. IT IS SWEET, STICKY AND DELICIOUS, AND THE FIGS ADD A REFRESHING TOUCH. SINCE IT IS QUITE RICH, PLAN ON CUTTING THE TORTE INTO FAIRLY SMALL DIAMONDS—GREAT WITH A CUP OF STRONG BLACK COFFEE.

MAKES 20–25 PIECES

INGREDIENTS
   6 tablespoons butter, melted,
      plus extra for greasing
   1½ cups walnuts,
      finely chopped
   1 cup ground almonds
   ⅓ cup sugar
   2 teaspoons ground cinnamon
   9 large sheets of phyllo pastry,
      thawed if frozen, each cut into two
      12 × 8-inch rectangles
   4 fresh figs, sliced
   strained plain yogurt, to serve
For the syrup
   1½ cups sugar
   4 whole cloves
   1 cinnamon stick
   2 strips of lemon zest

1 Preheat the oven to 325ºF. Generously grease a 12 × 8-inch shallow baking pan with melted butter. Mix together the walnuts, ground almonds, sugar and cinnamon in a bow and set aside.

2 Fit a sheet of phyllo pastry in the bottom of the baking pan. Brush with some of the melted butter and place another sheet of phyllo on top. Repeat until you have layered eight sheets.

COOK'S TIP
Paper-thin phyllo pastry is delicate and dries out quickly. Work with one sheet at a time, and keep the other sheets covered, or they will dry out.

3 Spoon half the nut mixture evenly over the phyllo pastry, right to the edges, and top with the fig slices.

4 Place two phyllo sheets on top of the figs, brushing each with more melted butter as before, then evenly spoon the remaining nut mixture over.

5 Layer the remaining phyllo sheets on top, buttering each one. Brush any remaining melted butter over the top of the torte, then score the surface with a sharp knife to give a diamond pattern. Bake for 1 hour, until golden.

6 Meanwhile, make the syrup. Place all the ingredients in a saucepan and mix well. Heat, stirring, until the sugar has dissolved. Bring to a boil, lower the heat and simmer, stirring occasionally, for 10 minutes, until syrupy.

7 Allow the syrup to cool for about 15 minutes, then strain it evenly over the hot torte.

8 Allow to cool and soak for 2–3 hours, then cut the torte into diamonds or squares and serve with the yogurt. Store the torte in an airtight container for up to 3 days.

VARIATION
If you like, replace the chopped walnuts with coarsely chopped pistachio nuts, or use finely chopped cashews for an ultra-rich flavor.

RED GRAPE <u>AND</u> CHEESE TARTLETS

FRUIT AND CHEESE IS A NATURAL COMBINATION IN THIS SIMPLE RECIPE. LOOK FOR THE PALE, MAUVE-COLORED OR RED GRAPES THAT TEND TO BE SLIGHTLY SMALLER THAN BLACK GRAPES. THESE ARE OFTEN SEEDLESS AND HAVE THE ADDED ADVANTAGE OF BEING SWEETER.

MAKES SIX

INGREDIENTS

12 ounces sweet shortcrust pastry, thawed if frozen
1 cup cottage cheese
⅔ cup heavy cream
½ teaspoon pure vanilla extract
2 tablespoons confectioners' sugar
2 cups red grapes, halved, seeded if necessary
¼ cup apricot conserve
1 tablespoon water

VARIATIONS

Use cranberry jelly or red currant jelly for the glaze. There will be no need to strain either of these. Also vary the fruit topping, if you like. Try blackberries, blueberries, raspberries, sliced strawberries, kiwi fruit slices, banana slices or well-drained pineapple slices.

1 Preheat the oven to 400°F. Roll out the pastry and line six deep 3½-inch fluted individual tartlet pans. Prick the bottoms and line with baking parchment and baking beans. Bake for 10 minutes, remove the paper and beans, then return the shells to the oven for 5 minutes, until golden and fully cooked. Remove the pastry shells from the pans and cool on a wire rack.

2 Meanwhile, beat the cottage cheese, heavy cream, vanilla and confectioners' sugar in a bowl. Divide the mixture among the pastry shells. Smooth the surface and arrange the halved grapes on top.

3 Strain the apricot conserve into a pan. Add the water and heat, stirring, until smooth. Spoon over the grapes. Cool, then chill before serving.

ONE-CRUST RHUBARB PIE

THIS METHOD CAN BE USED FOR ALL SORTS OF FRUIT AND IS REALLY FOOLPROOF. IT DOESN'T MATTER HOW ROUGH THE PIE LOOKS WHEN IT GOES INTO THE OVEN; IT COMES OUT LOOKING FANTASTIC!

SERVES SIX

INGREDIENTS

12 ounces shortcrust pastry, thawed
   if frozen
1 egg yolk, beaten
3 tablespoons semolina
¼ cup coarsely chopped hazelnuts
2 tablespoons turbinado sugar

For the filling

1 pound rhubarb, cut into
   1-inch pieces
⅓ cup granulated sugar
1–2 pieces preserved ginger in syrup,
   drained and finely chopped

COOK'S TIP

Egg yolk glaze brushed onto pastry gives it a nice golden sheen. However, be careful not to drip the glaze on the baking sheet, or it will burn and be difficult to remove.

1 Preheat the oven to 400°F. Roll out the pastry to a circle 14 inches in diameter. Lay it over the rolling pin and transfer it to a large baking sheet. Brush a little egg yolk over the pastry. Scatter the semolina over the center, leaving a wide rim all around.

2 Make the filling. Place the rhubarb pieces, granulated sugar and chopped ginger in a large bowl and mix well.

3 Pile the rhubarb mixture into the middle of the pastry. Fold the rim roughly over the filling so that it almost covers it. Some of the fruit will remain visible in the center.

4 Glaze the pastry rim with any remaining egg yolk and scatter the hazelnuts and turbinado sugar over. Bake for 30–35 minutes, or until the pastry is golden brown. Serve warm.

FRESH FIG PHYLLO TART

FIGS COOK WONDERFULLY WELL AND TASTE SUPERB IN THIS TART—THE RIPER THE FIGS, THE BETTER.

2 Using scissors, cut off any excess pastry, leaving a little overhanging the edge. Arrange the figs in the phyllo shell.

3 Sift the flour into a bowl and stir in the sugar. Add the eggs and a little of the milk and beat until smooth. Gradually beat in the remaining milk and the almond extract. Pour the mixture over the figs; bake for 1 hour, or until the batter has set and is golden.

SERVES SIX TO EIGHT

INGREDIENTS
    five 14 × 10-inch sheets phyllo
       pastry, thawed if frozen
    2 tablespoons butter, melted, plus
       extra for greasing
    6 fresh figs, cut into wedges
    ¾ cup all-purpose flour
    ⅓ cup sugar
    4 eggs
    1¾ cups whole milk or half-and-half
    ½ teaspoon pure almond extract
    1 tablespoon confectioners' sugar
    whipped cream or strained plain
       yogurt, to serve

1 Preheat the oven to 375°F. Grease a 10 × 6¼-inch baking pan with butter. Brush each phyllo sheet in turn with melted butter and use to line the prepared pan.

4 Remove the tart from the oven and allow it to cool in the pan on a wire rack for 10 minutes. Dust with the confectioners' sugar and serve with whipped cream or yogurt.

CREAMY YOGURT <u>AND</u> FIG CAKE

BAKED FRESH FIGS, THICKLY SLICED, MAKE A DELECTABLE BASE FOR A FEATHERLIGHT SPONGE.
FIGS THAT ARE A BIT ON THE FIRM SIDE WORK BEST FOR THIS RECIPE.

SERVES SIX TO EIGHT

INGREDIENTS

   6 firm fresh figs, thickly sliced
   3 tablespoons honey, plus extra for
     glazing cooked figs
   14 tablespoons butter,
     softened
   ¾ cup sugar
   grated zest of 1 lemon
   grated zest of 1 orange
   4 eggs, separated
   2 cups all-purpose flour
   1 teaspoon baking powder
   1 teaspoon baking soda
   1 cup strained plain yogurt

1 Preheat the oven to 350°F. Grease a 9-inch cake pan and line the bottom with baking parchment. Arrange the figs over the bottom of the pan and drizzle the honey over.

2 In a large mixing bowl, cream the butter and sugar with the lemon and orange zests until the mixture is pale and fluffy, then gradually beat in the egg yolks.

3 Sift the dry ingredients together. Add a little to the creamed mixture, beat well, then beat in a spoonful of yogurt. Repeat this process until all the dry ingredients and yogurt have been incorporated.

4 Beat the egg whites in a greasefree bowl until they form stiff peaks. Stir half the whites into the cake mixture to lighten it slightly, then fold in the rest. Pour the mixture over the figs in the pan, then bake for 1¼ hours, or until golden and a skewer inserted in the center of the cake comes out clean.

5 Turn the cake out onto a wire rack, peel off the lining paper and let cool. Drizzle the figs with extra honey before serving.

MELON AND STAR ANISE JAM

MELON AND GINGER ARE CLASSIC COMPANIONS. THE ADDITION OF STAR ANISE IMPARTS A WONDERFUL ASIAN FLAVOR TO THE JAM. IT'S SPLENDID ON TOASTED FRUIT-AND-SPICE MUFFINS.

MAKES 1 POUND

INGREDIENTS
2 charentais or cantaloupe melons, peeled and seeded
2 cups sugar
2 star anise
4 pieces preserved ginger in syrup, drained and finely chopped
finely grated zest and juice of 2 lemons

COOK'S TIPS
Use this jam in savory dishes instead of honey to add a spicy, noncloying sweetness. Jams require a large amount of sugar for proper jelling—don't cut back.

1 Cut the melons into small cubes and layer with the sugar in a large nonreactive bowl. Cover with plastic wrap and refrigerate overnight, so the melons can release their juices.

2 Pour the melons and juice into a large saucepan and add the star anise, ginger and lemon zest and juice.

3 Bring to a boil, then lower the heat. Simmer for 25 minutes, or until the melon has become translucent and the setting point has been reached. Test for this by spooning a small amount of the juice onto a chilled plate. If it wrinkles when you push a finger through the cooled liquid, it is ready to be canned.

4 Spoon the jam into hot sterilized jars. Seal, label and store in a cool, dry place. Once a jar has been opened, keep it in the refrigerator.

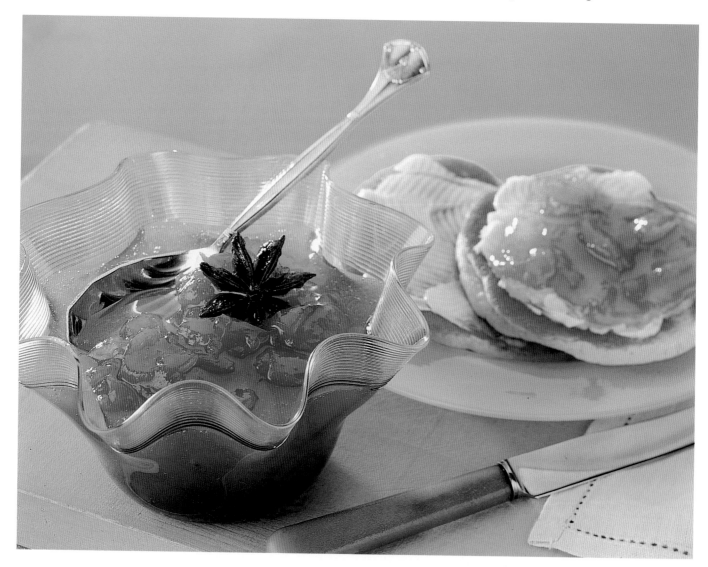

FIG <u>AND</u> DATE CHUTNEY

THIS CHUTNEY IS USUALLY MADE WITH DRIED FIGS AND DATES, BUT IT WORKS PERFECTLY WELL WITH FRESH FRUIT AND HAS A SUPERB FLAVOR. TRY IT WITH CREAM CHEESE ON BROWN BREAD.

MAKES 1 POUND

INGREDIENTS

    1 orange
    5 large fresh figs, coarsely chopped
    12 ounces fresh dates, peeled, pitted and chopped (2½ cups)
    2 onions, chopped
    2-inch piece of fresh ginger root, peeled and finely grated
    1 teaspoon dried crushed chiles
    1½ cups turbinado sugar
    1¼ cups cider vinegar
    ½ teaspoon salt

1 Finely grate the zest of the orange, then cut off the remaining pith and segment the orange.

2 Place the orange segments in a large, heavy saucepan with the chopped figs and dates. Add the zest, then stir in the onions, grated ginger, dried chiles, turbinado sugar, cider vinegar and salt. Bring to a boil, stirring gently until all the sugar has dissolved.

3 Lower the heat and simmer gently for 1 hour, or until the mixture has thickened and become pulpy, stirring often to prevent the mixture from sticking to the bottom of the pan.

4 Spoon the chutney into hot, sterilized jars. Seal while still hot and label once the jars are cool. Store for 1 week before using. Once a jar has been opened, keep it in the refrigerator.

VARIATION
If you would rather use dried figs and dates to make the chutney, you will need to increase the amount of cider vinegar by ⅔ cup to a scant 2 cups. Pit the dates and coarsely chop the figs and dates.

INDEX

ruby orange sherbet in ginger
    baskets, 194
rum and banana waffles, 230

S
salaks, 111
salustianas oranges, 80
Santa Rosa plums, 42
sapodillas, 110
satsumas, 78
sauces
    apple and cider, 146
    butterscotch, 134
    chocolate, 130
    cranberry, 67
    lime and cardamom, 226
    orange, 83
    toffee, 229
    see also coulis
sautéeing fruit, 14
seeds, removing, 13
segmenting
    citrus fruit, 13
    firm fruit, 12
Seville oranges, 81, 82
shaddocks, 72, 73
Shamouti oranges, 80
Sharon fruit, 104
sherbets, ruby orange, 194
shortcakes, raspberry and rose
    petal, 180
sloes, 47
snake fruit, 111
sorbets
    black currant, 179

lychee and
    elderflower, 216
soufflés
    cold lemon, 201
    cold mango, 214
    hot blackberry and
        apple, 171
    hot quince, 138
    iced gin and damson, 155
soursops, 91
Spanish limes, 95
Spartan apples, 23
spiced apple crumble, 132
spiced fruits jubilee, 151
spiced poached
    kumquats, 210
star anise
    coconut jelly with, 218
    and melon jam, 250
star fruit
    coconut jelly, 218
    exotic fruit sushi, 217
    exotic fruit tart, 233
    lemongrass skewers, 218
stewing fruit, 14
stone fruit, 36–49
    recipes, 148–167
storing fruit, 12
strawberries, 52–4
    berry brûlée tarts, 186
    buying, 54
    history, 52
    ice cream, 178
    jam, 189
    nutrition, 54
    preparing, 54
    serving, 54
    storing, 54
    summer berry crêpes, 172
    summer pudding, 170
    varieties, 52–3
streusel cake, 183
strudel, cherry and
    hazelnut, 157
Sugar Baby
    watermelons, 117
sugar bananas, 86
sultana grapes, 118

sultanas, 121
summer berry crêpes, 172
summer pudding, 170
sunberries, 59
sushi, exotic fruit, 217
Sweetie grapefruit, 72
syllabubs, peach melba, 152
syrups, port, 136

T
tamarillos, 111
    and mango
        pastries, 232
    tropical fruit gratin, 222
tangelos, 79
tangerines, 78–9
    canned, 79
    shells, 79
    varieties, 78–9
tangleberries, 60
tarte tatin, 140
tarts
    berry brûlée, 186
    exotic fruit, 233
    fig and walnut, 244
    French apple, 143
    fresh fig phyllo, 248
    fresh lemon, 205
    peach and red currant
        tartlets, 160
    red grape and cheese
        tartlets, 246
    tarte tatin, 140
    yellow plum, 162
tayberries, 59

Thompson seedless
    grapes, 118, 120
three-fruit marmalade, 210
Tientsin pears, 33

tiger watermelons, 117
toffee bananas, 228
toffee sauce, 229
Tommy Atkins
    mangoes, 100, 101
tree melons, 105
tree tomatoes, 111
trifle, Jamaican fruit, 224
tropical fruit gratin, 222
truffle loaf, 196
tummelberries, 59

U
ugli fruit, 73

V
Valencia oranges, 81, 82
vanilla desserts, 243
Victoria plums, 42

W
waffles, rum and
    banana, 230
walnuts
    and date brownies, 236
    and fig torte, 244
Washington Red apples, 24
watermelons, 117
    melon trio with ginger
        cookies, 242
whinberries, 61
white currants, 69
whortleberries, 61
Williams Bon Chrétien
    pears, 28
wineberries, 59
Winter Nelis pears, 30
Worcester Pearmain apples, 23
Worcestershire berries, 65

Y
yellow passion fruit, 102
yellow plum tart, 162
yogurt and fig cake, 249
youngberries, 59

Z
zesting, lemons, 74, 75

ACKNOWLEDGMENTS

Photographs are by Don Last and William Lingwood except those on the following pages: p25 ml Harry Smith Horticultural Photographic Collection (HSHC); p47 t Clive Simms; p53 tl HSHC; b/tr The Garden Picture Library (GPL); p54 br GPL; p56 br Clive Simms (CS); p58 m HSHC, tr A-Z Botanical/Bjorn Svenson; p59 br GPL, tl Derek St. Romaine (DSR), bl HSHC; p60 b HSHC; p64 t DSR; p65 bl/br DSR; p75 b CS; p77 b GPL; p86 l Peter McHoy; p91 l HSHC, b CS; p92 t HSHC; p94 b GPL; p97 t HSHC; p99 t CS; p104 t CS; and p110 t GPL.